ALLIES IN CONFLICT

'But the reality is that the way people and organizations and countries often approach difficult, delicate and conflict-laden situations is through the unspoken, unconscious conspiracy of signing each other's conflict certificates – by assuming in advance, that there will be a conflict in the first place.'

J. Edelman and M. Crain, *The Tao of Negotiation* (New York, 1993), p. 1.

Allies in Conflict

Anglo–American Strategic Negotiations, 1938–44

Steve Weiss
Visiting Research Fellow
King's College
London

in association with
KING'S COLLEGE, LONDON

First published in Great Britain 1996 by
MACMILLAN PRESS LTD
Houndmills, Basingstoke, Hampshire RG21 6XS
and London
Companies and representatives
throughout the world

A catalogue record for this book is available
from the British Library.

ISBN 0–333–67157–0

First published in the United States of America 1996 by
ST. MARTIN'S PRESS, INC.,
Scholarly and Reference Division,
175 Fifth Avenue,
New York, N.Y. 10010

ISBN 0–312–16431–9

Library of Congress Cataloging-in-Publication Data
Weiss, Steve, 1915–
Allies in conflict : Anglo-American strategic negotiations, 1938–44
/ Steve Weiss.
p. cm. — (Studies in military and strategic history)
Includes bibliographical references and index.
ISBN 0–312–16431–9
1. World War, 1939–1945—Diplomatic history. 2. United States–
–Military relations—Great Britain. 3. Great Britain—Military
relations—United States. I. Title. II. Series.
D752.8.W45 1996
940.53'22—dc20

96–24196
CIP

10 9 8 7 6 5 4 3 2 1
05 04 03 02 01 00 99 98 97 96

Printed in Great Britain by
The Ipswich Book Company Ltd
Ipswich, Suffolk

Contents

Acknowledgments vi

Abbreviations used in text and footnotes vii

Code-names ix

Conference Code-names x

Introduction 1

1 Introductory Strategic Talks 5

2 Conferences 37

3 Events Leading to a June Washington Conference 52

4 The SYMBOL and TRIDENT Conferences 69

5 QUADRANT: The Quebec Conference 92

6 TEHRAN: The Second Front, the French Resistance and the French Army 105

7 ANVIL, OVERLORD and the Italian Campaign 131

8 Conclusions 160

Notes 169

Bibliography 195

Index 207

Dedication

To Jean, the Petursson, Tunney, and Weiss families, and Helaine

Acknowledgments

I am grateful to the following men who served in the armed forces during the war, all of whom sat for interviews related to their areas of military expertise: Sir Ralph Kilner Brown (Logistics, OVERLORD planning, Law), General Sir William Jackson (British military doctrine and Staff planning in the Mediterranean), the late General James Doolittle (Army Air Force air crew replacement and training during 1944), Robert Reigle and Colonel Vincent Lockhart (Infantry hazards in Italy and France), Keith Sainsbury (Allied strategic possibilities in 1943–44), Sir Robin Brook, Sir Douglas Dodds-Parker, Geoffrey M. T. Jones and Arthur L. Funk (British and American clandestine operations), French Generals François Binoche, J-P de Lassus Saint-Geniès and Jacques Brule (the French Resistance and the French Army).

Some archivists who were most helpful during my period of research were Patricia Methven, Kate O'Brien and Marie Walsh (Liddell Hart Center for Military Archives), John Peaty and Sebastian Cox (Army and Air Historical Branches, MoD), John Taylor (NARA) and the staff at the Franklin D. Roosevelt Library.

Dr Michael Dockrill, my supervisor at King's, provided sound guidance, advice, humor and friendly criticism that was always both timely and appropriate. Professor Lawrence Freedman, head of the Department of War Studies at King's, was generous in providing financial support for my research. To Robin Kilpatrick, David London, Dr Ronnie Bregman and Dr Matthew Jones who were unstinting with their time and knowledge in most matters involving computer software, editing, history and language, my special thanks.

In closing, I hope that my children and grandchildren will not wait as long as I did to complete their education. As a former infantryman, I realize that there is much to be learned, much to be gained and so little time.

Abbreviations used in Text and Footnotes

AHB	Air Historical Branch
AAF	Army Air Forces (AAF US)
AAI	Allied Armies Italy
ABC	American–British Conversations
ABDA (COM)	Australian–British–Dutch–American (Command)
AFHQ	Allied Force Headquarters
AHB	Air Historical Branch, MoD, London
BL	British Library
C-in-C	Commander in Chief
CCS	Combined Chiefs of Staff
CEF	Corps Expéditionnaire Français
COMINCH	Commander in Chief, US Fleet
COS	Chief of Staff (British)
COSMED	Chief of Staff Mediterranean (British)
COSSAC	Chief of Staff to the Supreme Allied Commander
ETO	European Theater of Operations
FCNL	French Committee of National Liberation
FDR	Franklin D. Roosevelt
FDRL	Franklin D. Roosevelt Library, Hyde Park, NY
FO	Foreign Office (British)
GSD	General Staff Division (US)
IWM	Imperial War Museum, London
JCS	Joint Chiefs of Staff, (US)
JPS	Joint Planning Staff
JRUSSI	Journal of Royal United Services Institute
JSM	Joint Staff Mission (British Representatives of COS, Washington)
JSS	Journal of Strategic Studies
JSSC	Joint Strategic Survey Committee (US)
JUSSC	Joint US Strategic Committee
JWPC	Joint War Plans Committee (US)
KCL	King's College London
LoC	Library of Congress (Washington)
MAAF	Mediterranean Allied Air Forces
MoD	Ministry of Defence (British)
NARA	National Archives & Record Administration (US Archives)
OAFH	Office of Air Force History

OPD	Operations Division, US Army
OSS	Office of Strategic Services
PPF	President's Private Files
PSF	President's Secretary's Files
PRO	Public Records Office (British Archives)
RG	Record Group (US Archives)
RAF	Royal Air Force
SACAEF	Supreme Allied Commander Allied Expeditionary Force
SACMED	Supreme Allied Commander Mediterranean
SHAEF	Supreme Headquarters, Allied Expeditionary Force
SCAEF	Supreme Commander, Allied Expeditionary Force
SOE	Special Operations Executive (British)
USAAF	US Army Air Force
USACGS	US Army Command and General Staff College
WD	War Department, US
WSC	Winston S. Churchill

Code-names

ACCOLADE	Plan to capture the Dodecanese Islands, 1943
ANAKIM	Plan for seaborne invasion of lower Burma, 1943
AVALANCHE	Invasion of Italy at Salerno, September, 1943
ANVIL	Operation against southern France, 30 July, 1944
BAYTOWN	British Eighth Army Landing in southern Italy, 1943
BOLERO	Build-up of US forces in UK, 1942–44
BRIMSTONE	Plan to capture Sardinia, 1944
BODYGUARD	Overall strategic deception plan for 1944
BUCCANEER	British plan to capture the Andaman Islands in 1944
DIADEM	Allied Offensive, May 1944
DRAGOON	Changed from ANVIL in summer of 1944
FORTITUDE	Tactical Deception Plan for OVERLORD
GYMNAST	Plan for landings in French North Africa, 27 July 1942
HABAKKUK	British idea of constructing seadromes out of ice/wood shavings.
HUSKY	Invasion of Sicily, July 1943
IMPERATOR	British plan to take a Norman French seaport, summer 1942
MAGNET	Build-up of US forces in Northern Ireland, 1942
MASSINGHAM	SOE base near Algiers
MODICUM	US Mission to London 1942
OLIVE	British Offensive in Italy, August 1944
OVERLORD	Liberation of Northwest Europe by Allied Forces
ROUNDHAMMER	Improved version of ROUNDUP for May 1944
ROUNDUP	Plan for landings in Northern France, 1943
SHINGLE	Landings at Anzio, Italy, January 1944
SEXTANT	Cairo Conference, November–December 1943
SLEDGEHAMMER	Emergency landing plans in northern France, 1942
SUPER-GYMNAST	The final version of operation GYMNAST
SYMBOL	Casablanca Conference, January 1943
TORCH	Landings in French North Africa, 8 November 1942
WORKSHOP	Invasion of Pantelleria, June 1943

Conference Code-names

ARCADIA	First Washington Conference, December 1941, January 1942
EUREKA	Teheran Conference, November 1943
QUADRANT	First Quebec Conference, August 1943
RIVIERA	Argentia, Newfoundland Conference, 1941
SEXTANT	Cairo Conference, November–December 1943
SYMBOL	Casablanca Conference, January 1943
TRIDENT	Second Washington Conference, May 1943

Introduction

The Anglo–American Coalition

While the following study approaches certain controversial aspects of Anglo–American Second World War negotiations with a sense of 'mental self-liberation from the certain knowledge of their outcome',[1] it proposes to rectify distortions in the literature. This narrative is a critical study of the Anglo–American relationship between 1938 and 1944. It is primarily concerned with the unifying and destructive forces that affected the partners, as they searched for a strategic solution to the war in Europe. Focusing upon the series of high-level strategy meetings which took place from 1938 onward, there is revealed a growing divergence of strategic thought, a diminishment of mutual trust, and an awareness of unforeseen cultural barriers. An increasingly questionable negotiating process failed to match established civilian negotiations and codes of conduct or to produce comparable results. Further analysis highlights the interplay between the major participants within the civilian–military administrative structures in both countries. These dynamic structures, although not completely created by President Franklin D. Roosevelt and Prime Minister Winston S. Churchill, were shaped to an appreciable extent by these men. Roosevelt's and Churchill's methods of leadership are compared and contrasted, their personal relationship investigated. It is argued that the 'special relationship' between these two major political figures and their civilian–military establishments was a public relations myth whose intensity varied with time. Inherent American suspiciousness of British strategic intentions is seen as a major factor demonstrating against it, in spite of the Axis threat. Anglo–American tensions are disclosed and assessed with regard to clandestine warfare, special operations and rearming the French. The strategic divergence which culminated in the ANVIL debate reached its crescendo in July 1944 and marked the end of Britain's coalition dominance. ANVIL, the invasion of southern France, is examined, not only for its operational value, but as the embodiment, instrument and termination-point of the Anglo–American strategic conflict. Clearly, despite British and American aberrations, which included attempts to dominate the coalition, an Allied victory was obtained.

The ANVIL debate was a part of this greater controversy in which the search for an agreed, effective, war-winning strategy predominated. The coalition was disrupted by both the disunity and controversy within the American executive branch, which confounded and delayed British attempts to reach an expeditious, co-ordinated and mutually acceptable global strategy. During the early phases of the alliance, the Americans, suffering from a disorganized executive branch, failed to present a unified and coherent policy. Ill prepared, the virtual antithesis of British bureaucratic competence, the Americans undermined their negotiating possibilities. During early negotiations, American suspicions were frequently aroused when the British treated their new ally as a junior partner.[2]

Churchill's influence over Roosevelt determined Allied operations from 1942 to 1943, because the president, skeptical of General George C. Marshall's recommendation to invade northwestern Europe in 1943, sought other options.[3] Churchill and the British Chiefs of Staff (COS), haunted by the memories of the Great War's attritional battles, tried to protect their limited manpower from a direct collision with the Germans again after Dunkirk, preferring to attack the Italians in the Mediterranean instead. Having been driven from the Continent and losing her principal ally, France, Britain's options were severely limited between 1940 and 1941. Britain fought on alone, almost by reflex, without any rational prospect of final victory.

However, the American chiefs were opposed to Britain's tangential, 'soft-underbelly', 'closing the ring' approach to waging war.[4] They would seek and destroy the German Army in northwestern France once Western Hemispheric defence was assured. Feeling that Mediterranean military side-shows would only delay this purpose, the Americans grudgingly sanctioned British strategy, but remained wary of British imperial designs.[5]

John Erhman ascertained that, 'the area of Anglo–American consent remained larger than the area of dispute, and that, even when differing, the partners remained closely tied to each other.'[6] Erhman's assessment underestimates the partnership's insufficiencies that compromised its strategy and operations. The allied relationship was a marriage of expediency, more of a coalition than a 'grand alliance'. Alliances and coalitions are not the same thing, even though the terms are often used interchangeably.[7] 'An alliance is a more formal arrangement for broad, long-term objectives between two or more nations. A coalition is an informal agreement for common action.'[8]

> Necessity drives nations to form coalitions, as going it alone normally imposes serious limitations. Individual nations are usually insufficiently capable of addressing a given threat. Mobilization resources or time [sic] may not be available, and few factors contribute to public legitimacy like a coalition effort.[9]

Nor was it an entente, a friendly understanding between states, because that relates to a casualness and graciousness unheard of in wartime. One British official, stationed in Washington, wrote, 'Britain and America are partners, but they are also rivals, each anxious to prove that its views on policy, indeed its way of life is superior to that of the other. It is this element of competition which distinguishes the partnership.'[10]

Problems such as conflicting national interests, customary spheres of influence and historical balances of power, threatened collision between the two allied protagonists.[11] German Field Marshal Erwin Rommel said:

> A war of alliance always causes difficulty and friction between the allies, as each country tries to work for its own ends rather than the other's. The right thing in these circumstances is to air all differences openly and not to cover them with a cloak of silence.[12]

Both parties assumed that revelation would lead to further discord and loss of power, rather than closer collaboration, thus the assumption that hidden agendas existed. To the extent that an Anglo–American 'special relationship' existed, it was based on a common threat, not on sentiment. Although comrades in arms, their 'special relationship' was viewed as a 'common-law alliance',[13] that eventually revealed all the stresses of any protracted, intimate undertaking, however global in scope.

Another issue demanding attention is the correlation between the ascending power of one partner and the declining power of the other, the recognition of their changing roles and how that influenced strategy. Lt. General Sir Frederick Morgan, Assistant Chief of Staff at Supreme Headquarters Allied Expeditionary Force (SHAEF) wrote,

> As a British officer of SHAEF, serving an American Chief, I was well placed to watch the distressing drift apart, the growing impatience on American part with British bombast and bland assumption of superiority in so many fields. While on the British side there appeared all the evidence of a growing inferiority complex, jealousy of lavish American resources of all kinds and reluctance to acknowledge the scale of American achievement.[14]

At the administrative level, the managerial bureaus responsible for the allocation of resources (production and logistics), which proliferated within the American bureaucracy, performed well. Marshall remarked after the war, 'that it was the most complete unification of military effort ever achieved by two allied nations.'[15]

His assessment was disputed by General Montgomery, C-in-C British 21st Army Group, who wrote to Field Marshal Alan Brooke, Chief of the Imperial General Staff (CIGS), during the summer of 1944, 'that the British officers at SHAEF must realize that in addition to being good allied chaps, they must demonstrate definite loyalties to their side of the house; and on our side of the house, we must all pull together.'[16] Brooke kept a diary for most of the war, which summed up his doubts concerning the Americans, 'My God! What psychological complications war leads to! ... I am tired to death with humanity and by all its pettiness. Will we learn to "love our allies as ourselves"?! I doubt it.'[17]

1 Introductory Strategic Talks

A co-operative strategy, aimed at defeating Germany and Italy first, characterized the Anglo–American position when and if the United States entered the war. One historian labeled the 'Germany-first' approach the most important single strategic concept of the Second World War.[1] The position was expressed in a paper, *ABC-1*, produced by both parties at informal secret American–British conversations held in Washington, from January through March 1941. Both countries agreed that it was essential to co-ordinate joint action to meet and eliminate the German threat to the security of the North Atlantic and the British Isles. Clinging to their neutrality, the Americans proclaimed the paper to be hypothetical and non-binding in nature. Moreover, they insisted that the paper simply contained the force of 'professional predictability', and should not to be construed as a blueprint for future political commitments.[2] One of the officers defending this position was General Stanley D. Embick.

To Dissent or to Obstruct

Embick was General Marshall's senior advisor on strategy; as his pessimism about Britain's ability to survive increased, he objected to any British 'Germany-first' plans leading to operations in North Africa and the eastern Mediterranean.[3] An individual with 45 years of experience in national policy, diplomacy and grand strategy, he preferred to appease rather than oppose Hitler. In 1938, as Deputy Chief of Staff, he distributed and promoted the ideas of a prominent conservative anti-war and anti-military organization, The National Council for Prevention of War. Embick was a dissenter, but it is one thing to dissent, and quite another to obstruct.[4] During an interview in 1968, Eisenhower said, 'When they say that soldiers ought to make political decisions ... then they're showing their ignorance of what democratic government is. This is the kind of thing that makes Napoleons and Hitlers.'[5] Embick considered a general European war a colossal blunder and in April 1941 opposed an American declaration of war, because he thought that Britain's plight was less serious than his colleagues believed. Sent to Britain in 1941, he considered Churchill an amateur strategist, incapable of concentrating on the main issue. Although Marshall was less hostile, he was wary of dealing with a strategy motivated by British political interests.

Embick's eminent position on the Joint Strategic Survey Committee (JSSC) gave him a new and powerful forum for expression of his anglophobic views. Given extraordinary responsibilities and powers as advisors to the Joint Chiefs of Staff (JCS), Embick and the JSSC produced a series of papers which constituted the eventual JCS position on virtually every wartime issue.

Concurrently, within the General Staff Division (GSD), referred to as Marshall's 'Washington Command Post', the Operations Division's (OPD) Strategy and Policy Group (S & P), called the 'Brain Trust', formed similar views after studying British strategy and policy in the Mediterranean. S & P members served on various planning committees, but its head, General Albert C. Wedemeyer, Embick's son-in-law, was Marshall's Chief Strategic Planner from June 1942 to October 1943. Wedemeyer, a US Army graduate of the German *Kriegsakademie* in 1938, shared many of Embick's views. 'While not a member of the "America First" Committee he was "in accord" with many of its views, and immediately before Pearl Harbor found himself suspected of leaking the famous "Victory Program" he had helped author to the isolationist *Chicago Tribune.*'[6]

Both officers were representative of a large clique within the armed forces with similar beliefs. For example, they were convinced that Britain did not intend to invade Europe and defeat Germany, but would seek control of the Mediterranean in accordance with her traditional balance of power policy.[7] Perhaps the most comprehensive memo on British strategy and policy came from the Joint War Plans Committee (JWPC) in 1943 which reorganized and synthesized the various American viewpoints. It accused Britain of maintaining her world position at the expense of other countries, including the US. These ideas surfaced in statements and notes by individual chiefs, and in Stimson's presentations and warnings to Roosevelt. In August, Marshall offered his 'personal opinion' of British strategy contained in a 'formidable' S & P paper emphasizing that Anglo–American strategic divergence reflected very deep differences in national character and interests. Searching for other fundamental causes, it found these in the differing geographic positions, national structures and basis of power of the two countries.

Unaltered in their beliefs, Embick and Wedemeyer concluded that a slow, dispersed war of attrition centering on the Mediterranean would restore British control of that sea and avoid heavy casualties inherent in a cross-Channel attack. They believed that the British might attempt to delay a German defeat at Russian expense. If this policy were attempted, the Russians, fighting the bulk of the German Army, would surely have registered the strongest possible protest against Britain's behavior.[8] In accordance with Embick, Colonel Joseph McNarney, of the Army Operations Division (OPD) and Rear Admiral Richmond K. Turner, Navy Director of War Plans, collaborated to write the following,

> It is to be expected that proposals of the British representatives will have been drawn up with chief regard for the support of the British Commonwealth. Never absent from British minds are their post-war interests, commercial and military. We should likewise safeguard our own eventual interests.[9]

Although no plans were drawn up to involve American land forces in a major offensive against Germany, their build-up and employment was envisioned. The Joint Board, a corporate organization of American military chiefs, approved *ABC-1* on 14 May and sought the president's signature. Like Churchill, Roosevelt returned the paper unsigned, but the movement of approximately 100,000 men to Britain was not affected. *ABC-1* became the foundation upon which all future Anglo–American strategic meetings were based, despite an underlying American distrust of the British position.

Admiral King's Pacific Preoccupation

The incident that propelled the American 'Germany-first' strategy towards a coherent operational plan occurred at a meeting attended by both Marshall and King on 18 February 1942. King, 'who harbored a storm within him',[10] seeking increased action against the Japanese, requested that the Army provide ground and air forces to garrison a number of small Pacific islands. Marshall objected, predicting that if he acceded to King's request, it would dilute the Army's Atlantic strategy, minimize his influence with the president and weaken Army and Army Air Force personnel at the desired point of concentration. Moreover, King's proposal would subvert Chief of the Army Air Corps General Henry Arnold's attempts to create a separate air force.[11] Marshall viewed the Army's future interlocked with 'Germany-first'.[12]

Concerned that this request could lead to a full scale Army commitment in the Pacific,[13] Marshall demanded that General Dwight D. Eisenhower, as the new head of the War Plans Division, formulate a strategic analysis. He responded with a position paper, writing:

> We must differentiate sharply and definitely between those things whose current accomplishment in the several theaters over the world is 'necessary' to the ultimate defeat of the Axis, as opposed to those which are merely 'desirable' because of their effect in facilitating such a defeat.[14]

Defence of the Western Hemisphere

Many senior American and British officers having made a similar diagnosis, were fearful that the previous arrangements as expressed in *ABC-1* and listed in *RAINBOW 5*, a blueprint for defeating Germany first, which included an aggressive plan extending American security frontiers beyond the continental limits of the United States, would be abandoned in practice. Since the nineteenth century, the security and defence of the Western Hemisphere had always been a major consideration when defining American military policy. Even though the German Army was unable to cross the Channel to invade England in 1940, American planners were certain that it had the capability of crossing the Atlantic to invade the Americas.[15] Obsessed with this apocalyptic vision, the planners, reflecting traditional 'isolationist' doctrine, sought a line of defensive outposts to form a bulwark against a Nazi invasion: England and Iceland in the north and Dakar in the south. In 1941, General 'Vinegar' Joe Stilwell was ordered to plan a pre-emptive strike against the Azores, formative island links in the partially completed hemispheric defence. Distorted American perceptions of German designs on North and West Africa increased the already existing anxiety in Washington. Only 1,800 nautical miles separated Dakar from Natal, Brazil, a potential target for German air attack and airborne invasion.[16] The suppression of potential fifth column activities, Axis influence in, and German expeditions to South America, were subjects addressed by the planners.[17] Moreover, the Army doubted whether it could prevent a massive build-up of enemy ground and air forces in various collaborationist South American nations that would precede an Axis invasion of the US via Mexico or the Gulf and Atlantic coasts. It even considered plans to occupy Dutch Guinea a possibility, if only to protect the flow of Guinean refined oil, 95 percent of which was sent to the eastern American seaboard. To the British, American planners were obsessed with Latin America.[18]

Even after the Pearl Harbor attack, the American public desired hemispheric isolation, the majority of whom supported the war effort with an attitude of 'rational resignation'. Of the people questioned in a polling sample 45 percent admitted they did not know what the United States was fighting for; 25 percent of the population favored an immediate end to the war with Germany through negotiation, and 10 percent on any terms. Of those polled 59 percent were willing to fight an all-out war against Japan.[19] Many Americans were unwilling to support active military ground operations overseas. The President realized that his words were not enough to galvanize the public's martial spirit and its willingness to mobilize. Only military action focused on the German threat would reduce public indifference and increase its participation; if not, the whole war effort was imperiled. Projecting American power outward would have a twofold purpose: first, the occupation of West Africa and the Atlantic islands by American troops would prevent any hypothetical German seizure of those same areas; and second, it would also put the public actively in the war. Broadcasting to the nation on 9 December 1941, the President said, '…a German attack against Algiers or Morocco opens the way to a German attack against South America, and the [Panama] Canal.'[20]

President Roosevelt and Secretary of War, Henry L. Stimson recognized that the continued existence of Britain as a world power was essential to the security of the United States and that Britain's naval power secured the Atlantic frontier against aggressive German and Italian foreign policies. Roosevelt's willingness to co-operate with the British began as early as January 1938, was a result of a naval incident the previous year between the Japanese and the Americans in China, in which the *USS Panay,* a US gunboat, was sunk. These Anglo–American Naval conversations laid the foundation for later military co-operation, although they failed to achieve any integrated strategy.[21] During August and September 1940, further London conversations established the Anglo–American Standardization of Arms Committee.[22] Britain's declaration of war led Roosevelt to approach Prime Minister Neville Chamberlain's government, but only Churchill demonstrated any interest in the president's willingness to exceed the limits of co-operation by a neutral state. Churchill reckoned that the US would enter the war on the side of Britain in due course.[23] The Prime Minister received additional support from American Admiral, Harold R. Stark, Chief of Naval Operations, who warned his superiors against a 'Japanese first' policy in his 'Plan Dog' memorandum: '… if Britain wins decisively against Germany, we could win everywhere; but if she loses, the problem confronting us would be very great; and, while we might "not lose everywhere", we might possibly, not "win" anywhere.'[24]

Further, he objected to an 'unlimited' commitment in the Pacific, that would place severe limitations on aid to the British and the Atlantic defence. He feared that even a 'limited' commitment in the Pacific could turn 'unlimited', if only as a result of public impatience. Once this happened, the Pacific would take precedence, undermining American strategic emphasis.[25] Germany's defeat, therefore, would be primarily dependent upon the efforts of Britain and Russia, a daunting prospect. In the light of subsequent events, Stark was prescient.

American planners envisioned sending task forces overseas to co-operate with Britain and France in a war against Germany and Italy. As an offensive strategy, based on *ABC-1* and in agreement with the Joint US–Canada War Plan 2 (*ABC-22*), the first Army draft of *RAINBOW 5* was completed on 7 April 1941, and submitted to the Joint Board for approval by the Joint Planning Committee on 21 April.[26] Directed against the European section of the Axis, forces were to be increased in preparation for a predetermined Mobilization Day (M Day), which might precede a declaration of war or hostile acts.

In mid-June, 1941, instead of assaulting the Iberian Peninsula, invading North Africa and threatening the distant reaches of the Western Hemisphere, Adolph Hitler's armies attacked Russia. His action relieved the Americans of any immediate threat to the Western Hemisphere, lifted the danger of an invasion of the British Isles until 1942, and improved Britain's position in the Middle East. Hitler's attack on Russia stimulated Stimson to write in his diary on 5 March 1942 that

> Sending an overwhelming force to the British Isles and threatening an attack on the Germans in France; that this was the proper and orthodox line of our help in the war as it had always been recognized and that it would now have the effect of giving Hitler two fronts to fight on, if it could be done in time while the Russians were still in. It would also heavily stimulate British sagging morale.[27]

But what had been the preparations needed to reach these goals?

The American Victory Program: (The Brief of Strategic Concept & AWPD/1)

On 9 July 1941, Roosevelt requested that the Secretaries of War and Navy, Henry L. Stimson and Frank Knox estimate the overall production requirements needed to defeat America's potential enemies.[28] By 11 September the Joint Planning Committee of the Army and Navy's Joint Board submitted a strategic estimate, which provided a basis for future military production. Moreover, it asserted that Britain could only defeat Germany with American military participation, a reflection of Stimson's view; Germany was considered the prime enemy, and once defeated, Japan would retreat from the territory she conquered. The Board had no faith in the British idea that aerial bombardment could defeat Germany, concluding that only land armies could finally win wars, as an integral part of combined arms.[29]

Although the President had turned to Marshall to place America on a war-footing, a resourceful American supply policy was lacking. British competition for scarce resources and its demands for American assistance provoked an acerbic diary comment from Colonel Orlando Ward, Secretary General Staff: 'We are like a pointer pup. If someone with a swagger stick and a British accent speaks to us, we lie down on the ground and wiggle.'[30] Roosevelt's highly personal style of administrating included three small cliques within the White House whose advisors were not necessarily qualified to solve the major military supply problems. Ward promptly noted in his diary, 'GB [Great Britain] has asked Santa Claus for equipment totaling about 25 billion dollars. It is tragic that we can't shape our course on a long-range, clearly-thought out program.'[31] Adding six weeks later, 'The story of the British fifth column and how it captured our Govt. without anyone knowing it will be amazing indeed in the light of future history.'[32]

Concurrently, some British military leaders in Washington had concluded that America was not only utterly unprepared for war, but doubted its will to fight. This was not startling news to Marshall, who not only recognized the political divisions within the country, but had struggled to reorganize the Army since his accession as Chief of Staff in 1939. Marshall, having witnessed the Army's chaotic attempts to mobilize in 1917, hoped that the mobilization and training plans he presently envisioned would go far to reduce this disorder and dispel British prejudice. 'Gradualists' within the Army hierarchy were beginning to embrace the tenets of *ABC-1* and *RAINBOW 5*, which he advocated. They were also separating themselves from the isolationist position of Embick and his devotees.[33] The Chief of Staff was under no illusions. The White House cabal was seeking greater control of economic mobilization, which, if accomplished, would curtail War Department autonomy. To limit the demands by Britain, Russia, and China for American arms, which at times seemed excessive and unrealistic, Marshall's advisors and planners advocated the establishment of an agency in which the acquisition and disbursement of munitions would be placed under military control. Marshall clearly defined the need for a unified command over war orders, which, in part, would effectively assist the American Army to rearm in timely fashion.[34] The establishment of a central military agency would eliminate the chaotic 'blank-check' policy of supply as espoused by the White House. In a letter written to the Secretaries of the Army and Navy, Roosevelt stated, 'I wish you would explore the munitions and the mechanical equipment of all types which in your opinion would be required to exceed by an appropriate amount that available to our potential enemies.'[35]

Marshall felt that the British view of American participation was in the area of war production alone. If the Office of Production and Management was placed in charge of American production, the Army was under threat of not only becoming another claimant for its nation's arms, but a competitor against Britain and Russia as well. To neutralize this threat and counter the British effect upon White House thinking, Marshall, growing impatient with British arrogance, demanded a clear, orderly plan for the Army to follow in the months ahead. This and other deeper priorities, discussed between American military chiefs, were never shared with the British during the war; as Marshall stated, 'We discussed political things more than anything else ... But we were careful, exceedingly careful, never to discuss them with the British, and from that they took the count that we didn't observe these things at all.'[36] He reasoned that politics was the domain of the heads of government, but strategy was based upon policy. Therefore, ideas and assumptions could be excluded from Allied military discussions.

Recognizing the enormity of his task to transform a small pre-war army into a world-wide effective fighting machine in 18 months, Marshall assigned Major Albert C. Wedemeyer of the War Plans Division in July to produce a position paper on the subject. The paper, 'Brief of Strategic Concept', suggested that the two existing plans, that is, the inappropriate 'Protective Mobilization Plan' and its supporting 'Industrial Mobilization Plan of 1939' were outmoded and had to be replaced. Moreover, the administration needed to be provided with current data and estimates required for the mobilization of manpower, industry and shipping to defeat the Germans. Further, based on this information, these goals were to be achieved without causing the internal economy to suffer. The survey was not politically motivated by the president who, according to Stephen E. Ambrose, was more interested in post-war markets than full mobilization.[37] On the contrary, the president sought a formula by which victory could be achieved in the most cost-effective way, although he compounded the problem by failing to make distinctions between American and Allied supply priorities during the spring of 1941. Wedemeyer, the paper's author, in collaboration with personnel from the Navy and Army Air Corps, speculated that if Germany defeated Russia in 1941, Britain faced invasion and defeat in the spring of 1943, at the same time that American mobilization would reach its practical level of effectiveness. If Russia could hold on, he opined, Britain would survive, because American industrial capacity, productivity, and military forces, of a size and quality described and recommended in his paper would achieve its goals. The recommended estimates therein, combined with those of Britain's, would suffice to defeat the Germans.

Using the 'Brief of Strategic Concept' as its foundation, the paper, produced as a booklet in conjunction with the Army Air Forces estimate, 'AWPD/1', briefly defined the Army's approved strategy with regard to war plans, geo-politics, military philosophy and Army infrastructure. The 'Brief of Strategic Concept' and 'AWPD/1' originally lacked compatibility, because of their divergent views concerning the final battle of concentration and victory through air power. Wedemeyer accommodated both points of view in his final version, in an attempt to satisfy the proponents of either side, since there was too much at stake to do otherwise. With regard to British and American strategic theories, based on *ABC-1*, they varied for an additional reason, at one important point: the same American Army planners believed that the German Army had to be defeated on the battlefield and its will to fight broken in combat by future Allied armies; the British did not, relying instead on an overall German collapse, as defined in 'closing the ring'.[38]

Wedemeyer estimated manpower requirements, the probable size and composition of task forces, the possible theaters of operations, and the probable dates at which forces would be committed. 2,500 ships would transport five million men overseas. By 1945, bombers would have a 4,000 mile radius of action. Although criticized by segments of the tabloid press, it was popularly called the Victory Program upon completion in September 1941.[39] Henceforth, it served as a fundamental, albeit flexible,[40] planning document in preparing the country for war.[41] Matched against the reality of 1944, manpower proposals erred in three categories:

1. the men needed for the 'divisional slice' (the troops in support of the infantry);
2. provision for individual infantry replacements;
3. the amount of armored formations, anti-aircraft artillery, and tank-destroyers required.[42]

Originally, Marshall conceived of an US Army consisting of over 200 infantry divisions, but for political, economic and strategic reasons, the great expansion of the Army Air Forces being one, this number was changed to approximately 85. Therefore, theater commanders were always short of infantrymen, which placed great strain upon the generals and soldiers alike. On the ground, operations would suffer and more had to be accomplished with less.

How well the Victory Program succeeded can be judged by the following assessment: before the Japanese attack, US Army trainees were using broom sticks in place of rifles, and the gross national product was $100 billion dollars. By 1943, the American 'arsenal of democracy' produced more war material than all the other belligerents combined and its military budget alone would reach $100 billion dollars. The United States would reach levels of production within the next two years that were scarcely believable, for example, 45 percent of the world's arms, nearly 50 percent of the world's goods, and 66 percent of all the ships afloat.[43] In 1955, the Army staff calculated that Lend-Lease had equipped the equivalent of 101 US type divisions to eight of its Allies including the British Empire.[44] Japanese Admiral Soroku Yamamoto remarked after Pearl Harbor, 'We have awakened a sleeping giant and filled him with a terrible resolve.'[45]

Economics, the Victory Program and Lend-Lease

The battle for an acceptable Lend-Lease program was fought between the Secretary of State Cordell Hull and Secretary of the Treasury Henry

Morgenthau; the former demanded dissolution of British Empire's economic preference and economic nationalism, the latter demanded the defeat of Hitler's Germany without economic extortion. Morganthau saw Britain's fight against Hitler as just compensation for Lend-Lease.[46] Hull, as an anti-colonialist, wanted Britain to post $2 to $3 billion dollars of collateral in writing, believing that Britain possessed $18 billion dollars in Imperial wealth.[47] Both sides represented a portion of the president's thinking, but he replaced Morganthau with Hull during the final Lend-Lease negotiations. Instead of an outright subsidy for an ally admittedly fighting America's war, the Roosevelt administration wanted continuing assurance that Britain was fighting as hard as it could. As Britain's liquidity dwindled, her ability to buy arms on a 'cash and carry' basis diminished. Roosevelt indicated that Britain was ready to sell an estimated $7 billion dollars worth of privately owned British shares in American companies to continue her fight for survival. Both Secretaries and other cabinet members ardently supported the sale and English officials were advised to sell such direct investments as Shell Oil, Lever Brothers, and so on. Courtaulds, whose subsidiary, American Viscose produced 60 percent of all American rayon, and accounted for half of its parent company's income, was pressured by the American government to relinquish its control. Sold at a loss in order to protect American nominal national security, it was the American government who benefited financially.[48]

During the Lend-Lease negotiations, the Americans felt that Britain's policies had led to depression and war and these had to be changed to suit the American image. Calculations indicate that Britain received $27 billion dollars worth of Lend-Lease aid from the US , plus cash payments, and Britain, in her turn, provided America with $6 billion worth of Reverse Lend-Lease, a rarely mentioned amount. The official exchange rate then was four dollars to the pound, breakfast cereal cost just over three pence and petrol about nine.[49]

If Roosevelt fought for an improved post-war world, both he and Congress referred to more immediate and tangible matters, failing to admit to their economic exploitation of the British. Roosevelt delayed enactment of Lend-Lease policy, which increased the sense of drift,[50] while the British were vainly avoiding the barter of 'Imperial-Preference' in exchange for money and goods. Marshall awaited the formalization of Lend-Lease and its effect on the Victory Program, to which the Army's growth was tied. If he were successful, both programs would provide the US and its Allies with a substantive method of achieving maximum economic productivity and military effectiveness. Approved on 11 March, authorized Lend-Lease contracts served to establish major military production lines well before America went to war. Industry generally refused to convert to war production unless some sort of guarantee sustained production. Lend-Lease provided such a guarantee, and the War

Department found that an important segment of industry was already mobilized by 7 December 1941.[51] Speaking for Marshall, General Leonard T. Gerow, Chief of the War Plans Division said in 1941, 'Wars are won on sound strategy implemented by well-trained forces which are adequately and effectively equipped. The ultimate question was where military operations should be conducted in order to produce decisive results.'[52]

A Special Relationship

Churchill needed to produce decisive results too. Considering the need for a 'special relationship', as a politician he knew that American economic and defence interests were part reflections of its sovereignty. During 1940, Churchill failed in his attempts to convince the French defeatists of Britain's determination to fight on alone. Both American Ambassador to Great Britain Joseph Kennedy and Foreign Secretary Lord E. F. Halifax doubted Britain's ability to continue the fight at whatever the cost. Halifax wanted to ascertain Hitler's terms for ending the war after Dunkirk and Kennedy remained skeptical of Britain's chances of defeating Germany. Prior to Pearl Harbor, most Americans were convinced that Britain and France would defeat Germany without their intervention. Arrayed against Churchill was this linking of events and attitudes, of appeasing inclinations and isolationist bias, and military disasters. Against this panoply emerged the substance of Churchill's greatness, the recognition that the US held the key to Britain's survival. He knew that it would not be 'business as usual', if Hitler's attempts at world domination succeeded. To continue the fight alone required courage; to admit to reality, however distasteful, demanded mental tenacity and vigor. Unlike Chamberlain before him, he knew when to stop appeasing Hitler's insatiable appetite for conquest, but like Chamberlain, Churchill realized that the Americans would drive a hard economic bargain for their aid. Even if it included becoming an American warrior-satellite, in the real world, there would be no bugles, banners or payment for the months Britain stood alone, stretched to the breaking point. Rather than surrender, he went to Roosevelt with empty pockets. John Charmley, author of *Churchill's Grand Alliance* disparages Churchill, describing him as lacking resolve, 'putting a spine in a jelly fish',[53] because, according to Charmley, the prime minister's preoccupation with being free weakened his negotiating position and diminished his bargaining power with Roosevelt – that he gave 'away the store'. Charmley considered Churchill a sentimentalist and a dupe and then recants, but the inferential damage is done. He writes further of Churchill joining with Roosevelt and the Democrats, as an act 'of putting his eggs in one basket', rather than giving the Republicans and Senator Taft equal time.

It was the senator who said, 'Even the collapse of Britain is preferred to participation for the rest of our lives in European wars. Americans ought to determine their course entirely on what they believe to be the best for the US, whether nations like it or or disapprove of it.' Taft once declared 'that a Communist victory would be far more dangerous than a Fascist one.' [54] Charmley, by quoting the senator, inadvertently supports Churchill's astuteness and choice of remaining aloof from the isolationist Republicans; Charmley, like Taft, fails to remember that Churchill was at war with Hitler, not with Stalin. Churchill's appeals to Roosevelt were 'a matter of life and death.' [55] Charmley minimizes Roosevelt's predicament, and accuses him of wanting something for nothing, the British fleet. The president wanted it to join with the US fleet, if Britain were defeated in 1940; even then, war was to be avoided.[56] Unfortunately, Roosevelt could not overcome the mood of the country. However, to allow a fleet to fall into German hands was unacceptable; the Anglo–French sea battle at Mers el Kebir in 1940 and the scuttling of the French fleet at Toulon in 1942 are prime examples of the actions taken. Bradley Smith, author of *The Ultra Magic Deals*, discounts Charmley's description of Churchill as a man without negotiating clout:

> Anything approximating a 'buddy theory' of Anglo–American relations must be used with great caution, however. Churchill though desperate for American aid in 1940, was not prepared even then to play with an open deck or give away the store. Much of the crucial secret data about Britain's war effort was held back from the Americans in 1940–41, and there was little inclination to give way on what the British government saw as fundamentals simply in hope of securing American assistance.[57]

The Americans demanded British gold, 'new-world' bases and scientific secrets in payment for armaments; these assets were held hostage to protracted Anglo–American military trade negotiations, while Britain needed interim finance policies, on which its survival depended. Churchill addressed these concerns to Roosevelt with self-imposed restraint on numerous occasions, such as 'I am convinced that the assistance from the US on a far larger scale ... is essential, if we and you are to escape disaster, and we are fighting for our lives.'[58] London officials frequently assumed that a mutual identity of interests existed, to which the Americans were not always willing to agree. The British, dependent upon American goodwill focused intensely on the US, but the reverse was not nearly as vital. Discrepancies of strength and need are easily recognizable between nations.

Aware of Roosevelt's sympathy for Britain and his sensitivity to the mood of the American public in 1941, Churchill mused that, if Congress were asked to choose between peace or war, a lengthy three-month debate would follow.[59] A composite war and post-war strategy was needed to deal with Franco's Spain, Japanese Pacific expansion, commercial competition in Argentina, commodity arrangements, merchant shipping and civil aviation. For the British, it seemed as if the European war was once again enabling the New World to 'fatten on the follies of the Old.'[60]

Regrettably for both countries, as the president shifted between indecision and provocation, Churchill appealed for America's participation. Measured against accomplishment, Churchill could claim little, although he believed that the partnership had to be maintained at all costs with other considerations subordinated to it. He stated, 'that a complete understanding between Britain and the US outweighed all else',[61] and he told Eden, 'My whole system is based upon my partnership with Roosevelt.'[62]

Churchill believed he had created and furthered a special and personal alliance. This tie was not without discord, it became increasingly one-sided, and was subjected to the same pressures as the rest of international relations. For Britain to survive, Churchill needed to create and idealize an American relationship of mythic proportions. The result was a cobbled together 'special relationship', an attempt to improve Anglo–American public relations when little evidence existed to support it. Reporting to the War Cabinet, after Placentia Bay, he proclaimed that the president had ordered the US Navy to shoot German submarines on sight. Since no evidence exists proving that any order was issued, Churchill's statement smacked more of 'wish-fulfillment' than actuality.[63] He wrote to the president, 'Our friendship is the rock on which I build for the future of the world, so long as I am one of the builders.'[64]

Policy-makers in Washington did not attempt such intimacy, because British policy displayed short-sightedness, arrogance, even duplicity; Britain was needed for America's safety, not for its survival. Some British officials had warned as early as 1940 that too close an embrace with America would be akin to exchanging one master for another.[65] Churchill's 'special relationship', lacking a quorum of adherents, could not overcome British or American self-interest regarding modifications in military strategy, protectionist trading policies, spheres of influence, and colonial independence.[66] Assessing British prerogatives of empire, Roosevelt felt that, 'We will have more trouble with Great Britain after the war than we are having with Germany now.'[67]

Prior to America's entry into the war, American sensitivity in defence of its national interests took priority over any real or imagined kinship with Britain. When British warships severely damaged the German pocket cruiser, *Graf Spee*, during a sea battle off Uruguay in December 1939, the American State Department protested Britain's western hemispheric intrusion.[68] A small American minority encouraged co-operation on a personal basis, believing that the recognition of an earlier common heritage might lessen mutual distrust. However, Brooke, as CIGS, deduced that the manifestations of commonality were more of a hindrance than a benefit when both sides conferred.[69] Dill, assigned to Washington as Head of the British Joint Staff Mission in January 1942, was the exception. Marshall not only considered Dill to be the guarantor against the American perception of Churchill's imperial pretensions and strategic prejudices, but a facilitator in any forthcoming combined negotiations. Brooke described Dill's position as one that combined the duties of a deputy ambassador and deputy minister of defence. Marshall believed that Dill's search for an acceptable 'combined' global strategy, as a member of the JSM and the CCS, was never fully appreciated by Churchill. He reminded the prime minister of this in writing when Dill died in November 1944: 'I doubt if you or your Cabinet associates fully realize the loss you have suffered.'[70]

Roosevelt and his advisors defined their relationship with the British as a combative kinship. The popular image of a British ambassador neatly illustrated many of the unsavory qualities which millions of Americans held in contempt: wily, polished, and thoroughly unscrupulous, seeking to disadvantage his unsuspecting American counterpart.[71] Historically, an American sense of a special relationship had been paired with tension and distrust, as a reaction to the Revolutionary War, Britain's meddling in the American Civil War and British challenges to America's expression of 'manifest destiny' during the nineteenth century. Anti-British sentiments long existed in the US, and 'twisting the lion's tail' was not only expressed by Irish-Americans.[72] Therefore, the 'special relationship' may have been nothing more than a realization that the military and socio-economic competition between the two powers had to be subordinated to one of co-operation, in view of the Axis threat.[73]

At this stage of the war, although America moved towards industrial supremacy, there existed a rough equality between the British and Americans. Even if Britain were given the tools, Churchill knew that despite his rhetoric, it could not finish the job. Considering the fears and jealousies that exist between nations of equal stature, Britain's emerging relative weakness *vis à vis* America may have evoked a brief American paternal-benevolence that furthered co-operation between the two countries. Transcending the divination of a 'special relationship' was the real sympathy expressed and the military aid offered by Roosevelt and Marshall to Churchill when British-held Tobruk fell and its garrison of 33,000 men were taken prisoner by Rommel's forces on 21 June 1942 in North Africa.[74] If Lend-Lease were considered as America's most unsordid act, a questionable evaluation, the American offer of military assistance in the Middle East, at its own expense, was the most unconditional and immediate; the prime minister was deeply touched.[75] Brooke who was present at the White House that day, wrote later, 'I remember vividly being impressed by the tact and real heartfelt sympathy which lay behind these words. There was not one word too much, not one word too little.'[76]

The fall of Tobruk was a metaphor for the balance of power tipping ominously toward Washington. Churchill was realistic enough to create a belief system, albeit with limited but acceptable credibility and appeal, to which he and others could turn in an uncomplicated way. The title 'special relationship' was simple enough to cover aspects of personal relations, bordering on informality and transparancy, within the war's bureaucracies. Robert Sherwood, one of Roosevelt's speech-writer's, labeled the relationship a 'common-law alliance', joined by an unsigned integration of effort.[77] Nothing could compare to the color, emotion and connectedness that the term 'special relationship' evoked.

Churchill likened it to a love-affair between two people. They could be perceived visually, up close, a strong point in selling the idea. He suggested, 'No lover ever studied the whims of his mistress as I did those of Roosevelt.'[78] Two great democratic states, teeming with millions of inhabitants, were reduced to one loving couple. Churchill, his eyes twinkling, summarized America's change in status from peace to war: 'Oh that is the way we talked to her when we were wooing her, now that she is in the harem we talk to her quite differently!'[79] Churchill added a metaphorical variation to his original theme. The Prime Minister's nineteenth-century Romanticism described the relationship as a Grand Alliance, which he compared favorably with that of Marlborough and Prince Eugene of Austria. [80]

When addressing the House of Commons in 1940, Churchill alluded to the informality of Sherwood's Common-Law Alliance, 'These two great organizations of the English-speaking democracies, the British Empire and the United States, will have to be somewhat mixed up together in some of their affairs for mutual and general advantage.'[81] Nevertheless, he repeatedly returned to his favorite theme, marriage with all its vicissitudes. He told the King that after months of 'going out', Britain and America were now married.[82] Churchill's stratagem is poignant because the Foreign Office and the British Embassy in Washington were fighting rearguard actions in defence of position and prestige which was no longer supported by requisite power. Without this essential ingredient of successful diplomacy, relying on experience and maturity instead, the British discovered that their partner was more interested in tanks and gold than advice. Even if the old story that made the rounds in Whitehall at this time revealed that the two most important things in the world were 'love' and the 'special relationship', American officials were indifferent and rarely expressed the same interest. 'It was this cavalier treatment, this apparent indifference to relations with Britain that so infuriated, and the same time perplexed, those in London who were responsible for devising a British policy toward the United States.'[83]

Chief of Air Staff Sir Charles Portal, cast the relationship in a similar but more complicated mould a few years later at Casablanca. Churchill appealed to the public, Portal to the professional, 'We are in the position of a testator who wishes to leave the bulk of his fortune to his mistress. He must, however, leave something to his wife and the problem is how little in decency can he set apart for her.'[84]

This analogy relates to a conflict of resource allocation between the two major theaters of war; it distorts reality, and thus fails, because the British had little control over American resources. Portal implied that the British are the 'we' in the above. To the contrary, the Americans are the 'we', testator and wife combined, the British the mistress. The analogy may serve the additional purpose of identifying the subjective British negotiating position, that is, common-law alliances and mistresses are not recognized, and lack influence in many jurisdictions. Britain's influence declined when the enormous power and resources of the United States came to dominate the partnership.

Moreover, the idea of a 'special relationship', however ascribed, may have had more to do with British and American public morale rather than with the men who were in positions of leadership. A *Life* magazine poll revealed that Americans had no intention of fighting just to keep the British Empire intact.[85] Eisenhower wrote in January 1943,

> I am not so incredibly naïve that I do not realize that Britishers instinctively approach every military problem from the viewpoint of Empire, just as we approach them from the viewpoint of American interests. One of the constant sources of danger for us in this war is the temptation to regard as our first enemy the partner that must work with us in defeating the real enemy.[86]

Since competition, naval rivalry, tariff restrictions and war debts had almost precluded the possibility of any significant political and military co-operation, 'Churchill's idea of a lasting Anglo–American partnership ended in the dustbin of history.'[87] By 1944, not only did American infantry divisions outnumber those of the British and Canadians by a ratio of four to one in Europe, but American industry out-produced all the Allies combined. Churchill, demoted to junior partner, said, 'Up to July 1944, England had considerable say in things; after that I was conscious that it was America who made the big decisions.'[88] His comment was at variance with Neville Chamberlain's, who had expressed earlier, 'It is always best and safest to count on nothing from the Americans but words...'[89] To some extent that was true. However, the Japanese surprise attack on Pearl Harbor relieved Churchill of his immediate anxiety and deep concern for the future. He wrote, 'So we had won after all!... All the rest was merely the proper application of overwhelming force.'[90]

Inhibitors to Negotiations

Churchill's prediction of a future allied victory had little to do with the daily combined staff work required to achieve it. British and American senior officers, on whom the future of coalition policy came to rely in 1941, had the unenviable twofold task of not only achieving synthesis in negotiations, but achieving a viable working atmosphere. During the 1943 Casablanca Conference, British General John Kennedy discovered a remark in Oscar Wilde's, *The Canterville Ghost* that seemed appropriate to the discussions then in progress, in which the author suggested that the Americans and the British had everything in common except a language.[91] When British General Frederick Morgan was assigned to Eisenhower's Headquarters in early 1944 and received his first orders from the American General, he later wrote,

> But there came a terrifying shock, when his formal orders in writing were conveyed to me by his staff. It was a lovely job, no doubt, compiled according to the best War College standards. The words were all pure English but the whole document as it stood meant not a thing to any of us. So we began by getting ourselves instructed in US staff language and procedures. It is strange to think that less than twenty years ago the mutual ignorance of American and British fighting services was complete.[92]

Many senior American Army officers, were Anglophobic, anti-Empire, and isolationist; the word 'allies' was alien to them. Great War British strategy and 'generalship' were suspect and its military record inspired little confidence in 1939–1941. McNarney, considered to be an 'immediatist',[93] one who argued for increased American involvement, believed in the spring of 1941 that if Britain capitulated, the internal unrest created by this disaster could lead to a Communist take-over in the United States.[94] Like their British counterparts, the Americans were more fearful of Bolshevism than Fascism.

Most senior British Army officers were either 'pan Anglo-Saxonists' or 'Imperial isolationists'. Moreover, described as 'Easterners', in First World

War parlance, they advocated the peripheral or 'indirect approach', as the only pragmatic way of defeating the Germans.[95] Many criticized the American Army's lack of experience in modern war, discounted its officers because of limited overseas experience and questioned its performance in the First World War: the US raised large armies, but failed to equip them properly. Once fully mobilized, the Americans, defined as Westerners, planned to concentrate their unlimited resources and superior forces against the Germans, in the 'direct approach' [96]

Strategy dictated that a number of unforeseen operational and procedural points required reconciliation between the Allied services. For example, Britain described the first day of operations as 'D-Day', followed by 'D+1', 'D+2' and so on., whereas the United States used the version 'D.1', 'D.2', 'D.3', and so on. Thus there was a critical difference of one day in the operational dates. In signal procedure, the British used '12/2' to denote 12 February whereas the Americans used '2/12' to denote the same day. The British used GMT for all overseas operations, whereas the Americans used local time. When American officers of JPS Allied Force Headquarters Algiers were engaged in a planning study for post HUSKY (the 1943 invasion of Sicily) operations with their British associates, they were occasionally piqued by them:

> ... we were at work by 8 o'clock, took a short break for lunch, and knocked off at about 6:30. The British, however, began work about 9 or 9:30, took a long lunch break and worked until about 8:30. On a few occasions we would find on our desks in the morning a revised plan, prepared by the British after we had left, to conform to their views and altering our previous plan. The hassles that followed did little to promote international relations.[97]

Legal differences in contractual law arose during the 1942 London SLEDGEHAMMER meetings. Marshall surmised that the British operated on an 'agreement in principle' while the Americans depended upon the formal interpretation of written agreements. 'Agreement in principle' represented the spirit of the law and 'formal interpretation', the letter. Moreover, it can be presumed that each country had integrated its civil contractual behavior into its military ethos. British flexibility was regarded by the Americans as lacking in commitment and certainty, while American determination was regarded by the British as inflexible and over-determined. During the TORCH and ROUNDUP debates, the British soon learned that 'formal interpretation' could be just as frustrating as an 'agreement in principle'; it resulted in an American turn toward the Pacific in 1942.[98]

Sir Ralph Kilner Brown, a former British Colonel GHQ planner and retired Judge, concluded that 'agreement in principle', predicated on *caveat emptor*, 'let the buyer beware', originally applied to British real-estate law. Neither interested party was bound by the agreement, usually accomplished by oral approval and a hand-shake. As soon as agreement was arranged in writing and signed by both parties, in which both were bound by contractual liability if either defaulted, it changed from an 'agreement in principle' to one of formality. It followed that any Anglo–American strategic agreement could only bind by mutual good faith, and the usual civil financial penalties were inapplicable.[99] Specific to the April 1942 London Conference, a concerned Marshall wrote, 'Everyone agreed in principle, but many if not most of the participants held reservations regarding this or that. It would require great firmness to avoid further dispersions.'[100] During the August 1943 Quebec Conference, Brooke, frustrated by American intransigence, cited,

> ... the strain of arguing difficult problems with the Americans who try to run the war on a series of lawyer's agreements, which when once signed can never be departed from, is trying enough ... but I suppose that when working with allies, compromises, with all their evils, become inevitable.[101]

The problem with an 'agreement in principle', as in the case of SLEDGEHAMMER, was that it harbored a number of unwritten and unspoken British reservations. Since these concerns and objections were not revealed, Marshall assumed that agreement was reached. The cost of British subterfuge was high: alternate, viable strategies were delayed, trust was eroded, and the coalition weakened.

Churchill recalled the differences between the thinking processes of the two peoples in his post-war memoirs: the Americans felt that once the foundation plan had been established, all other stages would follow in sequence. The British assigned a larger importance to opportunism and improvisation, and sought to conquer as events unfolded.[102] Whatever may be laudatory and intuitive in Churchill's revelations, Eisenhower had a number of pre-D-Day administrative problems to face. Arriving in London on 16 January 1944, he spoke forthrightly to a gathering of some 50 or 60 British officers at SHAEF,

> Now I want you British to know that all Americans when they go to school learn in history that it was 'John Bull', the red-coat, who was always the nigger in the wood pile, and when Americans grew up they did not forget this teaching until they were put in contact and learned to know the British.[103]

Anglo–American Bureaucratic Structures

Each nation's administrative system varied, indicating that the search for and the acceptance and the application of a mutually agreed Anglo–American strategy would be an arduous and complex process. Article II, Section 2 of the American Constitution provided that the service Chiefs were to carry out the duties of their Commander in Chief. Under the president's direction, policy was to be determined by the civil authorities and strategy by the service chiefs. Unfortunately, effective American strategic planning was diluted by the divergent views of the Army COS, the president as C-in-C, and the absence of a much needed civilian-controlled staff-system.[104] By describing the power of C-in-C as an 'office' rather than a 'function', the Framers of the Constitution left undefined the C-in-C's specific powers and functions.[105] Unlike the British system, in which Churchill served as prime minister and minister of defence, the president could interpret his role accordingly without comparable intervention or assistance.[106]

Theoretically, the chain of command differed between the two allied systems, but in practice one aspect was common to both, that is, each system was interpreted and defined by the president and prime minister according to their idiosyncratic views of leadership, regardless of the table of organization. Both had created a small decision-making apparatus cut from his own cloth. Roosevelt rejected the idea of a war council, choosing instead to surround himself with a clique of personal advisors on war strategy set between him and his regular military advisors.[107] The service secretaries were relegated to the periphery by an executive decree, Military Order of July 1939.[108] Although each system provided for advisors and planners at every level of fact-finding, consultation, and decision-making, both Churchill and Roosevelt manipulated the system to their advantage. This is not to imply a whimsical disregard for the office of high command within the political process; it simply demonstrated that these men were flexible and inquisitive enough to maximize their own investigative and strategic techniques and abilities collaterally. As national leaders and politicians, they demanded timely responsiveness and expertise from their subordinates on demand, but on occasion they by-passed the accepted chains of command.[109] Lacking clear rules of compliance, some sensitive personalities might disapprove, but the leader's recognition of accepted political custom and practice within a war-time frame of reference kept that within reasonable limits.[110] Theoretically, there was a difference in power between the president and the prime minister. Roosevelt formulated foreign policy whenever he chose, whereas Churchill directed foreign policy subject to the decisions of the War Cabinet. However, in practice, the differences were not as great, since Churchill frequently led the Cabinet and Roosevelt often deferred to the wishes of his advisers.[111]

Without benefit of a Secretariat or a linkage to a Chiefs of Staff Committee, the president's unorthodox approach to and formulation of American military strategy was handicapped by his limited use of professional military opinion.[112] Both Marshall and Stimson were concerned, because, unlike Churchill and Brooke, Roosevelt and Marshall rarely met.[113] Misperceptions and assumptions were bound to occur between them, but until April 1942, Marshall had few alternatives to counter Roosevelt's strategic predilections and his demand for action.[114]

The American Joint Chiefs of Staff

In 1939, the exigencies of the coming war led to an expansion of the Army–Navy Joint Board, the center of American military power since 1903. On 5 July 1939, Roosevelt transferred the Board and several other military procurement agencies from the service departments to the newly established Executive Office of the President.[115] With the signing of this executive order, the Board was superseded by the JCS, but formal legalization to this structural change did not follow, adding to the jurisdictional confusion. In the end the JCS emerged by reason of semantics: whenever the services chiefs met, they simply called themselves the JCS.

Lacking authorization as a separate entity, its status and power obscure, the JCS was left to interpret its role from within, relying on presidential guidance. Permission granting the JCS to function rested simply on an exchange of letters between the president, Marshall and King. Functioning with subsidiary groups and specialized committees, it kept the president informed on all common Army and Navy matters of policy, strategy, and production. JCS presidential recommendations required unanimity and any JCS directives that set operations in motion required presidential approval.[116] Provoked by a series of military disasters in 1942, the American press and Congress clamored for a Department of National Defense under a civilian secretary reporting directly to the president. King opposed the idea, claiming that he and Marshall, in their individual capacities as service chiefs, always had authorization to confer directly with the President on all military matters.[117] Churchill gave a brief summary of Roosevelt and his Administration when he returned to Britain in early 1942:

> The President had no adequate link between his will and executive action. When the President saw the Ministerial heads of the Fighting Services, who were little more than private secretaries and responsible to him only,

> meetings were quite informal ... Harry Hopkins played a great part in helping the President to give effect to his policies...'[118]

The JCS's close identification with the president rested upon his concept of executive control. He preferred quasi-formal legal positions coupled with informal personal relationships. However, top army and navy commanders were chosen for their statesmanship and experience, in readiness for the political as well as the purely military aspects of the global situation.[119]

> The JCS became, next to the President, the single most important force in the overall conduct of the war, the level and scope of their activities far transcending those of a purely professional body. As a result, the JCS ended the war with no experience in functioning simply as a military organization. Four years of war had given them a political tradition and role.[120]

Although King could lay claim to the above, his personality did little to facilitate negotiations. When they met in Washington in 1942, British Admiral A. B. Cunningham believed King to be,

> ... a man of immense capacity and ability, quite ruthless in his methods, he was not an easy person to get on with. He was tough and liked to be considered tough, and at times became rude and overbearing ... He was offensive and I told him what I thought of his method of advancing allied unity and amity ... he could hardly be called a good co-operator. Not content with fighting the enemy, he was usually fighting someone on his own side as well.[121]

Liaison between the White House and the Joint Chiefs was unreliable and faulty; needed decisions were delayed, papers lost. Field Marshal Sir John Dill, head of the JSM described their functioning as follows.

> There are no regular meetings, and if they do meet there is no secretariat to record their meetings. They have no joint planners and executive planning staff ... Then there is the great difficulty of getting the stuff over to the President. He just sees the Chiefs of Staff at odd times, and again no record ... The whole organization belongs to the days of George Washington.[122]

Marshall convinced the President, over King's objections, that Roosevelt's affable and trusted friend, retired Admiral and former diplomat William D. Leahy, would be an excellent choice as his personal chief of staff. Leahy joined the JCS in that capacity, becoming its extra-legal chairman through seniority, and remained an equal among equals without any command authority. From the summer of 1942 onwards, the JCS consisted of King, Marshall, Leahy, and Arnold.[123] Lacking the power that their quasi-legal status imposed, they solicited for an Executive Order to rectify the situation. Roosevelt refused, insisting that it would inhibit their flexibility. Left to serve solely at the president's pleasure, basing their authority on his approval and tacit consent, the JCS sought self-identification and failed.

Since Roosevelt wanted to control American war policy, he disallowed the creation of a civilian–military council. Henceforth, the civilian departmental secretaries of War, Navy, and State were refused entry into any organization dealing with policy. Without the additional contribution of civilian–political viewpoints, the JCS, as arbiter, lacked the experience and qualification necessary to originate and advise on strategic possibilities; to that extent an imbalance existed and policy-making was distorted.

Leahy, as go-between, briefed the president on the committee's findings as well as the actions of the JCS, who sometimes joined Roosevelt to discuss the concepts of grand strategy privately. Usually it was Marshall who maneuvered the other Joint Chiefs into a unified position on particular issues. In effect, the president determined the general objectives, the JCS worked out the policies and logistics, and the theater commanders determined the details. Whatever its shortcomings, the JCS provided the president with the support he needed.

The Wider Role of the JCS

As a substitute for a war council, the JCS was forced to extend its activities into areas of diplomacy, politics, and economics. Although it dealt with military issues such as the evacuation of sick and wounded from overseas, naval escort operations in the Atlantic, and munitions assignments, the JCS also considered the appropriation of critical raw materials. As the war progressed, more and more political questions had to be addressed and decided. The formulation of American policy preparatory to the great inter-allied war conferences, for example, was normally done by the military and the president. The JCS dominated the established system, discovering that the lack of a formal charter and close alignment to the president tended to expand its interests and power, as his expanded. To its surprise, no rival agency, therefore, could juridically accuse the JCS of exceeding its authority.

So far as the major decisions in policy and strategy were concerned, the military ran the war the way the American people and American statesmen wanted it run. On the domestic front, control over economic mobilization was shared between military and civilian agencies.[124] On 11 September 1941, two months before America's entry into the war, the Joint Board compiled a list of major national objectives. They were western hemispheric integrity, continuation of the British Empire, regional balances of power, and establishment of friendly regimes. Although Marshall and Stark added their signatures to the above declaration, it represented pre-war limited executive military thinking, which underwent an inexorable change, influenced by the president's interpretation of wartime foreign policy.[125] The JCS exchanged the accepted military views of balance of power and military security for two others: first, military victory was to be the overriding goal; second, the requirements of military strategy were to be decisive in national policy, thereby acceding to the president's assumptions and values of civilian thinking.[126]

Clausewitz and the JCS

If the purpose of war is to express a nation's political will by an admixture of other means, the American military was not prepared to apply Clausewitz's basic tenet, that of the interplay between political Ends and military Means.[127] During the early phases of the war, the JCS concentrated on the military Means and referred the political Ends to the White House. Floundering without any clear notion of government policy, the JCS was dependent on the president's guidance and direction, but this was rarely forthcoming. The JCS failed to see that strategy and statesmanship were synonymous at the highest levels, or that violent means were the mere servants of political deliberations. 'No war was better recorded than World War II, but all too often the historian who has struggled through mountains of paper finds the trail disappearing, at the crucial point of decision-making, somewhere in the direction of the White House.'[128]

Nevertheless, the basic outline for the destruction of the enemy in battle was the president's. Roosevelt would reject any JCS proposal if it were in conflict with the animating principles of the American effort. The edifice he created mirrored his view of governance: he liked to work in an unstructured and competitive environment in which he held all the strings and made all the final decisions.[129]

Roosevelt's Use of Secrecy

Roosevelt arbitrarily cloaked his affairs in secrecy and frequently chose, when sending a message to Churchill in London, to withhold its contents from Marshall. British administrative policy, by contrast, required that written copies be supplied to designated governmental officers on a 'need to know' basis. Roosevelt's methods of confidentiality, excessively misplaced here, were disruptive and time consuming. At great risk, Dill supplied COS copies of secret Roosevelt–Churchill correspondence to Marshall, his trusted friend.[130] Fortunately, so supplied, Marshall not only knew what was happening, but for what reasons.[131]

Roosevelt had done much to create an administration whose weaknesses were those of informal and overlapping confusion rather than rigidity, by which he chose to keep everybody guessing. Reminiscent of the pre-war New Deal years, Roosevelt formed committees of men with divergent views and invited them to seek consensus. He dissolved and reconstituted his own committees, and sometimes neglected their proposals. Although he had admired President Wilson's systematic attempts to secure peace in the world, Roosevelt was determined not to entrap himself in position papers, as did his predecessor. Roosevelt, perhaps the finest intuitive politician of modern times, had learned to solve problems not by reasoned analysis but by intuition. Bored by administrative procedures, he left clear and precise directives unwritten; as a consequence, his own office was not tightly organized and his bureaucracy was often chaotic.[132]

He strove to do many things simultaneously, even though this meant keeping all parts of the war effort going at varying tempos in all directions. While he tended to compartmentalize military and political affairs, the JCS could not. Scheduled JCS/presidential meetings diminished from 1942 onwards, in sharp contrast to Churchill's almost daily meetings with the COS Committee.[133]

The British Chiefs of Staff

The chaos that beset the wartime American government searching for and designing a military/executive administrative system did not affect the British to the same extent. However, a major problem that distinguished the British system from the American was Churchill, as noted by Brooke,

> ... Marshall never seemed to have any difficulties in countering any wildish plans which the President might put forward... Winston never had the slightest doubt that he had inherited all the military genius from his great ancestor Marlborough! His military plans and ideas varied from the most brilliant conception at the one end to the wildest and most dangerous ideas at the other. To wean him away from these wilder plans required superhuman efforts and was never entirely successful in so far as he tended to return to these ideas again and again.[134]

Britain's system possessed a level of accountability, realism, flexibility, and systematic co-ordination unknown to the Americans. Churchill took immediate action to establish and consolidate his position as prime minister in May 1940, by making some changes in Lord Maurice Hankey's (minister without portfolio) existing bureaucratic structure. Even if Churchill had achieved his position through a spontaneous Parliamentary revolt, which reflected Britain's mood, rarely had a prime minister in a time of crisis grasped unlimited power. Much like Roosevelt, he excluded his service ministers from the War Cabinet, a body consisting of five members of whom he was one. The War Cabinet acted as an occasional court of last resort for his ministers and committees, before he decided. The Prime Minister's domination of foreign policy was clear and complete, and in effect, his direction, leadership, and action obtained. Furthermore, Churchill added to his power by creating and assuming the post of Minister of Defence. To achieve the most flexibility, he deliberately kept the powers of this post imprecise. He wanted to force a highly structured bureaucracy into more energetic action as part of Britain's war effort. Churchill made a subtle and ill-defined change rather than a legal and constitutional one, affording him great power without any interference from any other lawful supervisory authority.[135] As both prime minister and minister of defence, he supervised the war effort, and became its chief director through the exercise of political authority and the formulation of defence policy.[136]

In addition to the permanent machinery of government, Churchill made a practice of establishing *ad hoc* committees over which he presided whenever he wanted to focus dramatically on a particular aspect of the war effort, for example, the 1941 U-boat menace. In other similar organizational efforts, he demonstrated a pragmatic flexibility, searching for the most efficient ways to direct total war.[137] Churchill established the post of Minister of State, a position accountable to the War Cabinet, with direct access to the prime minister, created to provide the local British Commanders-in-Chief with the political guidance not hitherto available. The appointment of Harold Macmillan as Cabinet-ranked Minister Resident to Eisenhower's Allied Headquarters in North Africa, demonstrated Churchill's need to have the British point of view placed before the American commander.[138] Restraint was not one of Churchill's virtues: during March 1944 he attempted to wrest the Joint Planners from the COS Committee arguing that they belonged to his staff all along and not to the COS. Brooke rejected any change of structure, commenting that,

> To suggest, as the Prime Minister was doing, that the 'Planners' were part of his staff and not that of the COS Committee, was the equivalent of depriving the headquarters of command of its Operational Branch. The idea was fantastic for even if he did complete a plan with the planners the

> plan would still have to come before the COS Committee. All that he was doing was wasting the planners time, and they were very busy people...[139]

In the end, Britain's organizational machinery for prosecuting the war achieved an important balance between Churchill's application of leadership and the Defence Committee's ability to restrain him by a variety of military and civilian resources. Churchill and the Defence Committee or the War Cabinet met frequently to address an endless number of political–military issues, to prepare for eventualities and to determine policies associated with total war.[140]

The Chiefs always attended Defence Committee (Operations) meetings, as did other ministers when required; it was this organization, as well as Churchill himself, that became the focal point where the political–military elements of power were synthesized. The Defence Committee (Supplies), usually chaired by the Prime Minister, separated the many detailed logistics issues from policy and operations, ensuring that this important link was addressed.

In another brilliant move, Churchill placed the military wing of the War Cabinet Secretariat under him, as his own machinery for action rather than a Ministry of Defence. Thus actual power soon shifted from the War Cabinet to Churchill, even though it had represented the supreme executive authority. As its influence waned, the Chiefs of Staff Committee, subordinate to the Defence Committee (Operations), presided over by the Prime Minister, gained ascendancy.

With the clear lines of a unified command structure established, Churchill was free to form an intimate relationship with his Chiefs, something Roosevelt failed to accomplish with his own. The Chairman chaired the meetings, acted as spokesman for the Chiefs before the Defence Committee or Cabinet, and advised on matters concerning his service. The strategic questions as well as the day-to-day running of the war devolved upon the minister of defence, the Chiefs and those ministers whose jurisdiction covered a particular problem or issue. These changes represented practical improvements to the original system's functioning commensurate with total war.[141] Demand for an independent principal strategic adviser never arose, which suited Churchill, who always believed in straightforward dealing with the responsible professionals.

To operate this organization, Churchill relied on what he termed his 'handling machine', General Hastings Ismay, called 'Pug', who became his representative on the COS Committee. As head of the Cabinet Secretariat, Ismay was a hard worker, of unchallenged reliability, a consummate bureaucrat, and a negotiator who could elicit decisions and compromises without antagonisms.[142] Brooke comments,

> ... He bore all the brunt of the first storms which some of our papers created, and was able next morning to warn us as to what the reactions were. He was kept up practically every night by Winston, was abused and sworn at, and seldom received any word of encouragement, and yet he went on serving Winston with utmost devotion.[143]

In his capacity as Principal Staff Officer to the MoD, Ismay qualified for full COS membership on the basis of this position, but the right to sign the Committee reports was disallowed.[144] Analogous in function to Dill in Washington, he had influence but not final responsibility. Finally, Ismay resisted any attempts on Churchill's part to fill the Office of the Minister of Defence with such well known court favorites as Professor Lindemann and Major Desmond Morton.

By 1942, Churchill and the Chiefs of Staff were now running the war. Their relationship was never precisely defined, but it was close and constant. He met the three service chiefs and Ismay once a day, and more often on an informal basis as well. At first, Churchill had some difficulty getting service representatives with whom he was comfortable, but when CAS Air Chief Marshal Sir Charles Portal in 1940, CIGS General Sir Alan Brooke in 1941, and the First Sea Lord Admiral Sir Andrew Cunningham in 1943 replaced their predecessors, the membership was set. Vice Admiral Lord Louis Mountbatten, Chief of Combined Operations, participated as needed. The actual running of the services was left to the vice chiefs, who like their superiors, met together daily. The work of COS was to advise the Government through the Prime Minister on all questions of British military policy and strategy. The COS or its Mission combined with the American Chiefs of Staff to form the CCS who advised the president and prime minister together on matters affecting American and British forces jointly.[145]

The British had developed a blueprint for a system of sequential responsibility and accountability, which included the military leadership, the War Cabinet, and Parliament. Thus a collective body rather than an individual exercised supreme authority, allowing it to approach decision-making realistically. This was achieved as a result of the COS being given broadly defined powers and having excellent information on which to base decisions. The British system was resilient; it maintained centralized control, but there was considerable appreciation for versatility between the British nerve center and the war theaters.[146] For most of the war Churchill's organization was rational and efficient, creating, as he claimed, 'a stream of coherent thought capable of being translated with great rapidity into coherent action.'[147]

This is theoretically true, but it was a Churchillian exaggeration. Even though the COS expressed a remarkable degree of unity, it suffered from persistent, strong inter-service disagreements. To its credit, the chiefs remained friendly, not allowing argument to degenerate into acrimony, sublimating special service interests to the needs of victory. In this, both Ismay and Portal played an important part. As the war progressed, the Chiefs achieved a higher level of solidarity, tempered by time and experience. They approached and confronted strategic problems, in like manner, as highly trained intelligent professionals, despite their varied temperaments.[148]

However, in practice, Churchill breached the jurisdictional subdivision of responsibility when he formed a small inner cabinet, over which he presided as minister of defence; the COS was left without a civilian chief in the War Cabinet who could champion their specific point of view. Jurisdictional boundaries were also breached by the prime minister when he insisted that either he or his personal representative, General Ismay, attend Chiefs of Staff meetings on a regular basis. This prevailing situation limited the Chiefs' opportunities to consult in private, to view matters from their own perspective, and to co-ordinate a strategy against the prime minister should they fundamentally disagree with him. The Chiefs could only fight it out directly with either Churchill or Ismay on a day-to-day basis. Under this system, Churchill as Minister of Defence could not remain dispassionate or critical regarding plans, which as Chairman of the COS he had helped to formulate. It was a system that favored Churchill's demanding personality and strategic perceptions, and limited the Chiefs' ability to parry and counter.[149]

> ... Thus it was that the framework of decision making constituted a triangle with Churchill at its apex. It was he who directed and managed British 'grand strategy' by means of an intimate dialogue ... with the Chiefs of Staff on one hand and Eden on the other.[150]

Some Churchillian Relationships

Churchill's relationship with his Chiefs of Staff was heavily dependent on personality factors, a condition manifest throughout the war by the taking of strong adversarial positions. One of Admiral Dudley Pound's methods of diffusing Churchill's wilder schemes was to delegate planning officers to undertake a full-scale investigation of his proposals; this would result in a detailed refutation of the project followed by its quick demise.[151] Neither Pound's successor as First Sea Lord, Cunningham, nor Dill, as CIGS, ever achieved the same kind of acceptability, regardless of talent or professionalism.[152] Dill wrote, shortly after assuming the position of Chief of the

Imperial General Staff (CIGS) on 27 May 1940, 'I am not sure that Winston isn't the greatest menace. No one seems able to control him. He is full of ideas, many brilliant, but most of them impractical. He has such drive and personality that no one seems able to stand up to him.'[153]

Three years later, Dill had not changed his mind, and in a letter dated 26 August 1943, he wrote, 'I often wonder if the people will ever know of the difficulties and the dangers of Winston. It may be a great privilege to work with a genius, but my Lord it is difficult and terribly wearing. I wonder where we should be now if Winston had his untrammelled way.'[154]

Field Marshal Archibald Wavell, whose fortunes as a commander had reached their nadir in the Mediterranean in 1941, wrote to Brooke after the war that, '...I know how much the success of our strategy owed to your personal efforts and direction, and to your ability to handle with patience and yet firmness that very difficult personality, Winston.'[155]

Churchill's irascibility had been too much for Dill and Wavell, as representatives of military organization and methodology. Both men found it difficult to work with the him; Wavell could be inarticulate in his presence and Dill lacked self-confidence.[156] Even though he could be considerate to members of his inner professional circle, Churchill did things to suit himself, regardless of how he inconvenienced others. Lacking the capacity to develop close friendships, he used people for the immediate service they could render and replaced them according to need.[157]

Churchill and Portal had little difficulty forming a relationship that included a corresponding admiration and affection for each other, in which no serious disagreement, professional or otherwise, ever occurred. Portal recognized that though the prime minister's incessant probing might be a nuisance, or on any other given occasion, wholly unfounded, it was the prime minister's right and duty to probe, and that by such energy at the top the war would be won.[158] On one occasion, when Portal violently disagreed with Churchill, he apologized. A broad smile appeared across Winston's face, and he said to Portal, 'You know, in war you don't have to be nice, you only have to be right.'[159]

Brooke, promoted to CIGS after an exhausted Dill was relieved in November 1941, reassessed his relationships between the COS Committee and Churchill as prime minister and minister of defence, recognizing that the best method of getting along with him was to give way on non-essentials. When a matter of vital importance arose, the CIGS would say to the prime minister, 'I am your subordinate. I'll only carry out what you wish if you give it to me in writing and sign it.'[160]

On these occasions, Brooke heard nothing more about the matter; Churchill had dropped it. With Brooke's ascendancy, Churchill discovered that he admired his intelligence, his ruthlessness in dealing with unsuccessful commanders, and his strategic sense. Moreover, the new CIGS was also quick, decisive, methodical and not afraid to decentralize.[161] However, Brooke suffered from an underlying vein of pessimism and uncertainty that was an invaluable complement to Churchill's constant self-confidence and occasional euphoria. Brooke's reaction to his appointment as CIGS was in direct contrast to Churchill's ebullient acceptance of his office in May 1940:

> I had never hoped or aspired to reach those dizzy heights, and now that I am stepping up onto the plateau land of my military career the landscape looks cold, bleak and lonely, with a ghastly responsibility hanging as a black thundercloud over me.[162]
>
> ... I have felt that every day of this war was taking off a month of my life.[163]

Churchill's self-confidence was misleading, because he suffered from recurrent fits of depression and mania. This behavior, manifested by ceaseless activity and obsessive thinking, lessened his 'black dog' mentality and lassitude. Relaxation was out of the question and the relationship between him and his professional staffs suffered. Although the prime minister achieved a number of successes functioning this way, Brooke bore the brunt of Churchill's incessant mental pounding and persistent energy. The CIGS tried to parry the prime minister's strategic requests by keeping him on a tight rein,[164] and constantly rebuked him in his diary, dwelling on Churchill's overbearing and inconsiderate nature.[165] Admiral Cunningham wrote of Churchill, 'No decisions were reached; in fact, a thoroughly wasted day. What a drag on the wheel of war this man is. Everything is centralized in him with consequent indecision and waste of time before anything can be done.'[166]

Part of Brooke's outbursts was certainly due to the constant efforts by the Chiefs throughout the war to dissuade Churchill from his penchant for tangential enterprises that dissipated the energies of staff and his commanders. Planning staffs, for example, were ill-used, wasting time on either secondary or wholly irrelevant objectives, particularly when there was a lull in the war's action: Operation WORKSHOP (an invasion of Pantelleria), Operation JUPITER (a Norwegian expedition) and Operation ACCOLADE (an invasion of Rhodes).[167] None of these plans was activated, because the Chiefs opposed him on strategic grounds, and Churchill, at heart a compromiser, however recalcitrant, grudgingly respected their judgment.[168]

> All those who worked with Churchill paid tribute to the enormous fertility of his ideas, and the inexhaustible stream of invention which poured from

him ... They agreed that he needed the most severe of restraints, and that many of his ideas, if activated, would have been utterly disastrous.[169]

The prime minister's demanding behavior increased Marshall's wariness of Churchill. Without benefit of an American joint staff mission in London and without the access the prime minister afforded to the COS, Marshall took Churchill's pronouncements seriously and literally. To him and his colleagues, Churchill appeared to be unpredictable and unreal, his talk extravagant. Moreover, stirred by a blending of distrust and appeal, the American Chiefs approached him with caution, because they were unable to place his strategic imagination within the context of practicability. When he advocated the occupation of Norway's North Cape, the Americans thought him mentally unsound, although their British counterparts recognized the idea simply as the exploration of his manifold thoughts. Portal considered the American mind to be pedestrian and practical; this increased the difficulties of understanding Churchill:

> ...they were susceptible of his personality, because they were frightened of being carried away by him and so they tended to oppose from him ideas which they might have willingly accepted from a more restrained and less captivating personality. They admired and respected him, but they were doubtful of his strategic judgment and suspected his political motives.[170]

2 Conferences

Between December 1941 and August 1944, eight major summit conferences convened: two were held at Quebec, two at Washington, two at Cairo and one each at Teheran and Casablanca. The designated conference participants met to discuss strategy and the war's crucial issues. Cities in foreign countries were preferred, because neutral ground offered a more relaxed atmosphere in which to work, away from the intrusive, easily available, self-serving bureaucratic machinery. Summits usually occurred when strategic planning had reached a point at which decisions on Allied strategy and policy demanded resolution at the highest levels.[1] They were designed to hammer out strategy based on the approved grand strategy, although this was not always adhered to. In attendance were the JCS, the COS and their retinues, followed by the presence of the civilian leaders, Roosevelt, Churchill (and occasionally Stalin), whose final approval was required. Left behind were the American Secretaries for State, War, and Navy, and their British counterparts. Preceding the arrival of the major participants, Washington and London based staffs prepared the ground-work.[2]

The General as the Negotiator

The members of the CCS were inexperienced negotiators, although Marshall, politically intuitive, had learned rudimentary negotiating procedures in dealing with Congressional committees. During 1941, he lobbied extensively for a bill extending the Selective Service Act, which passed the House of Representatives by a single vote. Without Marshall's tireless and non-partisan efforts, it would have been defeated.[3]

Marshall and his service colleagues had reached the pinnacle of their military careers in a hierarchy of limited dissent and cultural, service and personal eccentricities that affected their approaches to problem-solving. Since the JCS and the COS rarely met in executive session, unfamiliarity conspired against optimum results, although a few co-operative members helped to contain the friction.[4] Envy, distrust and prejudice, acting as catalysts for protracted debate, inhibited the speed of deliberations and undoubtedly affected their outcome.

John Maynard Keynes, the British Treasury's expert on external finance, considered the Americans as wayward Anglo-Saxons, who mangled the English language into what he openly and contemptuously referred to as 'Cherokee'. Keynes warned the British Cabinet, upon his return from

Washington in 1941, that negotiating with the Americans was provisional until the last moment, and that an orderly progression in the quest for a final settlement was non-existent.[5]

Placentia Bay and ARCADIA

The August 1941 meeting at Placentia Bay, Newfoundland, code-named RIVIERA, was held against the backdrop of a British victory over the Italians in Libya, the neutralization of the French fleet in North Africa, the British loss of Greece, and the possibility of further German Mediterranean attacks. Churchill, seeking American aid, hoped to achieve a joint declaration of war aims. Roosevelt demanded two preconditions for the meeting: no discussions regarding a possible American declaration of war; and no economic or territorial deals for a post-war world. Sumner Wells, Assistant Secretary of State, was concerned about rumors of secret deals between Britain and the deposed Greek and Yugoslav monarchs in return for their wartime support.[6]

British Organizational Skills and American Corporate Disunity

The Americans were impressed with British negotiating and organizational skills. One of their favored techniques was to present a 'united-front'. Having recently visited Britain, Arnold had been impressed with British thoroughness and felt the Americans were going into the RIVIERA conference cold.[7] The COS never admitted to internal dissension, and disagreements between government and military, between the services themselves, were resolved in advance or obfuscated within formidable studies. King and Marshall, by contrast, publicly stated their differences and disunity.[8] Roosevelt withheld guidance and remained evasive, awaiting assurance from an American public doubtful of going to war. By keeping his strategic intentions private, by maintaining a nebulous national policy, little could be accomplished during the forthcoming military discussions.[9]

Churchill's party included General Sir John Dill, CIGS; Admiral of the Fleet Sir Dudley Pound, the First Sea Lord; Air Vice Marshal Sir Wilfrid Freeman, VCAS; Sir Alexander Cadogan, Permanent Under-Secretary of State for Foreign Affairs; Professor F. A. Lindemann, scientific adviser and Lord Moran, Churchill's personal physician. These men were assisted by an array of deputies, all ready with position papers and supporting studies. If British staff work were not necessarily better, it was certainly more comprehensive.

The American delegation, by contrast, was small, with few aides and planners. Joining Roosevelt in the American delegation were his three military chiefs, Marshall, Stark, and Arnold; besides King, Sumner Welles, Under-Secretary of State and two civilian advisors, Harry Hopkins, Personal Assistant and Special Advisor to the President and Averell Harriman, Director of the Lend-Lease program. Staff arrangements were so limited that AAF Captain, Elliot Roosevelt, the President's son, was asked to perform as a recording secretary during military discussions.

Placentia Bay offered the first opportunity for many of the British and American senior officers to assess each other's professional abilities, but the anti-British attitudes, expressed by several senior American staff planners, did not bode well for the future. However, when Marshall and Dill met for the first time at Placentia Bay, they formed a close professional friendship that bode well for Allied co-operation. Both sides were less apprehensive than ambivalent, the construction of a coalition dependent upon how each side assessed the other. Warned by Churchill that Marshall, in his quiet way, meant business, Lord Moran considered Marshall the key to the situation. 'If we are too obstinate', the prime minister observed, 'he might take a strong line. That would avail us little, because neither side could contemplate going forward without him.'[10]

Only by working closely together would personal antagonisms or questionable abilities be exposed.[11] Attempts to form a coalition were considered ill-conceived, if not impossible to these senior officers, because of their disparate backgrounds. King, for example, while not openly hostile like Embick, was distinctly cool toward Britain, whom he had considered a maritime adversary during the inter-war period. Even the ship on which the Americans traveled, the *USS Augusta*, had been a pawn in the United States–British rivalry over the definition of 'cruiser' during the early 1930s. He epitomized the prevailing attitudes of the previous 20 years, that is, indifference, suspicion and bitterness. Regarding Britain's national, imperial and balance of power concerns, Roosevelt was to say shortly after Pearl Harbor that, '...I've been trying to tell Churchill that he ought to consider it; it's in the American tradition, this distrust, this dislike and even hatred of Britain.'[12] Questions of trade, shipping and naval strength had precipitated Anglo–American tensions during the inter-war years, and Britain was regarded as a serious and dangerous competitor.[13] The English, not to be outdone, went so far as to break at least one of the US State Department codes.[14]

Divergent Strategic Philosophies

Churchill and the COS believed that the Germans could be defeated without a huge invasion army striking at the Continent and that the war could be won by a combination of blockade, propaganda, armies of liberation, and strategic bombing. Moreover, modern armored divisions accompanied by a popular Continental uprising, secretly armed from without, would ultimately defeat Germany.[15] When the British landed troops in Europe they would 'go as policemen', Europe would be re-occupied, not liberated.[16]

In essence, what Britain needed was America's productive genius.[17] and not another American Expeditionary Force. The British recognized America's wish to remain neutral for the time being, and even encouraged it, preferring that it supply Britain with the vast amounts of military hardware it needed. Marshall and some of his planning staff thought otherwise. Disturbing was the British emphasis on strategic bombing versus the American emphasis on massive ground assault at the chosen point of concentration. Even their diplomatic colleagues, Alexander Cadogan, Permanent Under-Secretary at the Foreign Office and Sumner Welles had difficulties resolving certain issues, such as Japanese encroachments in the south-western Pacific. Too strong a warning could lead to war in the Far East, one that the Anglo–Americans were in no position to wage; for the British, war in the Pacific would divert desperately needed assets from Europe. Waving a number of British military proposals aside, the American admirals agreed to convoy all shipping, including Britain's, from Newfoundland to Iceland. The British were stunned by American concerns about western hemispheric defence and their 'Monroe Doctrine' approach, concluding that the American military planners were too parochial in their outlook and lacked an appreciation of global strategy. To them America's preoccupation with the defence of the Panama Canal seemed misguided at best, when the Suez Canal was threatened.[18] Admiral Richmond Kelly Turner believed that, if they became allies, American interests would be subordinated to those of Britain's, because the British did not understand or appreciate the fundamental policies and strategic necessities of the US.[19]

Variation of National Interests

The meeting revealed each nation's position and their divergent perceptions regarding the war's priorities, which had strategic implications. Britain was engaged in a war; while the US was neutral, although wobbling on the edge. Before the meeting, the Americans had the temerity to send a series of cables to London arguing that if the British did not fight the American way, they might not win at all.[20] However intrusive, Anglo–American suppositions were based on a conflicting set of expectations: would America simply be an arsenal of productivity or would it actively engage and defeat the Germans with an army of its own? Only the president could clarify America's grand strategic and political view, without which little progress could be made. Dill was disturbed by the American emphasis on protecting their own hemisphere.[21] Even if the American position were over-determined, Marshall looked beyond it to a strategy that culminated in a northwest Europe campaign. In summation, many of those present protected their national and service interests and their professional reputations, all of which combined to affect the extent to which they were prepared or willing to co-operate. Although Marshall yearned for action, he was well aware of American unpreparedness. At the time 40 tanks were apportioned between four armored divisions. Air enthusiasts, including Roosevelt, eagerly awaited the massive production build-up of air forces as envisioned in *ABC-2*, thereby eliminating (according to the theory) the need for large ground forces. Germany would be bombed into submission.[22] Churchill could defend his willingness to invade the Continent in the bombers' wake, executed only after Germany's total collapse. British General Morgan summed up the American viewpoint:

> On the US side there were several considerations. They were forming one hell of an army, navy and air force. A big navy had plenty of uses, so had a big air force, but when you came to look for a theatre of war where you could deploy such an army there weren't many. That factor was dominant from an early stage. The best theatre for such an army was western Europe...[23]

Within this maze of opinions, the conflict between a British peripheral strategy and an eventual American battle for the 'heartland' remained; therefore, a mutually acceptable strategy seemed a distant goal.[24]

A Question of the United States Assuming Power

The result of the meeting resulted in a combined political document, entitled the *Atlantic Charter*, that included war aims, democratic ideals, and an eight-point contract for world peace once Germany was defeated.[25]

Beyond that, the US maintained its neutrality. Churchill could not lead America into war at Placentia Bay, however hard he tried, although many people in Britain expected it. During the previous year, in an exchange of letters between Harvard University President, James B. Conant, and Budget Director, Lewis W. Douglas, both men agreed that not only must the US become the dominant world power, but an expression of that dominance had to be its willingness and capacity to fight to maintain that power when necessary. They concluded that if the American people did not think the assumption of that power was worth it, all would be lost.[26] There was little sympathy in America for the cost Britain was paying in human and economic terms. Roosevelt, aware of that reluctance, understood that American public opinion was deeply pacific and isolationist. Recognizing that obduracy, he used hemispheric defence as an excuse to rearm. Moreover, until the prevailing mood changed, the US left Britain to fight the war alone. Aid moved slowly, but on 23 February 1941, the United States and Britain decided to exchange British bases for American war material.[27] Moreover, hundreds of tanks and planes were destined for the Middle East, some American shipping would be shifted to British control, and 150,000 antiquated rifles were ear-marked for Britain's Home Guard.[28] American reluctance to accede to British increased material requests was used as a ploy to assess Britain's actual needs; meanwhile Britain agreed to overhaul its purchasing mission in Washington to achieve greater co-ordination. Finally, the 'shoot on sight' order regarding the protection of Atlantic convoys was soon to be announced by the president, but Congress would not revoke the Neutrality Act of 1939, containing its 'cash and carry' provision, until the first week of November, one week after the sinking of the American destroyer, *USS Rueben James* by the German *U-562*, six hundred miles off the coast of Ireland.[29] Returning from a supply allocation meeting in Washington, Lord Beaverbrook reported to the British War Cabinet in London, 'There isn't the slightest chance of the United States entering the war until compelled to do so by a direct attack on its own territory, and it seems that this could not happen until Britain and Russia have been defeated.'[30]

Even if Beaverbrook was prescient and Churchill bewildered as to how America would come in on Britain's side, Roosevelt had taken a step closer towards active belligerency. Hitler regarded Roosevelt's avowal of the Lend-Lease agreement and the extension of the Atlantic neutrality zone as an American declaration of economic warfare. As a retaliatory measure, on 25 March Hitler extended the North Atlantic war zone as far west as Greenland. Japan and Germany would solve Roosevelt's dilemma four months later.

American Public Opinion and Presidential Efforts

In spite of the president's efforts, the American public considered the meeting a failure. The meeting had little effect upon the level of American aid designated for Britain. Originally low, the increase was minimal. Immediately after the meeting became public knowledge, a Gallup poll on 18 August inquired, 'Should the United States enter the war against Germany today?' The respondents revealed that 20 percent supported entry, 74 percent were opposed, and five percent were undecided.[31] Welles felt that by the time the public's mood shifted, the Allies could have lost the war. Roosevelt adhered to an American political tendency, to follow rather than lead public opinion; it was no match for the German *Blitzkrieg*.

Returning to London on 19 August, Churchill revealed the depth of Roosevelt's concern for Britain, admitting that the American people and particularly Congress were determined to remain neutral. Contrary to the president's perceptions of the American public's mood, the prime minister chose to discount the polls, regarding them as less than representative. He sensed a lack of urgency in Washington, feeling that if Roosevelt were to put the issue of peace and war before Congress, there would be a sluggish three-month debate. He had warned the president that he could not answer for the consequences if Russia collapsed while the US remained neutral. Although dependent upon the opinion polls as a guide for executive action, Roosevelt hoped to provoke the Germans into hostilities by creating an incident in the Atlantic naval war.[32]

ARCADIA

Two weeks after the Japanese attack on Pearl Harbor, Roosevelt, Churchill and their military staffs met at a second Anglo–American series of meetings held from 22 December 1941 through 14 January 1942 in Washington (code-named ARCADIA). The American COS were ill-prepared to cope with such an abrupt entry into war. With the nation reeling after the disaster at Pearl Harbor, with a public clamoring for revenge, American administrative procedures were criticized by an incredulous Dill, writing to his superior, Brooke in London,

> They have no joint planners and executive planning staff ... Then there is the great difficulty of getting the stuff over to the President. There are no regular [Joint Chiefs of Staff] meetings, and if they do meet there is no secretariat to record them. He just sees the JCS at odd times, and again no record. There is no such thing as a Cabinet meeting, and yet the Secretaries for War, Navy, etc. are supposed to function ... Eventually they will do great things...[33]

Even before the ARCADIA Conference began, Churchill and his Chiefs of Staff, traveling from Britain aboard *HMS Duke of York*, telegraphed the Americans that they wished to discuss the following five main topics:

1. Fundamental basis of joint strategy;
2. Interpretation of the joint strategy in terms of immediate military measures;
3. Allocation of joint forces to conform with (1);

4. Long-term program based on (1), including forces to be raised and equipped;
5. Establishment of joint machinery for implementing (2) and (3), and (4).[34]

Churchill had reason for traveling to Washington so soon after Pearl Harbor. He needed reassurance that Roosevelt and Marshall would remain steadfast to their *RAINBOW 5* strategy even after Pearl Harbor. During US neutrality, he had said to his son, Randolph, in the summer of 1940, 'I shall drag the United States in.'[35] Now, he hoped that wooing the Americans no longer required his previous customary caution. [36]

Desperate for American assistance, a determined Churchill wished to discuss future collaborative ventures in the Mediterranean and French North Africa, a reiteration of the defensive Anglo-French basic war plan of 1939. In turn, American strategists, in 1941, viewed German control of West Africa as a major threat to American Atlantic communication lines and considered such 'peripheral' areas as Brazil, the Azores, Morocco, and Dakar as posing a more immediate threat to American security than a German victory in Europe.[37]

At ARCADIA, the Americans clearly enunciated their position: joint war plans recognized the North Atlantic as the principal theater of operations, the first essential of which was the preservation of communications across the North Atlantic using the British Isles as a fortress covering the British Fleet. The decision to establish an American force in Britain was immediate.[38]

Withal, the prime minister's proposals for a combined British and American amphibious operation in North and West Africa (GYMNAST) in 1942 interested the president. He considered operation SUPER-GYMNAST, the final development of operation GYMNAST a distinct possibility. Benefits would follow: the American people, bruised and angered by Pearl Harbor, would back the war effort and support their troops in action. Discussions of the British agenda and the American paper, 'Estimate of the Military Situation' did not result in a detailed plan of operations at ARCADIA, but a comprehensive memorandum entitled 'WWI' emerged before the conference closed in March.[39] ARCADIA was a most difficult conference with little pattern, because a new alliance of so-called equals was in process. The resulting discussions were long and wearisome, [40] but the following was thought necessary to defeat the Axis in Europe:

1. to achieve an armaments program for victory; to defeat the U-boats, to close and tighten the ring around Germany by supporting the Russian front, supplying Turkey with arms and military supplies, increasing our strength in the Middle East, and retaking all of the North African coast;

to wear down German resistance by air bombardment, blockade, subversive activities and psychological warfare.

2. The inexorable goal of offensive action, even though it can not be achieved on the scale in mind for 1942, may become a reality in 1943 as exemplified by a return to the Continent, a). via the Mediterranean, b). from Turkey into the Balkans, or c). by landings in western Europe.[41]

Preoccupied with the latest events in the Pacific, the Americans were ill-prepared to question the British proposals. Although they had signed the document, having made only slight changes, it remained largely a British design. The Americans were uneasy, and in the ensuing months their uneasiness was to increase.[42]

Strategy and the New System

Marshall believed that the military should be in charge of its own supplies; although a firm defender of civilian control of the military, he opposed the creation of a two-man civilian resource board, as originally conceived by Roosevelt and Churchill, that could interfere with established military plans and operations.[43] The negotiated inter-allied preliminary agreement, which became permanent over time, favored Marshall's view. During a White House meeting at the end of the conference, Roosevelt recommended that in case of disputes, the civilian board members could appeal to the president and prime minister. Churchill reluctantly agreed, and on 14 January 1942 the Munitions Assignments Board became responsible for the allocation of munitions, under CCS supervision.[44] For the first time, finished war material would be allocated in accordance with strategic needs. The economic boards (Assignment, Shipping, Raw Materials, Production and Resources, and Food) were soon established under the direction of the president and prime minister.

If these new boards and committees were organized to successfully prosecute the war, to what extent did ARCADIA formulate a strategy translated into action? The British and Americans had independently concluded, then mutually agreed, that 'holding the line' against Japan was in the interest of both nations. If the Japanese could be held by a minimum of means, the president wanted to position overwhelming allied naval power in the Atlantic and defeat 'Germany-first'. However, the combination of interlocking global concerns and limited military resources demanded immediate attention: such was the need for basing an air force in Australia, increasing strength in the Pacific, reinforcing British troops in the Middle East, acquiring bases on the Atlantic Islands, Brazil, and Africa, and relieving

British forces in Northern Ireland and Iceland.[45] Churchill and Roosevelt exchanged ideas, Marshall and Roosevelt disagreed over priorities: the president wanted American troops in action during the year, but the prime minister sought to avoid any action that would echo the attritional battles of the previous war. ARCADIA represented the beginning of a concerted search for a practical European invasion plan,[46] which included a spectrum of thought that ranged from the British 'peripheral strategy' to a direct American 'cross-Channel assault'.[47] The effect of increased American focus on the Pacific or heightened British interest in the Mediterranean upon strategic deliberations remained unclear.

Active Participation of the CCS

Within the same period that the political leaders conferred, the American and British Chiefs of Staff met 12 times. Not surprisingly, the two air chiefs, Arnold and Portal, were agreed proponents of winning through air power, but the two admirals, Pound and King, fighting two different naval wars – one in the Atlantic against the U-boats, the other in the Pacific against the Japanese advance; espoused different strategic priorities and had little in common. Marshall and Brooke's differences reflected Marshall's interest in logistical and organizational considerations in support of an eventual concentrated effort across the English Channel, while Brooke's centered on battle experience, understanding the *Wehrmacht*'s abilities, and the traditional British maritime strategy of 'closing the ring'.

During the conference, the British repeated their strategic theme for the summer of 1943 in Europe, first expressed at Placentia Bay. Churchill stated,

> In principle, the landings should be made by armoured and mechanised forces capable of disembarking not at ports but on beaches, either by landing-craft or from ocean-going ships specially adapted. The potential front of attack is thus made so wide that the German forces holding down these different countries cannot be strong enough at all points ... expeditions should be marshalled by the spring of 1943 in Iceland, the British Isles, and, if possible, in French Morocco and Egypt. The main body would come direct across the ocean.[48]

The majestic sweep of Churchill's sense of strategy is noted in the above quotation, because it not only contained the essence of future amphibious operations, but included expectations far beyond the scope of allied ability, even at full mobilization and production capacity. Claiming to be a proponent for an invasion of northwest Europe, Churchill could point to his own definitive role in the pioneering and development of landing craft, although his support of the landing shifted precariously as the war progressed.[49] No wonder that the Americans remained skeptical of his strategic concepts and usually feared the worst when he and the president met in closed session. Even though they were both highly talented, each man required the balancing restraint of carefully organized staff advice, which they avoided at times.[50] Under Churchill's guidance, Roosevelt usually succumbed to Churchill's strategic rhetoric, leaving much to be undone by a concerned Marshall. For instance, on Christmas Eve, 1941, Roosevelt agreed to a Churchill suggestion for 1942 Pacific operations, that if a convoy of American reinforcements and planes sent to the Philippines could not break through the Japanese blockade, it should be re-routed to Singapore, described by the prime minister as an 'impregnable fortress'. Marshall, upon receipt of this memo, fearing a dangerous precedent, protested its method and content to Stimson. Shocked and angry, the Secretary of War considered it improper to discuss such matters with the leader of a foreign country while the fighting in the Philippines continued. Protesting to Harry Hopkins, he argued that if the president continued to make such arbitrary decisions on matters of extreme urgency without benefit of his COS present, he and other top-level War Department personnel would resign. Faced with the actual British report, advised by Hopkins to be careful about the formality of his discussions with Churchill, the president recanted and never by-passed Marshall again.[51]

Global War, a Supreme Commander and British Misgivings

Stung by the president's incursion into strategy without consultation, Marshall proposed that a supreme commander be designated for the Pacific. Negotiations between the British and American Chiefs began immediately and resulted in the existing British–American Chiefs of Staff committee, headquartered in Washington, being installed as the Combined Chiefs of Staff. Brooke thought it a bad idea, criticizing false arrangements made in Washington.[52] The CCS was created not to originate, but to inform and assist both political leaders on strategic requirements, prosecute the war on a global scale, and to direct the ABDA theater commander in timely fashion. The Combined Chiefs were not the ultimate decision-makers, that prerogative was reserved for both Roosevelt and Churchill, but it served them as a decision-making body.[53] Representing the strategic will of both countries, the CCS expected the theater commander to follow its directives. Moreover, the CCS would allocate vital supplies as needed through the Munitions Assignment Board, functioning under its control. Marshall said,

> We had to come to this in the First World War, but it was not until 1918 that it was accomplished, and much valuable time, blood, and treasure had been needlessly sacrificed. If we could decide on a unified command now, it would be a great advance over what was accomplished then.[54]

It was a vital achievement for Marshall, and Stimson hoped that the Pacific example could be applied to other theaters of operations.[55] The British thought otherwise, calling the proposal 'wild and half baked'; and Brooke felt its emphasis on the western Pacific rather than the Indian Ocean was misplaced; the more the COS looked at their task the less they liked the American proposal, and even the British Cabinet doubted its value.[56] Dill feared that it would be fatal to have a British commander responsible for the disasters looming in the Pacific.[57] To counter the American stroke, Brooke sent well-instructed British representatives to Washington to present the British staff's case. Unfortunately, this procedure of direct confrontation by London-based military emissaries was not always carried out. Additionally, Brooke sought London as the base for military planning and strategy, not Washington, at this stage of the war.[58]

> Ever since Portal and Pound came back from the USA, I have told them that they 'sold our birthright for a plate of porridge', whilst in Washington, they had up to now denied it flatly. However, this morning they are at last beginning to realise that the Americans are rapidly snatching more and more power with the ultimate intention of running the war in Washington. However, I now have them on my side.[59]

Concerning strategy, both the Roosevelt and Marshall agreed that the first American combat venture against the Germans had to succeed, because failure would have an extremely adverse effect on the morale of the American people, particularly in an election year.[60] Seeking to assist the Russians, Marshall viewed the North African operation as a threat to his idea of pushing as many men and arms across the Atlantic in 1942, preparatory for a cross-Channel attack. He believed that the battle of northwest Europe would be the final battle of the war; therefore, Marshall viewed the Mediterranean theater as subsidiary to it, in which the enemy was to be simply 'held' without inhibiting operations soon to be identified as BOLERO and ROUNDUP.[61] Rather than fight a war of attrition when one had the wherewithal to fight a war of annihilation, American planners were determined to apply the concepts of mass and concentration in the manner of the American Civil War's General Ulysses S. Grant. A stalemated war was unacceptable to them.[62]

Before negotiations ended, the British gave way on two counts: rather than an integrated command structure, they wanted theater commands and staff to be composed of one nationality and the war perceived as a whole unit, thereby eliminating geographical divisions based on national responsibility. The Americans refused. The British COS wrote the following memo and sent it to Washington:

> This system, arbitrarily laid down on a geographical basis, would be dangerous and wrong ... The strategy of war must be looked at as a whole, and predominant roles in the fields of operation allocated in accordance with the general strategic situation and the resources of the allies.[63]

During the conference's sessions, Naval captain, John L. McCrea, one of the president's aides, wrote of the British, 'They all talked exceedingly well and made much sense, and the staff organization was superb ...'[64] Although the British were less suspicious of American aims, most of the American planners distrusted British strategy, believing it was based on an ulterior design, the preservation of the British Empire. Unperturbed, the British may have thought that the Americans were not smart enough to worry about.[65] Laurence S. Kuter, a talented young AAF colonel, observed at a number of meetings, that if a controversy reached boiling point between the participants a few cooler heads prevailed:

> ...with Admiral King red in the neck and inarticulate, General Arnold apparently furious but quiet, Brooke equally red-faced and inarticulate, it was Portal on the British side and General Marshall on the American side that calmed things down in very simple language: 'We can't blow up on things like this. Something has to be done ... let's get on with it.'[66]

Divergent Views of GYMNAST

Preliminary planning for the North African operation, code-named GYMNAST, reached impasse, because of the divergent views expressed by either side regarding,

1. the size of the force;
2. the level of French assistance and German reaction;
3. air support;
4. the practical use of Casablanca as a seaport.

Maximum forces that could be landed after the initial embarkation totaled approximately 180,000 evenly divided.[67] Shipping, in short supply, was the critical factor; cargo vessels needed to stem the Japanese in the ABDA theater injuriously limited and delayed operations. Once the Pacific crisis was past, the president and the prime minister wanted North Africa revived.[68]

ARCADIA succeeded in creating needed administrative structures. The Combined Chiefs of Staff Committee, the Joint Chiefs of Staff, the US Joint Planning System, a unified theater command structure, division of responsibility among theaters, a fixed, but not necessarily rigid, distinction between the terms 'Joint' and 'Combined' were created or defined during the conference. The CCS, assigned to meet continuously rather than periodically, was to be served by several subordinate and permanent staff sections identified by 'combined' as the first word in their title: Planning Staff, Intelligence Committee, Secretariat and the Military Transport Committee.

Churchill's Domination at ARCADIA

ARCADIA closed with Churchill dominating allied strategy, both in theory and practice: bombing, blockade, aid to Russia, and clandestine European operations were emphasized. Co-operative allied naval ventures in the Atlantic, exchanges of American for British units in Iceland and Northern Ireland were organized, against the background of an inexorable war. For the Americans, harsh reality outstripped wishful thinking. Ill-prepared to fight a global war, it would take more than a year after the traumatic events at Pearl Harbor to mobilize, equip, train, and deploy its forces in any appreciable numbers.[69] No agreement had been reached to use Britain as a base for future amphibious operations. Marshall's plan for a cross-Channel attack to relieve Russia in 1942 was substituted for a North African blocking action against a possible German threat to Spain, Portugal, and Morocco. The CCS asserted, 'In 1943 the way may be clear for a return to the Continent, across the Mediterranean from Turkey into the Balkans, or by landings in western Europe.'[70]

Roosevelt and Churchill had said little to their Chiefs about national policy on which strategy could be based.[71] Killing more and more Germans, victory at all costs, and demanding total enemy capitulation were not war aims on which an improved and peaceful post-war world could be built. Strategic planning suffered, because Allied political objectives remained unclear.[72] Politically, the conference produced the *Declaration of the United Nations*, which reaffirmed the principles of the *Atlantic Charter*: the war was being fought to defend and perpetuate life, liberty, justice, and human rights throughout the world. No nation would make a separate peace, and the resources and energy of all were to combine until the enemy was defeated. Twenty-six nations signed on 1 January 1942.[73] General Sir Leslie Hollis, second in command of the Prime Minister's Defence Office, considered the ARCADIA Conference to be,

> ... the most difficult of all conferences, for the Anglo–American alliance was still untempered steel. The Americans were reeling under the disaster of Pearl Harbor, and possibly a little nervous that the war-tried British might try to tell them what to do. We, on the other hand, were anxious to show that we had no desire to act as senior partners in the new formed alliance, but as equals. We had no pattern to guide us, and the discussions were therefore long and wearisome.[74]

General Hollis who collaborated with the author, James Leasor, after the war, was correct regarding American reactions during the conference, but naïve to think that the British, from the prime minister on down, did not want to impose their will upon the newcomers regarding strategy and experience. As the conference closed, the British succeeded in selling their plan to the Americans, who lacked a plan of their own on which to base a 'Germany-first' policy. 'Trust me to the bitter end', were Roosevelt's final words to Churchill when they parted;[75] that trust was to be sorely tested, as the war intensified.

3 Events Leading to a June Washington Conference

Prior to the 19–25 June 1942 Washington meeting, top-level conversations were held in London with V. M. Molotov, Stalin's Foreign Commissar, from which two disparate points emerged. Britain was prepared to meet its obligations under the Second Protocol, an Anglo–American Lend-Lease agreement extending aid to Russia, but chose to remain non-committal on a second front. Refusing to guarantee that a landing would take place in September 1942 on the Continent, Churchill offered to continue planning for one.[1] Interpreting this as Churchill's intention to abandon a second front, Molotov cabled his views to Stalin, '...consequently the outcome is that the British Government does not accept an obligation upon itself to establish a second front this year; and declares, and that conditionally, that it is preparing some kind of experimental raiding operation.'[2]

Doubting they could fulfill supply obligations to the Soviets under the agreement, due to shipping losses on the Murmansk run to Russia, Roosevelt, in contrast to Churchill, promised to open a second front in 1942, if Russia would accept a reduction in tonnage. After Molotov's visit to Washington, a communiqué issued on 12 June indicated that he and Roosevelt had reached full agreement regarding the establishment of a second front in Europe in 1942.[3] Roosevelt reasoned that since Anglo–American strategy for 1942 and 1943 remained inconclusive, an American–Russo agreement might force the issue.[4] The JSM had warned the COS that progress toward the formulation of an acceptable Anglo–American strategy had proved disappointing. One cause centered on American unwillingness to pursue the strategic argument to any logical conclusion, specifically that one theater of war was more important than another.[5] To settle these problems and any other difficulties that could not be satisfactorily dealt with by correspondence, Churchill decided on another personal visit to Washington.[6] Roosevelt agreed to meet between 17–21 June.

Mountbatten's Meetings with Roosevelt

Admiral Lord Louis Mountbatten, Churchill's emissary, conferred privately with the Roosevelt and Hopkins ten days before the prime minister arrived. Meeting with Roosevelt, at the exclusion of Marshall and King, Mountbatten expressed Churchill's views concerning his disenchantment with SLEDGEHAMMER, a proposed landing on the Norman coast of France in

1942; as an alternative, Mountbatten tried to convince the president that the strategic advantage lay with GYMNAST. Marshall and King, having learned of the meeting and its agenda, expressed concern that without their professional advice, the president would be at a disadvantage.[7]

Fascinated with royalty, Roosevelt was infatuated with Mountbatten, the King's cousin, who had been a social success on his last trip. The newly appointed Chief of Combined Operations, holding exalted rank in each service, an ambitious Beaverbrook protégé and a Churchill 'front-man', was considered to be more skilled in public relations than in naval operations by the COS.[8] As a master in verbal gymnastics and a consummate weaver of epic tales, Mountbatten captivated the American president by suggesting that a 1942 TORCH (formerly GYMNAST) was a fair exchange for a 1943 ROUNDUP. The stakes were high. If he failed to convince the president, Britain would lose its influence over war production and weapons allocation.[9]

Mountbatten argued that SLEDGEHAMMER was limited by a shortage of landing craft and short-range fighter aircraft arrayed against a powerful enemy force of 25 German divisions. Before Mountbatten's arrival, the President had begun shifting his support from SLEDGEHAMMER, as advocated by Marshall and Stimson, to GYMNAST. Accepting Mountbatten's views without the benefit of those of his Joint Chiefs, the President compounded their sense of isolation.

Mountbatten, after favorably impressing the president, sent a summary of their five-hour meeting to his superiors in London who relayed it to the Joint Staff Mission in Washington. The JSM passed it on to the American Chiefs at a 19 June CCS meeting. Roosevelt remained silent.[10] Previous studies have omitted the CCS/Mountbatten meeting of 10 June, at which he failed to reveal his aversion for SLEDGEHAMMER.[11] From Dill's intelligence, Marshall and the JCS were well aware of Mountbatten being economical with the truth, having secretly received two views of his meeting with Roosevelt: Marshall had a copy of Mountbatten's letter to the president, which included a summary of their talk, and an account of their conversation from Hopkins. In this case, Dill, an honest broker, was trying to prevent something stupid from happening that would not only prolong the war, but disrupt the fragile sense of Anglo–American unity.[12] American entrenched suspicions of British intent and purpose were aroused.

Roosevelt's Desire to Help the Russians

Moreover, Dill, as Churchill's agent as head of the British Joint Staff Mission in Washington, informed the COS of a conversation he had with Hopkins, that included the president's desire to help the Russians in 1942 with an

American North African military operation.[13] Even before Churchill arrived, Marshall guessed from Dill's information that Mountbatten had influenced Roosevelt to accept GYMNAST and reject SLEDGEHAMMER. Mountbatten considered this to be his most important assignment of the whole war.[14] Both Marshall and Stimson restated their positions to the president by letter, in which they attacked GYMNAST and endorsed SLEDGEHAMMER; while Stimson and Marshall enclosed a 'letter of concurrence' signed by informed members of their staffs, Hopkins, discouraged by Roosevelt's change of mind, thought that the US deserved to get into the war on the basis of its growing military strength.[15]

CCS Meetings in Opposition

The results of the president's meetings with Mountbatten at the White House and Churchill in Hyde Park were in direct opposition to the CCS series of meetings held concurrently in Washington. Brooke, who disliked SLEDGEHAMMER and feared any North African amphibious operation that would reduce supplies to the threatened Middle East, preferred to continue planning for a 1943 landing in northwest Europe. Failing to convince Brooke of SLEDGEHAMMER's value, Marshall agreed with the British Chief of Staff that GYMNAST was not a viable operation in 1942, because of successive Russian defeats, the weakness of BOLERO's strategic reserves and the British Eighth Army's continuing retreat in the western desert. The CCS concluded that even if amphibious attacks against Hitler's western European fortress contained certain hazards, they would be preferable to GYMNAST.[16] Even if the CCS reported their findings to the president and the prime minister, it is doubtful whether Roosevelt and Churchill would have altered their conclusions. Moreover, they agreed that BOLERO served as a bulwark against a German invasion of Britain and an Allied launching pad for an invasion of the Continent, the application contingent upon the battles in Russia. Allied Intelligence estimates indicated that by early winter Russia would either thwart German aggression or be defeated. The prime minister hammered away at the president by asking,

> But in case no plan can be made in which any responsible authority has good confidence, and consequently no engagement on a substantial scale in France is possible in September 1942, what else are we going to do? Can we afford to stand idle in the Atlantic Theatre during the whole of 1942? Ought we not to be preparing within the general structure of BOLERO some other operation by which we may gain positions of advantage and also directly or indirectly to take some of the weight off

Russia? It is in this setting and on this background that the operation GYMNAST should be studied.[17]

Churchill insisted that if there were any alternative American plan whose immediate employment would achieve comparable results to GYMNAST, he would listen. The Americans had nothing to offer but SLEDGEHAMMER. Politically committed to the Russians, Roosevelt refused to wait for a 1943 BOLERO/ROUNDUP, even though a cross-Channel invasion of such magnitude might have been the most expeditious means of winning the war.[18] Unlike GYMNAST, SLEDGEHAMMER, as a threat, would have directly helped Russia. Scarcity of manpower was not an overriding problem for Marshall, in the long term, as it was for Brooke. The Americans could absorb the losses attendant to a sacrificial operation like SLEDGEHAMMER, even if the odds were unfavorable; the British could not.

Martin Blumenson, in a recent journal article, criticizes the coalition for concocting a strategy whose primary purpose was to liberate territory rather than destroy the German Army in France during 1942. Doubting the quality and effectiveness of their own forces and fearful of a direct confrontation in northern France, they chose a Mediterranean strategy, which, he concludes, prolonged the war beyond 1944. Blumenson fails to define the Anglo–American strategic controversy, as considered here, which resulted in an additional move to the periphery.[19] Moreover, by failing to draw a distinction between the British and American strategic positions, as did Michael Howard, Blumenson disregards Churchill's awareness of the prevalent American attitude: its military leaders, suspicious of British intentions, favored a massive cross-Channel attack and suspected that GYMNAST (renamed TORCH) would serve to protect British interests rather than to defeat Germany. Churchill pressed Roosevelt for a full and irrevocable commitment to British strategy.[20]

The Americans realized that the British would remain intransigent, even if Russia collapsed in 1942.[21] Marshall might have argued that if SLEDGEHAMMER and IMPERATOR (a divisional strength three-day hit-and-run raid in France) were abandoned, nothing could convince the Germans (or the Russians) that a second front landing was imminent.[22] The German High Command, free from this threat, could then transfer, as it did, more of their ground and air reserves to the Eastern Front with impunity.

Defining a second front in the broadest practical terms, Roosevelt concluded that American forces could be in action sooner and in greater strength in the Mediterranean than in northern Europe. The benefit of employing green American formations afforded an opportunity to gain combat experience on more favorable terms, because German strength and fighting-power in North

Africa was only a fraction of what it wielded in Europe. Moreover, American troops, engaged in a less intensified Mediterranean 'side-show', would gain in experience gradually and take fewer casualties. However distant from the main theater of war, German defeats in the Mediterranean might affect the stability of the German regime. Thus, by engaging American troops in combat before 15 September in a relatively safe operation set in French North Africa, Roosevelt surmised that he would gain public support for the war effort, lessen the strain on Russia, and win the November congressional elections for his political party.[23]

America had only been in the war 11 months, poorly armed with scant, archaic equipment and a small peacetime military cadre. Daunting was the task to transform it into a large, modern and aggressive fighting force capable of amphibious combat operations.[24] Marshall was to say in 1956,

> We failed to see that the leader in a democracy has to keep the people entertained. The people demand action. We couldn't wait to be completely ready. Churchill was always getting into side shows. If we had gone as far as he did we never would have got out. But I could see why he had to have something.[25]

Churchill and Mountbatten succeeded in turning the weaknesses of the American system to their own advantage, that of gaining the president's attention and arguing for the acceptance of GYMNAST, as the centerpiece of British strategy. Roosevelt's self-confidence sometimes precluded the use of balanced inquiry, and inadvertently contributed to the outcome his visitors were seeking. The foregoing informal American process, seemingly flexible and expeditious was defined by a president capricious in his decision-making, who discounted the participation of qualified observers and advisers, like Marshall and King, appointed to safeguard the nation's strategic interests. Marshall recognized that the source of the problem stemmed from the president's interpretation of his role as Commander-in-Chief, his lack of accountability and his intermittent use of the JCS.[26]

Lack of Administrative Accountability

The President had made military decisions for political reasons without the benefit of professional advice. Two months later, to avoid a recurrence of this error, the JCS recommended to the CCS that where military and political considerations were both involved, it must be accepted that no military commitment should be entered into on the political level without prior consultation with the CCS.[27]

With SUPER-GYMNAST neutralized by the loss of Tobruk, with BOLERO, not an action in itself but the logistical build-up that would lead to action, with SLEDGEHAMMER failing because of a lack of resources, GYMNAST was revived. Two years later, shortages of landing craft continued to plague the Allies. In a telegram to Marshall, Churchill remarked that, 'history would never understand how the plans of two great empires should be so hamstrung and limited by a hundred or two of these particular vessels.'[28]

Marshall and King argued in a memo sent to the President that 'the advantages and disadvantages of implementing the GYMNAST plan as compared to other operations, particularly 1942 emergency BOLERO operations, leads to the conclusion that the occupation of Northwest Africa this summer should not be attempted...'[29] During an August meeting of the CCS, Cunningham stated that GYMNAST, renamed TORCH, was intended to relieve German pressure on the Russians by clearing the Mediterranean for Allied shipping, relieving the threat to Malta, and by securing Egypt. Once this was achieved, North Africa would become a departure point for the invasion of Europe. King and Marshall disagreed with Cunningham's interpretation, believing that the British had designed TORCH to relieve the Middle Eastern convoy routes and to deny naval bases to the enemy from which they could attack Allied South Atlantic convoy routes. Moreover, the Americans and Russians believed that only a cross-Channel attack in 1942 could provide the relief Russia sought. BOLERO leading to SLEDGEHAMMER in 1942 and ROUNDUP in 1943 were the operations required; anything else was a dispersion of force, an abuse of resources and tangential to Russian demands and needs.

If the landings were compared, TORCH was less fraught with danger than SLEDGEHAMMER, because the bulk of German military strength lay primarily in Russia, along the northern coast of Europe, and not in Vichy controlled French North Africa. Approximately 200,000 German troops were stationed in Tunisia, but only a small German Armistice Commission was based in Algeria and French Morocco.[30] Moreover, Marshall, arguing against TORCH, revealed that its failure would bring only ridicule and loss of public confidence, while a failure in SLEDGEHAMMER, for which the public had been adequately prepared, would have been more acceptable. This did not square with Roosevelt and Churchill's mutual conception of the Channel being made red with the blood of Allied dead, if a landing were attempted.[31] Leahy concluded that since the reputation of the American armed forces was at stake, success in TORCH was essential. If they failed, he warned, plummeting American prestige would result in appalling political consequences for the patriots and peoples of China and Russia. Leahy did not raise similar concerns for SLEDGEHAMMER.[32] Both JCS and the

COS extolled the virtues and discounted the hazards of their pet operation, in an attempt to sway the other, all to no avail.

MODICUM

The Washington Conference was representative of the British attitude towards negotiations, in which the application of the 'Yes/But' method was applied. The following is an example:

> ...Plans and preparations for the operations in this theater (western Europe) are to be pressed forward with all possible speed, energy and ingenuity ... If a sound and sensible plan can be contrived, we should not hesitate to give effect to it. If a detailed examination shows that despite all efforts, success is improbable, we must be ready with an alternative.[33]

The wording smacks of double-talk, with the unmentioned alternative, GYMNAST, preferred. Mixed messages on 'Grand Strategy', as related above, contributed to the conference's inconclusive outcome. It was moot in any case, as Churchill knew that Roosevelt favored GYMNAST, as a means of hustling American troops into action. Before GYMNAST became formalized, however, the president sent Marshall, King and Hopkins to London once again – their mission: to settle the controversy on which Allied strategy had seemingly foundered. It was as if he were directing them to perform in a calculated charade of his own making, since the president had secretly decided upon North Africa beforehand. The difference between the two American visits to London, within the space of four months, must have been a cause of concern for the three of them, as they flew across the Atlantic.

Marshall and Hopkins had previously flown to London in early April 1942, taking with them a plan, originally conceived by Eisenhower, detailed by his operations staff and re-shaped by Marshall; it defined an operation that would threaten the Germans directly in northwest Europe and relieve pressure on the Russians. Known as the 'Eisenhower Memorandum' of 25 March, it emerged with modifications in its final form, as the 'Marshall Memorandum' of 1 April.[34] The plan, presented by Marshall at a White House meeting the following day, was supported by Stimson and Hopkins, and approved by the president, who immediately authorized both his Chief of Staff and Chief Advisor to by-pass the newly organized CCS, 'where it would simply be pulled to pieces and emasculated.'[35] Taking it directly to Churchill and the COS in London, negotiating on the president's behalf,[36] Marshall would by-pass the CCS in the name of expediency. The circumvention failed, because Dill notified his superiors in London on 5 April that, 'You may shortly be seeing a paper from a high US source on operations in western Europe which we have today been able to glance at unofficially.'[37]

The informer's name was omitted, but it did contain a summary of the American plan three days before Marshall and Hopkins arrived, time enough for Churchill and the COS to explore it thoroughly and prepare for their rebuttal. Alex Danchev, in his biography of Dill, attributes certain appellations to him, but 'operative'[38] is not included. At the same time, both American representatives were buoyed by the prospect of not only showing something new to the British, but having it approved. The author, Brian Loring Villa, wrote:

> The arrival in April of General Marshall and his advisors, who were determined to keep alive the possibility of an emergency landing in Europe in 1942, gave Mountbatten his opportunity by reopening the question of what operations should be undertaken in that year. What followed turned out to be the most important strategic debate of the war.[39]

Soon after Marshall and company arrived on 8 April, the meetings, code-named MODICUM, began. Differing from earlier British SLEDGEHAMMER and ROUNDUP proposals, which depended upon a severe German collapse before attempting a Channel landing, the American proposal recommended forcing that collapse with their own military formations.[40] There were two main considerations: first, the continuance of Russian resistance; and second, that northwest Europe was the place where the expanding American Army and Air Corps could engage in active operations and gain war experience. To the Americans, ROUNDUP was their major war effort, and, once agreed upon was considered irreversible. The plan described the following operations:

a. BOLERO, a logistical build-up in Britain of 30 American divisions, plus air power within 12 months, and,
b. ROUNDUP, the deliberate invasion of Europe by 30 American and 18 British divisions in Normandy, supported by 5,800 combat planes in 1943.

Marshall gave his reasons for the choice of western Europe:

1. The shortest route to the heart of Germany passed through France.
2. The theater in which the first major Allied offensive could be staged.
3. Effective results could be obtained more rapidly than elsewhere.
4. Nowhere else could the Allies attain the overwhelming air superiority vital to success.

5. The United States could concentrate and maintain a larger force in that area than it could in any other.
6. Combined Allied combat power could be employed, and maximum support given to Russia in 1942.
7. SLEDGEHAMMER, an emergency landing of approximately five divisions with supporting air on the Cotentin peninsula on 15 September 1942.[41]

The British were skeptical, setting the stage for a prolonged Anglo–American strategic debate that began here and reverberated throughout the war. Although the British found the American ROUNDUP acceptable, they harbored reservations and objections regarding SLEDGEHAMMER's practicality and timeliness in 1942, but remained non-committal regarding its defects. Brooke wrote, 'With the situation prevailing at that time it was not possible to take Marshall's "Castles in the Air" too seriously. His strategic ability was of the poorest! It must be remembered that we were literally hanging on by our eye-lids!'[42]

A British Ruse

Fearful of an American move toward the Pacific, the British resorted to subterfuge in order to irrevocably involve America in defeating 'Germany-first'. An agreement would establish an American concentrated production effort, an increased material allocation program, an intensification of training and Britain-bound troop movements, a contribution specifically geared to fighting directly across the Channel. If they accepted Marshall's proposals, the British would achieve their goal of supply and theater priority. By comparison, Marshall who consistently viewed British operations in the Far and Middle East as secondary and diversionary, relied on BOLERO to refocus British interests and eliminate such dispersions. He urged that operations on the Continent 'not be reduced to the status of a residuary legatee.'[43] Measured against this main effort were the calculated risks taken at the expense of the Middle East and the Pacific where further Japanese incursions would have to be stopped with the current level of resources.[44]

On 14 April the COS accepted the American proposal 'in principle', agreeing that planning in London should begin immediately for a major offensive in Europe in 1943 and for an emergency landing, if necessary, in 1942.[45] However, the British wavered over SLEDGEHAMMER. The inclusion of the phrase 'if necessary' in the agreed document signaled that the COS considered SLEDGEHAMMER subject to further negotiations, if future conditions demanded other alternatives. Marshall knew that the substantive 'agreement in principle' remained a treacherous problem with regard to SLEDGEHAMMER. Churchill's post-war memoirs reveal that the prime minister harbored grave doubts regarding SLEDGEHAMMER's feasibility, but chose to say little regarding the plan during the meeting. Butler, writing in the British Official History, ascribed an unreserved concurrence:

> British officers gathered that in spite of our efforts and intentions to do the contrary, the Americans thought we did not mean to really do business on their plan – this because of our insistence on the seriousness of the situation developing in the Middle East and Indian Ocean.[46]

This does not square with the feelings of the British planning staff who advised the COS. They considered Marshall's proposition strategically ridiculous, a pipe dream of colossal proportions, produced in a mood of totally unjustifiable self-confidence. They concluded that he was far too optimistic in thinking that green American troops could defeat the veteran Germans in late 1943 or even early 1944.[47] Sir Ralph Kilner Brown, one of the British planners, said in a 1993 interview,

> The month of June 1942 saw the relationship between the British and the Americans strained and stretched almost to the breaking point. It was only the personal friendship between Roosevelt and Churchill, and the admiration each felt for the other, that enabled them to overcome the mutual suspicion which existed between the British and American service Chiefs, to build upon the shaky foundations of the Allied war effort...[48]

Motivated by their need for American supplies, filled with doubts regarding Marshall's plan and fearful of reprisals if they rejected it, Churchill and the COS defaulted. Although problems of shipping, landing craft and experienced troop manpower shortages, which were far more crippling to SLEDGEHAMMER than the Americans envisaged, remained unresolved, Marshall and Hopkins assumed that a military settlement had been reached.

The British, having failed to address most of SLEDGEHAMMER's problems openly, not only evaded their responsibility to the alliance, but helped to distort and perpetuate American delusions by their duplicity. The Americans believed SLEDGEHAMMER to be possible and necessary. The British did not, but feared the Americans would abrogate the 'Germany-first' agreement and turn unilaterally towards the Pacific, leaving Britain to fight on alone. Eisenhower had recommended a Pacific alternative if the British rejected the Marshall Memorandum.[49] During the evening of 14 April, at the end of a War Cabinet Defence Committee meeting attended by the Americans, Churchill formally accepted Marshall's proposal.[50] Churchill wrote to Roosevelt on 17 April, 'We wholeheartedly agree...' as the meetings in London concluded.[51] There would be no more thrashing around in the dark, or so it seemed.

The British conferees in London deliberated over SLEDGEHAMMER from the time the Americans had left in mid-April and on 8 July they reached a decision. The prime minister informed the president by letter, the first paragraph of which read,

> No responsible British General, Admiral or Air Marshal is prepared to recommend SLEDGEHAMMER as a practicable operation in 1942. The Chiefs of Staff have reported 'The conditions which would make SLEDGEHAMMER a sound sensible enterprise are very unlikely to occur.'[52]

With the April agreement repudiated, Ismay said of that time,

> Our American friends went happily homewards under the mistaken impression that we had committed ourselves to both ROUNDUP and SLEDGEHAMMER ... When we had to tell them that we were absolutely opposed to it (SLEDGEHAMMER), they felt that we had broken faith with them...[53]
>
> We should have come clean, much cleaner than we did, and said, 'We are frankly horrified because of what we have been through in our lifetime ... you see, we are not going into this until it is a cast-iron certainty.'[54]

While the British equivocated, even if, as Brooke claimed, Marshall was strategically naïve, Churchill and Brooke were less than candid, were manipulative and chose avoidance over direct confrontation. Between Marshall and Brooke there was always something of a temperamental barrier, the British General reserving his true feelings over SLEDGEHAMMER for his diary. By not arguing for his strategic beliefs, Brooke missed an opportunity to be forthright. He could have said that 'agreement in principle' only applied to ROUNDUP and not to the plan as a whole, with SLEDGEHAMMER requiring further study. On 29 April Churchill, unknown to Marshall and Hopkins, said to the War Cabinet, 'While preparations should proceed on the basis that we should make a resolute effort to capture a bridgehead on the Continent in the late summer (of 1942), we were not committed to carrying out such an operation.'[55] The War Cabinet agreed. Thus the euphoria of a 'noble brotherhood of arms' disintegrated into an atmosphere of mutual suspicion and distrust that increased the danger of the coalition unraveling.

Before Marshall and company's second journey to London on 16 July, the president insisted that if SLEDGEHAMMER was definitely canceled, they were instructed to work for an absolute co-ordinated use of British and American forces in 1942. Roosevelt was convinced that only a second front would ease the German pressure on Russia; he said,

> It must be constantly reiterated that the Russian armies are killing more Germans and destroying more Axis material than all the twenty-five united nations put together. Therefore it has seemed wholly logical to support the great Russian effort in 1942 ... to develop plans aimed at diverting German land and air forces from the Russian front.[56]

Nevertheless, in late June the president doubted if a second front could be established with the means available before the upcoming November congressional elections. Without either viable Pacific or the Middle East alternatives, the president leaned toward GYMNAST as the only economical choice in the war against Germany. Churchill and Brooke knew that not only did Roosevelt secretly want a September GYMNAST, but that the American conferees were in disarray strategically: King preferred action in the Pacific, Hopkins in Africa and Marshall in Europe.[57] The concatenation of events in Russia and divergent American attitudes proved insurmountable to Marshall. If Churchill and Brooke remained steadfast, and at the same time supported BOLERO, GYMNAST would become a reality.[58]

A united Churchill and COS conceived of a tactical plan to use against the Americans: they would not mention GYMNAST, but allow the Americans to make their case for the cross-Channel attack. Once the plan was rejected, the Americans, charged to follow presidential instructions, would be forced to agree to GYMNAST. Meeting in closed session, the American conferees and their London staffs, seeking ways to overcome British reticence, revised SLEDGEHAMMER to mean a landing on the Cherbourg peninsula. The British had prepared a revision of their own, that is, their government required permanent landings, a condition that the COS believed impossible to satisfy. Alone, this condition would defeat Marshall.

GYMNAST Prevails

The meetings began on 20 July and lasted four days. The Americans presented their case, the theme of which was support for Russia in the guise of a cross-Channel attack either as a 'sacrifice operation' or the 'first-stage' of ROUNDUP; the British considered that a 'sacrifice' operation against the Pas de Calais, if it were to absorb German forces and help the Russians, would end in disaster with the loss of six divisions, and furthermore, as a 'first-stage' operation, the landing could not be maintained, because of rapid intervention of 15 German divisions, limited Allied fighter support over Cherbourg and poor Channel weather after September. Churchill and the COS, sure of success, rejected the American proposal as unrealistic and requested that Roosevelt be informed of the impasse, as a means of considering alternative operations.[59] The president responded a few hours later, instructing that his American representatives reach consensus quickly, insisting that GYMNAST be considered for immediate consideration. Roosevelt compared an Allied invasion of North Africa with the German invasion of Norway, an operation that returned a large dividend on a small investment. Marshall was under no illusions; GYMNAST would have little or no direct effect upon any critical front of the war, but it did have the full support of both the president and prime minister, controllers of vast supplies and forces. He and King maintained that,

> ...Great Britain is the only area from which the combined strength of the United Nations can be brought to bear against our principal enemy – Germany, so that no avoidable reduction in our preparations for ROUNDUP should be considered as long as there remains any reasonable possibility of its successful execution.[60]

Roosevelt responded to a second Hopkins cable by requesting an invasion date no later than 30 October, then commanding, 'full speed ahead'.[61] The American conferees noted that without active Russian participation and the continuation of BOLERO, they were left with a defensive line of action against Germany as their only option. The British insisted that GYMNAST, now renamed TORCH, did not break with *ABC-1*'s combined strategic concept of sea blockade and air operations. The Americans disagreed, because unlike ROUNDUP, GYMNAST was a defensive operation. They were also concerned that approval of TORCH would delay a 1943 ROUNDUP until 1944, a conclusion already reached by the British chiefs. On 24 July, although Marshall had complied with his Commander-in-Chief, and both sides had agreed that a second front in Europe should be postponed until 1943; 'CCS-94', the combined statement of policy, read as if it were Marshall's creation:

> ...if the situation on the Russian front by 15 September indicates such a collapse or weakening of Russian resistance as to make ROUNDUP appear impracticable of successful execution, the decision should be taken to launch a combined operation against North and North West coast of Africa at the earliest possible date before December 1942...[62]

Marshall requested that preparations for SLEDGEHAMMER continue for the purposes of deception or exploitation, but activated if either an emergency arose or the Germans collapsed. In addition, with British approval, he withdrew 15 US Army Air Force groups and a division's worth of assault shipping from Europe for use against the Japanese.[63] Because it would take over three months of planning and preparation to mount a North African operation, Marshall and King sought a definite decision on TORCH from the president and prime minister. Contrary to their thinking, Dill and Leahy thought that both political leaders had decided favorably, but Marshall and King believed that both Roosevelt and Churchill had to acknowledge the consequences of choosing TORCH and dooming ROUNDUP: as a consequence, left unchallenged in the West, free from a cross-Channel attack for at least a year, the Germans could shift formations elsewhere at little cost to themselves. Moreover, TORCH would increase the strain on limited Allied resources because of longer shipping distances, additional tonnage requirements and repetitive shipment of manpower between Britain and the Mediterranean.[64] Marshall and Stimson tried to prolong the strategic debate as long as possible by accepting GYMNAST as the operation of last resort. As recorded by General Walter Bedell Smith, Roosevelt ended all speculation at a White House meeting attended by the JCS on 30 July:

> The President stated very definitely that he, as Commander-in-Chief, had made the decision that TORCH would be undertaken at the earliest possible date. He considered that this operation was now our principal objective and the assembling of means to carry it out should take precedence over other operations as, for instance, BOLERO ... we are now committed to the provisions of 'CCS-94', which calls for the final decision to be made by September 15.[65]

The After-Shock of Roosevelt's Decision

As usual, none of the major American participants were taken into the president's confidence prior to his decision. Rather than discussing the relative merits of his strategic options with his Chiefs in London, he informed them of his decision after the fact. Contrary to Marshall and King's thinking, Roosevelt, ignoring the need for further inquiry, insisted that his TORCH decision would not prevent ROUNDUP in 1943.[66] Although Churchill and Brooke had been initially divided on GYMNAST, by 17 June they agreed that the North African operation offered the only alternative for an allied offensive that year.[67] Taking comfort in their unified viewpoint, supported by Dill's confidential information, Churchill and Brooke exploited American strategic fragmentation to their own advantage throughout the conference.

Frustrated, Marshall and King sought refuge in 'CCS-94', in an attempt to lessen the effects of the decision. No sooner had the agreement been reached, than they considered 'taking up their dishes and going away', a figurative description of increased American participation in the Pacific, and a de-emphasis of *ABC-1*.[68] Although the president had contributed to the scuttling of both SLEDGEHAMMER and ROUNDUP, he refused to allow any such reprisal, proclaiming that TORCH remain pre-eminent. Marshall considered it to be a momentous change in grand strategy and Eisenhower considered it to be the blackest day in the history of the war.[69]

During the controversy in London, the Pacific theater was in no way being treated as a backwater. The Americans increased the intensity of the conflict in the Pacific to such an extent that the Japanese realized that their adversary had the means and determination to defeat them. As the British could not be held directly accountable or liable for abrogating the SLEDGEHAMMER agreement, the Americans could not seek redress in binding arbitration. However, they could exact penalties. Direct sanctions applied against an ally were unconscionable, but with rearranged priorities and limited shipments to Britain, the effect was the same. For the rest of the year, resources flowed as fast to the Pacific as they did to the Mediterranean; while supplies to Britain slowed to a trickle.[70] As a result of the TORCH decision, the American Army had more troops deployed against Japan by the end of 1942 than deployed against Germany. Both in an attempt to limit the feared dispersion of forces and in the belief that the turnabout was fair play, Marshall and King adopted the British technique of interpreting a contract on the basis of 'agreement in principle' (in spirit) rather than on 'formal interpretation' (the letter). Dill made the distinction in a personal letter to Marshall, 'To what extent does "CCS-94" alter *ABC-4*/CS.1? ... it certainly covers TORCH ... At present, our Chiefs of Staff quote *ABC-4*/CS.1 as the Bible, whereas some of your people, I think, look upon "CCS-94" as the revised version!'[71]

Although Brooke admitted that an African operation involved a necessary dispersion of forces which would otherwise have been available for ROUNDUP, he felt TORCH was the only worthwhile operation. Stressing that strong forces were always needed in Britain, he added that they should be poised to re-enter Europe as soon as possible.[72] When that would happen was questionable, but as late as 27 July, after the agreement had been reached, Churchill telegraphed Roosevelt: '...as I see it this second front consists of a main body holding the enemy pinned opposite SLEDGEHAMMER and a wide flanking movement called TORCH...'[73]

The TORCH plan, even the later cautious American version, based on concerns over a shortage of shipping, mistrust of Spanish intentions and a reluctance to commit their green troops to a fierce initiation fitted easily into British strategy, whereas American strategy had to be fitted into TORCH.[74] Some of the more cynical amongst the American planners felt that they had been deceived by 'perfidious Albion'. They thought that Britain, leaving the defence of her island to the Americans, was free to pursue its imperial policies and post-war settlements elsewhere. Stimson, embittered over the decision to land in North Africa, forcefully expressed his dissatisfaction to the president. The Secretary's behavior encouraged army officers in the War Department to reveal their doubts and opposition to this change in strategy. Roosevelt's response was swift in coming: the Secretary was ostracized for several months. The importance of the London negotiations were expressed by Brooke at the end of the conference, 'It has certainly been a trying week! The major strategy of the war had been at stake, and the Americans intent on carrying out an attack that could only result in disaster, and might well vitiate the whole of our future strategy.'[75]

Churchill's Meeting with Stalin

Approximately one month later, Churchill met Stalin in Moscow to report on the TORCH agreement reached in London. Stalin's reaction differed from Brooke's. The Soviet leader concluded that his western allies had invalidated their arrangement with him for an Anglo–American landing in northern France. He said on 15 August 1942:

> ...the refusal of the Government of Great Britain to create a second front in 1942 in Europe inflicts a moral blow to the whole of Soviet public opinion ... prejudices the plan of the Soviet Command ... deteriorates the Military situation of England and all the remaining Allies ... most favorable conditions exist in 1942 for a second front in Europe, because almost all the forces of the German Army have been withdrawn to the Eastern Front ... the creation of a second front in Europe is possible and should be effective...[76]

TORCH not only delayed the cross-Channel invasion until the spring of 1944, but exceeded its original operational estimates because of Hitler's decision to fight for Tunisia. TORCH denuded the European theater of operations of men and material – leaving it as a standby theater manned by a skeleton crew.[77] If it were Roosevelt's intention to pit American combat units against the Germans, he failed. French, not German, troops opposed the Americans during the TORCH landings in November 1942. TORCH not only failed to give Stalin the relief he needed, but it allowed Hitler to move 27 divisions, including 5 armored divisions, from northwest Europe to

Russia.[78] When the Allies rejected SLEDGEHAMMER, either as a landing or the threat of one, the Russian Army, which represented the only force capable of defeating or containing the German Army, faced near destruction. The 25 German divisions in France would have contained and eliminated a 1942 SLEDGEHAMMER operation, but the threat of one almost certainly would have kept them in place. While the German armies in Russia intensified their unrelenting pressure on the Soviets, the Germans in Tunisia were preparing to teach the Americans an unforgettable combat lesson, but not before another summit conference assembled at Casablanca, Morocco in late January 1943.

4 The SYMBOL and TRIDENT Conferences

On 7 January 1943, one week before the Casablanca Conference, Roosevelt and the JCS met at the White House to discuss future strategic options. Asking if they were united in advocating a cross-Channel operation, he discovered that consensus was non-existent and division existed between them and their planners. Marshall discounted further Mediterranean action on the basis of logistics and shipping demands, advocating a cross-Channel attack.

> The losses in northwest France would be in troops, but to state it cruelly, we could replace troops, whereas a heavy loss in shipping which would result from the BRIMSTONE (Sardinia) operation, might completely destroy any opportunity for successful operations against the enemy in the near future.[1]

Marshall had failed to raise this argument during the two London meetings of April and July 1942, when he had proposed SLEDGEHAMMER as a sacrificial operation to satisfy both Russian demands and American military thinking. If he had lobbied further for SLEDGEHAMMER, he might have either exposed, limited or neutralized British dissent, but binding agreements were nearly impossible to attain throughout 1942 and 1943, largely because the president continued to equivocate on the issue of a European grand strategy. The impasse between the British and American strategies was described, 'as one thing or the other with no alternative in sight'. As Commander-in-Chief, pressed to choose between a European or Mediterranean strategy, he felt wary of domestic political adversaries who could convert any executive military recommendation into a partisan political issue. He warned that the British would have a comprehensive plan at Casablanca, but he offered nothing as comparable. A hobbled JCS could only fight a rearguard action against the COS.[2]

Casablanca was the 'watershed' conference of the war, because its decisions politicized the war in an utterly irretrievable manner.[3] Casablanca developed a military strategy based on attrition rather than maneuver and on the acquisition of space rather than the elimination of the German Army.[4] Incompatible differences increased the tensions between the British who advocated a war of opportunity ending with a landing in France as the *coup de grâce* and the Americans who advocated a war of concentration beginning with a collision of forces.

Roosevelt, Churchill and their staffs, with Marshall and Brooke as the chief protagonists, met at Anfa, near Casablanca from 13 to 23 January 1943.

Roosevelt's mood was optimistic and carefree, as if he were delighted to be out of the intemperate politics and cold weather of Washington. Sub-tropical Casablanca offered superb accommodations to the visiting dignitaries. Harold Macmillan wrote soon after arriving,

> ...I christened the two personalities [Prime Minister and the President], the Emperor of the East and the Emperor of the West, and indeed it was rather like a meeting of the later period of the Roman Empire ... there was a curious mixture of holiday and business ... in these fascinating surroundings.[5]

During the life of the Conference, the major participants attended 31 meetings, some of which were presided over by the president and prime minister. Stalin had declined his invitation, because of the critical situation in Russia. The British arrived at the conference feeling confident, having learned beforehand that the JCS had approved of their agenda. [6] The CCS assembled and later agreed to thrash out problems of combined strategy before informing the prime minister and president of the work in progress. For the summit meetings at least, the two Chiefs of Staffs Committees were able to negotiate face to face, without having to resort to an exchange of trans-Atlantic cables to resolve their strategic differences.[7]

Since Dill had informed his superiors in London that the Americans lacked a 'united front', Churchill decided to apply the same inexorable approach at Casablanca that had worked so successfully during the previous July in London. He waited until the Americans exhausted themselves talking, before applying the logic of British Mediterranean strategy.[8] Unlike the out-classed Americans, whose preparations were incomplete, the British conferees arrived with a headquarters ship, the *HMS Bulolo*. It contained a full planning staff with elaborate secretarial, telecommunication, library and cipher facilities, organized to present the British position and to counter American arguments.[9] Brigadier Ian Jacob, military assistant secretary to the War Cabinet, intimated that he never could have foreseen a result so comprehensively favorable to British ideas which prevailed throughout most of the conference.[10]

Fearing that Russia might collapse or sue for a separate peace and concerned about the defence of the British Isles, Churchill pleaded concurrently for greater allied activity in the Mediterranean and a rapid BOLERO build-up at home. Since BOLERO's pace had slowed as the American shift to the Pacific increased, he concluded that Marshall was penalizing him for abandoning SLEDGEHAMMER, postponing ROUNDUP and promoting TORCH: late November War Department directives decreed that Lend-Lease supplies and materials formerly ear-marked for BOLERO's expansion were being cut back. Churchill, as a junior partner, had to plead his case with Roosevelt on 24 November 1942.

> ...This has caused us very great concern, not so much from the standpoint of Lend-Lease but on the grounds of grand strategy. We have been preparing under BOLERO for 1,100,000 men, and this is the first intimation we have had that this target is to be abandoned ... I do beg of you, Mister President, to let me know what has happened. At present we are completely puzzled.[11]

At a 16 January presidential meeting, King, doubtful of British strategic intentions, informed the president that the JCS had attempted and failed to obtain the COS's concept of how the war should be won. He concluded that the British had definite ideas as to what the next operation should be, but doubted that they had an overall plan for the conduct of the war.[12] Later the same day, King demanded that the British state how the war was to be conducted and what were the overall plans and the percentage of the war effort required for the defeat of Germany, of Japan.[13]

Although Churchill admitted that TORCH was no substitute for ROUNDUP, and agreed that it ought not be abandoned, he and his Chiefs offered the Americans the strategy they had recently constructed, to defeat the Italians as the first priority for 1943. Even though the British plan was riddled with contingencies and ineffectual compromises, the COS hoped that its design might eliminate the need for ROUNDUP altogether. Action in the Mediterranean would have top priority, but sufficient resources would be allotted to the Pacific, and BOLERO would be slowly resuscitated.[14] The British were obsessed with preventing ROUNDUP and on 22 January, the British Joint and Combined Planning Staffs offered two position papers, 'CCS-167' and 'CCS-169'. 'CCS-167', the first document examined various cross-Channel operational landings in the light of existing German morale and levels of disintegration, with a target-date of August. The second paper, 'CCS-169', proposed an organization of command, control, planning and training for a cross-Channel operation in 1943. Raids would be considered on a contingency basis, and although ROUNDUP was declared dead for 1943, it was recommended that preparations and planning for it be continued.[15] No American paper was offered in rebuttal. Wedemeyer, as one of the attending American planners, concluded that the JCS lacked executive support, leadership and a clearly defined strategic position. 'They never discovered how to convince the British of the danger of frittering away our combined resources on indecisive, limited operations'.[16] Wedemeyer paid tribute to Dill's ability to state the American position on innumerable occasions during the Conference. The following is an example of how Dill reported the American position to Churchill, as if the Field Marshal were part of the JCS and privy to its intimate thoughts.

> 15 July 1942 ... Marshall is convinced that there has been no real drive behind the European project. Meetings are held, discussions take place, and time slips by ... King's war is against the Japanese ... May I suggest with all due respect that you must convince your visitors that you are determined to beat the Germans, that you will strike them on the continent of Europe at the earliest possible moment even on a limited scale, and that anything which detracts from this main effort will receive no support from you at all?[17]

Dill, portrayed as a man who garnered immense respect and affection in Washington for his efforts to state the American case, caused Wedemeyer to lament, 'We had no Dill of our own in London. Even had we had one, it is doubtful that he could have penetrated the glacis set up by the British conviction that their decisions were beyond argument.'[18]

General John Kennedy, Assistant Chief of the Imperial General Staff, had written of the Conference that,

> ...We were still convinced that they [Americans] were wrong and we were right. Now our problem was to get them to accept our strategy, without causing them to lose interest in the priority of operations against Germany. We all felt that the Americans had bigger ideas than ours and more drive; but we had as yet no great respect for the quality of their staff work, and did not regard their strategical conceptions as being based on realities, but we found the American officers difficult to know.[19]

For the first week, no progress was made. Opposing arguments were repeated *ad nauseam*.[20] King and Roosevelt sought to shift to the offensive against Japan, and as soon as US productivity increased, more and more resources would flow to the Pacific.[21] On 15 January, the British conferees realized that neither ally could afford to delay the assault on Germany, because of Britain's diminishing resources and the American public's demands for revenge in the Pacific. British policy had by no means been decided before the Conference, but there was general agreement between members of the COS that some Mediterranean operation should be mounted. When enough steam had been blown off, Brooke wrote of the Americans,

> It is a slow and tiring business, which requires a lot of patience. They can't be pushed and hurried ... It is a slow and tedious business, as all matters have to be carefully explained before they can be absorbed ... I was in

despair and in the depths of gloom ... It is no use, we shall never get agreement with them.[22]

Dill, armed only with the power to influence and persuade, advised Brooke that it would be a mistake to allow a catalogue of unsolved problems to fall into the hands of the president and prime minister. If Brooke were willing to demonstrate some flexibility, he could break the stalemate and secure the agreement he sought. Brooke agreed.[23] Surprisingly, the CCS accepted Brooke's progam for consideration the following day with only a few trifling changes, allowing practical planning to begin.[24] Nevertheless, the negotiations ended without an agreement on the percentage of resources required for each of the major theaters. The sailors and airmen mirrored the needs of their political superiors, a strategy that would open the Mediterranean to shipping, employ an expanding army and establish air bases from which southern Europe could be attacked. Withal, the British view prevailed: Japan would be held in check with the existing forces in the Pacific, with limited aggressive action planned, while Germany was defeated.[25] They saw the Mediterranean theater gaining in prominence in which opportunistic military operations after Torch would continue. Marshall maintained that only a head-on collision of forces would eliminate the Germans from the war, and insisted that 'land-liberation' was both more costly and more time-consuming than 'force-concentration'. Wedemeyer complained that the British test of friendship placed a limited value on loyalty and reciprocity, more on enticement and manipulation. He blamed the British for their lack of flexibility, seeking to take more than they gave, as epitomized in negotiations by the voluble prime minister and his sensitive Chief of Staff.[26]

The American Handicap

Even if the Americans had come to Casablanca with a well-conceived strategic plan, and equipped with an excellent administrative structure, it is unlikely that they could have recommended ROUNDUP as a viable option in 1943. Roosevelt, seeking further operations in the Mediterranean, was against it and Marshall's planners disagreed over ROUNDUP's feasibility. Eisenhower, deliberating further, believed ROUNDUP could not be staged before August 1944.[27] After post-Torch conversations with Eisenhower, Marshall considered fighting a strong rearguard action in ROUNDUP's defence rather than risking a direct confrontation between the British and the reluctant members of his own team. However, Roosevelt found that unacceptable and both he and Churchill eliminated that option, believing that the Allied armies in North Africa should not remain idle while the Russians were engaged in titanic battles in the East. Inaction in 1943 would not, indeed could not, be tolerated, even if it meant abandoning ROUNDUP.

Privately, some top American officers had lingering doubts about British intentions, and they expressed little appreciation for Britain's war effort, battle experience and strategic planning. If differences of opinion between the Americans had not weakened their negotiating position, and if Brooke were less formidable and convincing at the conference table, the results at Casablanca might have limited future Mediterranean operations, thus benefiting ROUNDUP.[28]

'Unconditional Surrender'

On 24 January, Roosevelt demonstrated a form of state-craft that was at best casual and at worst irresponsible. His controversial policy of 'unconditional surrender', consented to by Churchill with feigned surprise, was proclaimed to the world at the final press conference. Since Stalin, King, Marshall and Hull had not been consulted or notified beforehand, their surprise was genuine. The President first aired his notion at a White House Meeting on 7 January.[29] No discussion followed concerning the political–military ramifications of the formula. Subsequently, Churchill and a few members of staff were notified between 19–21 January. They responded approvingly, but objected when the formula failed to include Italy.[30]

'Unconditional surrender', immortalized by Union General Ulysses S. Grant during the American Civil War, could be argued to be the appropriate tactic during the siege of Ft. Donelson in February, 1862. To appropriate the term as a slogan 81 years later did not suggest a sound strategic policy, however dramatic.[31] Churchill notified the War Cabinet and offered his interpretation: the Germans were to be completely disarmed, to stand trial for atrocities, and pay reparations. The entire German Army and its General Staff were to be disbanded.[32] Goebbels called it 'total slavery' and 'castration for the whole male population.' And the German population believed him, accepting that a total war was being waged against the German nation, not just the Nazi party; and consequently, the formula nearly destroyed six years of work by the anti-Nazi opposition.[33] Eisenhower requested that the formula be softened before the Normandy landings in 1944.[34]

The president's abhorrence of the Axis narrowed his war aims to simple destruction of the enemy regime, and discouraged consideration of policy once the fighting stopped. He believed that the United Nations, controlled by the victorious 'Big Four', would supersede the previous balances of power in the post-war world. Winning the war and punishing the enemy became his administration's eventual political and military objectives, with all other political considerations becoming irrelevant. Churchill and Eden were willing and enthusiastic collaborators.[35] The president remarked that he as 'Dr. Win-the-War' had replaced 'Dr. New Deal'.[36]

Stephen Ambrose wrote that, 'Unconditional surrender was a brilliant stroke of policy, because by keeping this and other war aims vague, Roosevelt prevented bickering among the Allies.'[37] This observation is debatable, because even before Roosevelt's announcement, the Allied leadership was already treating each other with doubt, suspicion, and mild contempt. The evidence suggests that the president's views on policy were vague all along; and his decision to speak out, without prior consultation, was a manifestation of that vagueness. The unconditional surrender statement can be understood as a means of reassuring Stalin. However, Roosevelt failed, because Stalin could not be assuaged with words alone, particularly when the second front remained still-born. A more plausible reason emerges, that of soothing an American public outraged over Eisenhower's dealings with Admiral Jean Darlan, commander of all Vichy forces in French North Africa, which resulted in the French agreeing to a cease-fire that saved American lives. Realizing again that to jump too far ahead of his constituency was politically dangerous, Roosevelt pitched his declaration to the folks back home and achieved the desired result.[38]

The Allied leaders lost an opportunity to deeply reflect on the question of 'whether total victory is necessarily the surest foundation for a lasting peace.'[39] Understanding Russian intentions regarding Roosevelt's notion was difficult to assess, but ten months later, in late October they acceded to its principles. 'Unconditional surrender', made public as an Allied war aim, had deleterious effects: it stiffened the enemy's will to resist, it delayed Italian armistice negotiations at a most critical time, and it contributed much grist to the German propaganda mill. Whatever Roosevelt's deeper reasons, for example, to avoid a repetition of Wilson's 'Fourteen Points', to quiet the public over the Darlan deal, to change the geographical and social map of Germany, to convince Stalin that his western allies were not intending a separate peace with Germany and to prevent him from doing the same, it smacked of vengeance. However, if it had been Allied policy (rather than Roosevelt's), a modified 'unconditional surrender' could have contributed to the attainment of security from post-war German ambitions. William Cavendish-Bentinck held a senior position in the Foreign Office in 1943. He stated,

> When news of the unconditional surrender formula came through from Casablanca I told Cadogan, 'There are two old men out there who have done this without thinking while they were full up with rough red Moroccan wine.' Later my view was that this formula did make the Germans fight

> harder; on the other hand it led to the complete break-up of the German officer corps and their being absolutely discredited.[40]

It failed even to demonstrate that the war's mission was for 'good' to triumph over 'evil', because the inclusion of Stalinist Russia as part of the Grand Alliance had already corrupted that perception.[41] The time to fight a different kind of war for different ends was long past because primary war aims with regard to Germany had never been clarified, and both Britain and Russia had hidden agendas. Nevertheless, the scourge of the Third Reich had to be obliterated, and if Russia was the vehicle with whom to proceed, Churchill and Roosevelt recognized that her participation was crucial.

On 10 March 1944, The JSSC enclosed a proposed memorandum, 'Effect of Unconditional Surrender' Policy on German Morale to be approved and forwarded by the JCS to the President. The committee recommended that the President make a statement, following a large-scale bombing raid and before OVERLORD, that would reduce the existing level of German morale increased since the original formula was announced more than a year before. Hopefully, it would separate the Nazis from the German people, free the population from its criminal leadership and ease Allied entry into Germany.[42] Roosevelt refused.

The Giraud–de Gaulle French leadership problem

The President and General Charles de Gaulle, leader of the fighting Free French forces, met for the first time in Casablanca. Roosevelt was already prejudiced against him, because of his involvement in the ill-fated Dakar expedition and his involvement in seizing Vichy-held islands off the Canadian Atlantic coast. Little is known of what de Gaulle said when they met in private, because he spoke in low tones, recorded as grunts by both Elliot Roosevelt and Captain John L. McCrea waiting outside.[43] In this, Churchill colluded, sometimes behaving as Roosevelt's henchman against de Gaulle.[44] Putting both French generals, de Gaulle and Henri Giraud, together at Casablanca, in what seemed to be a 'shotgun wedding', turned out to be a poorly stage-managed affair, that soon ended in divorce. Roosevelt commented in a letter to Hull,

> We delivered our bridegroom, General Giraud, who was most co-operative on the impending marriage, and I am sure was ready to go through with it on our terms. However, our friends could not produce the bride, the temperamental lady de Gaulle. She has got quite snooty about the whole idea and does not want to see either of us, and is showing no intention of getting into bed with Giraud...[45]

Thinking that Giraud, High Commissioner of French Africa, and de Gaulle would accept and execute an Allied policy concerned with those parts of the French Empire free of Vichy control, both the President and the Prime Minister failed to realize that an insurmountable political and military gulf existed between the Frenchmen. The meeting, at which the two generals posed shaking hands, was nothing more than a charade that ended with a vague declaration of Gallic resolve. Grudgingly, the Prime Minister knew that de Gaulle would not sacrifice his country's dignity in his dealings with the President the way he had over TORCH. This combination and interplay of prejudicial attitudes and concrete intransigence between Roosevelt, Churchill, and de Gaulle added little to the speed of French revival or getting on with the war.[46]

Impressions at Casablanca hardened rather than softened Roosevelt's opinion of Churchill. 'On specific issues, [Roosevelt] could also be more acerbic toward him than he was toward Stalin.'[47] He had concluded earlier that Churchill was an old fashioned imperialist bent on protecting the Empire. With a certain disregard, he decided that it was pointless to discuss political issues with him. Although Roosevelt was a steadfast ally in the war against Hitler, he opposed rather than shared Churchill's 'imperial' point of view. When the *Atlantic Charter* was being formulated, Roosevelt wanted it to apply, not only to Europe, but everywhere, including the colonial areas. Churchill and the British War Cabinet rejected the suggestion out of hand, insisting that the *Charter* was not intended to deal with the internal affairs of the British Empire ... or the Philippines.[48] Roosevelt commented to his son, Elliot, at the conference, 'The English mean to maintain their hold on their colonies. They mean to help the French maintain their hold on their colonies. Winnie is a great man for the *status quo*. He even looks like the *status quo*, doesn't he?'[49]

Attritional Warfare–The Chances of a Normandy Invasion in 1943

Fighting a lonely rearguard action over ROUNDUP, Marshall's only recourse was to agree to the reduction of the Tunisian bridgehead from which no armed forces were to be deflected.[50] Its destruction was given 'top priority' at Casablanca, thereby eliminating any consideration for other timely, more rewarding, opportunistic actions with a higher rate of profitability. Allied victory in the desert and mountains of Tunisia followed victory in the Mediterranean and Atlantic, and not the other way around. Once a strategy for action elsewhere was applied, Mediterranean operations would be used as 'a threat only'. According to historian John Grigg, Axis action in the bridgehead ceased to exist on 13 May. Grigg concluded that the Germans defending the bridgehead gained the time needed for their countrymen in northwest Europe to construct and improve Channel fortifications along the French coast. With impunity, they transferred 17 divisions from western Europe between November 1942 and February 1943 which added, not relieved, pressure on the Russians. American disunity precluded closing in on and attaining an important 'glittering' prize, the reasonable possibility of winning the war one year earlier.[51]

Grigg's view is an oversimplification because TORCH, regarded as the first major amphibious assault planned and executed by the Allies, posed problems of unknown dimensions. The whole range of amphibious procedures and the utilization of inter-service communications, air power, close-in naval supporting-gunfire, regimental combat teams, combat-loading logistics, controlled by an overall commander, were in their infancy and lacked the proficiency a Normandy invasion demanded. An evaluation of two recent smaller amphibious operations can be drawn. Guadalcanal, an island in the South Pacific, and Dieppe, a French port on the English Channel, were costly, stark reminders that if the enemy in North Africa had been Japanese or German fierce and protracted fighting would have followed and every foot of ground contested.

It does not follow that a released Mediterranean Allied force could have accomplished a beachhead in Normandy. Even though Sicily was the largest amphibious assault in history, an operation which included 3,000 ships, over 200 air squadrons, upwards of 500,000 men and two airborne divisions, there were only 200,000 Italians soldiers of questionable fighting ability and 62,000 assorted German troops on the island to offer resistance, a far cry from the 15 to 30 German divisions obstructing entry into northwestern France. Unlike Normandy, the loss of Sicily presented no threat to Germany, regarding the outcome of the war in the West.[52]

Grigg's recommendation for a 1943 cross-Channel attack is plausible if viewed as a sacrificial SLEDGEHAMMER operation to assist the Russians, regardless of cost; otherwise, OVERLORD demanded time, will and technology in order to succeed. Lt. General Frederick Morgan's directive of 15 July 1943, addressed to the Secretary, Chiefs of Staff Committee at the QUADRANT Conference made the comparison between the two operations:

> ...operation HUSKY and operation OVERLORD. the two expeditions could hardly be more dissimilar. In HUSKY the bases of an extended coastline were used for a converging assault against an island; whereas, in OVERLORD it is necessary to launch an assault from an island against an extended continental mainland coastline. In the Mediterranean the

tidal range is negligible and the weather reasonably reliable, in the English Channel, the tidal range is considerable and the weather capricious.[53]

The tactical lessons learned off the North African shore and on its beaches may have prevented greater loss of life in subsequent operations such as HUSKY. Competence demanded that failed procedures, unreliable equipment and poor leadership be changed before the next amphibious operation. TORCH revealed that the operation was hastily organized and carried out under very difficult sea conditions, that the troops were inadequately trained and that planning was more theoretical than practical. The problem was compounded with odds favoring the defenders, particularly if they enjoyed the benefit of interior lines and land-based air power.[54] Moreover, Normandy may have been compromised in another way.

During the summer of 1943, General James Christiansen, Army Ground Forces COS, criticized Marshall for freezing the Army at 7.7 million men. From that amount, he allocated 3.2 million of the 'best and the brightest' to the Air Force. Marshall had made a fateful decision that is, that an Anglo–American air offensive plus a Russian ground war would produce a decisive victory. Marshall's revision of the existing Victory Program increased the immoderate pressures upon the regimental combat teams, revealed a flaw in his expectations and questioned his commitment to a head-on collision with the enemy. By reducing the Army from 200 divisions to 80, he gambled with the future of the US and placed the responsibility of success on 750,000 front line soldiers.[55] The replacement problems in northwest Europe, during the fall and winter attritional battles of the campaign, fought under ferocious conditions, would reveal this gross error in judgment: 'In Lorraine, General George Patton "drafted" five percent of army and corps troops for retraining as infantry, and when bloody fighting along Germany's Westwall sent infantry losses soaring, he "drafted" an additional five percent.'[56]

The Results of the Conference

The Casablanca conference ended in enfeebled compromise. Churchill and Roosevelt felt that the agreement fell short of great-power capabilities, although British strategy remained pre-eminent. Stalin's demands for a second front were once again delayed. Both Allied leaders insisted on further action in the Mediterranean, and Marshall and the JCS agreed to a Sicilian operation, defined as an expedient action dictated by current circumstances.

On 19 January the essentials of the agreement were revealed:

1. To assault and occupy Sicily, allowing for the safe and economical passage of shipping through the Mediterranean.

2. To force Italy to leave the war.
3. To divert German pressure from the Russian Front.
4. To seek Turkey's active support.
5. To increase the bombing of Germany from Britain, and to prepare for re-entry on the Continent, if Germany weakened.
6. To defeat the U-boat and win the war at sea.
7. Due to a shortage of landing craft, time constraints, and inadequate planning, HUSKY, the code-name for the Sicilian assault, not ROUNDUP, was the landing of choice.[57]

The Americans considered the above agenda as defensive 'pin-pricking', the British as aggressive action.[58] In addition, the Mediterranean was split into two commanded structures, one British, one American, which was to prove impracticable.

Further Reactions and Considerations

According to Michael Howard, not all American ideas suffered: the British delegates approved of Admiral King's Pacific policy and General Arnold's bombardment program for Germany. Even though ROUNDUP 1943 was a major loss to Marshall and tacitly dead, Morgan was designated Chief of Staff to the Supreme Allied Commander (COSSAC) and a special Allied Inter-Service Planning Staff was created to plan for the execution of a cross-Channel attack, with the vague proviso, 'as soon as circumstances allowed.'[59] Brooke summed up British policy to include continuing actions in the Mediterranean, and proposed returning to the Continent *en masse* in 1944. This subject reminded some Americans of SLEDGEHAMMER's loss and the meetings held in London the previous July.[60]

The American Chiefs recognized their ineffectiveness when arguing their case against British logic, reality and preparedness; sensing their inferiority did not lend itself to co-operation and goodwill even while co-signing with the British. General Sir Ian Jacob, Ismay's deputy, stated,

> They had left most of their clubs behind ... On thinking it over, I do not believe that this was an unreasonable result. After all, we were not two business opponents making a deal in which one was bound to profit at the other's expense. We were partners, trying to hammer at a common line of action.[61]

The Americans regarded Churchill's Mediterranean intentions with increased suspicion as the year progressed. The more he shoved Brooke's Mediterranean policy at them, the more they attributed his aggressive behavior to be a manifestation of self-serving imperialistic designs. Sometimes, he could be withering, as he was toward Eisenhower.[62] Frustrated, the Americans were as irritated with themselves for succumbing to British pressure as they were with the British, whose blandishments did little to soften the inevitable. Howard, although even-handed, cannot deny the American feeling of being gulled at Casablanca, a feeling which persisted long after the event. In the last analysis, fruitful negotiation depends upon the capacity of each party to threaten the other with damage if acceptable compromises are not made and to withhold that damage if acceptable compromises are.

Marshall was convinced 'that every diversion or side issue from the main plot acts as a suction pump.'[63] His metaphor of the Mediterranean as a 'suction pump' comes close to Howard's conclusion that Casablanca legitimized attritional warfare.[64] Marshall strongly opposed any campaign that would absorb untold amounts of men and equipment, that could result in unacceptably high casualties, exhaustion, and wastage. War is an act of attrition in absolute terms, but, in relative terms, a war can be defined either as a war of attrition or one of maneuver. Both sides must determine what is an acceptable level of attrition when measured against its strategic goals. Any commander must ask himself whether the attrition he is imposing on the enemy will be worth the attrition he is imposing on his own forces.[65]

The American historians Matloff and Snell have alluded to the Casablanca's aftermath with a mixture of reticence, reprimand, and renovation. The use of 'rearguard', and 'counteroffensive' are battlefield words associated with action against enemies, words not necessarily descriptive of actions around the negotiating table between partners:

> The indecisiveness of the Casablanca Conference on basic strategic issues ... brought home to the Army strategic planners the need to adjust themselves to a new phase of coalition warfare. The effect of General Marshall's rearguard action at the conference was to give them the time they badly needed to regroup for a 'counteroffensive' in their dealings with the British in 1943 ... the Army strategic planners would have to start anew in 1943 to plan for victory.[66]

'In many ways, the Casablanca conference was a low point in the co-operation between the president and his military advisers.'[67] In sum, the Americans were handicapped in negotiating with the British for most of the war,[68] but, the Casablanca Conference tolled the death knell for the American 'either–or' school of strategic thinking. It was now 'this-and-that'. No longer would considerations, choices, and decisions be as simplistic as they once were prior to the conference, that is, a Mediterranean versus a northwest Europe policy. From now on the strategic view would encompass all theaters, and would therefore be global in reach. Each theater, considered as part building-block of the total, would be connected and interrelated, its problems surveyed, its needs assessed. Precise relationships involving the combined air offensive, and the European and Mediterranean theaters, however, would remain the lynch pin and have top priority in American strategic planning. The strategic 'lode star' remained as always, the cross-Channel attack in 1944.[69] The JCS searched for presidential approbation in their quest for an inescapable British commitment to a cross-Channel invasion in 1944.[70] The counter-attack had begun.

American Attempts to Break the Casablanca Agreement

Dispirited, Marshall and King tried to thwart the enactment of the Casablanca agreement. During a CCS meeting in late April 1943, the JCS presented a paper, 'CCS-199' which sought to clarify the Casablanca decisions and to serve as a guide for future American actions. The key to the paper was the so-called differentiation between 'commitments' and 'undertakings'.[71] The COS was perplexed, since the precise wording of the agreement, 'CCS-155/1', had been discussed with meticulous care and unanimously approved at Casablanca. Although the same language was used, the British admitted that shades of meaning were sometimes interpreted differently, requiring further discussion. Having resolved similar problems at past conferences, the British failed to understand why an entirely new document was required, unless the Americans wanted to change something in the mutually approved strategy. If necessary, the British suggested, 'CCS-155/1' could be safeguarded by a line-by-line interpretation or by agreed textual amendments. The COS affirmed that nothing would be gained by the production of a new paper, which could hardly fail to have its own shades of meaning different from those of the original. If changes were made in the existing manifesto, the COS would need time to carefully consider any new interpretations and proposed amendments; these changes, in turn, had to be agreed by the CCS before being referred to their political masters, the president and the prime minister, for approval – a time consuming process.[72]

Unlike civil law, an ally could not be compensated for breach of contract. Free of sanctions, neither side was immune to re-interpreting an agreement when it suited its purpose, whether it was the Americans over the Casablanca arrangement or the British over SLEDGEHAMMER.[73] Attempts to amend an agreement in the event that circumstances change may not sound like much of an agreement. Contractually, on the one hand, the British regarded American determination as inflexible behavior, exaggerated and insufferable.

On the other, the Americans regarded British flexibility as equivocal, lacking both assurance and commitment.

TRIDENT

Five months passed before another major conference, code-named TRIDENT, convened in Washington to confirm earlier decisions, to clarify Anglo–American planning and to specify long-term military goals. As the conferees gathered, they were informed of Allied dominance in North Africa, the Pacific, the Aleutians, at Stalingrad and in the Atlantic. The conference, originally suggested by Eden, recommended by Churchill and confirmed by Roosevelt, convened on 12 May; in attendance were the president, the prime minister and their military staffs. Brooke, representative of his British colleagues, was apprehensive of the American drift towards the Pacific since the Casablanca Conference, and in Washington he would seek reassurance that the 'Germany-first' formula remained intact. Nor did he envisage an easy time of it, because, in his view, King continued to divert large forces to the Pacific with Marshall's implicit support. Brooke dreaded the up-coming meetings, knowing that they would entail hours of argument with an ally trying to depart from the agreed basic strategy. Strained and depressed at the thought, he reasoned that if the Americans were allowed to succeed, if the Pacific were to absorb the bulk of the Allied effort, the war could go on forever.[74] Even though the Americans disagreed with his Mediterranean strategy, Marshall counted on Brooke to blunt some of Churchill's impractical schemes and Roosevelt was determined to see 'Germany-first' through to the end.[75]

The Americans Continue to Reorganize

Prior to TRIDENT, the American military establishment was in the midst of a major administrative reorganization, which, it was hoped, as one of a number of outcomes, would manifest itself in a more favorable negotiating stance against the British. Innovative procedures were applied by the military and business communities, both understanding that mobilization and production had to be linked to national policy and strategic planning. Since scientific management was first developed and widely applied in the United States early in the century, experience determined the appropriate mix of management, machines and manpower, the combination of which improved and grew as the war continued.[76] However, certain army doctrines impaired military effectiveness, specifically, the emphasis on daylight bombing and the de-emphasis of infantry, as evidenced in the European air and ground campaigns that followed. As part of the overall effort, increased efficiency demanded that the JCS authorize studies covering standard policy procedures for all of its sub agencies. Moreover, it instructed the Joint Staff Planners to prepare, recommend and submit a study on the organization of a Joint General Staff to function under the JCS.[77]

A Plethora of Committees

Although the Joint Strategic Survey Committee (JSSC), led by Embick,[78] had been established in November 1942 to advise the JCS on broad, long-range strategic planning, steps were taken to improve the effectiveness and co-ordinating functions of the Joint Staff Planners (JPS), related to strategy.[79] The Joint War Plans Committee (JWPC), established in April, subordinate and responsible to the JPS, was empowered, in part, to develop joint outline plans, papers and studies for future operations.[80] These recommendations were to serve as a basis of agreement for the JCS, on which unified policy could be reached, defended and addressed in consultations with the British. Many of the impending changes were directed toward offsetting the COS.[81]

During a JCS meeting on 8 May, four days before the conference convened, the Americans expressed their apprehension of British inter-service co-ordination and the abilities of its negotiators. A composite of pre-conference JCS meetings revealed that the JCS continued to suffer from inferior negotiating skills and limited cohesion. Time was spent searching for the most effective method, such as sticking to fundamentals and eliminating as many of the details as possible in order to avoid complications. Wedemeyer contended that the JCS remain non-committal on global strategy until the British revealed their intentions regarding post-HUSKY (Sicily) operations and European strategy in general. Presented papers, such as 'Conduct of the War in 1943–44' (JCS 290), were to be brief, listing an opening recommendation, followed by a discussion. In addition, the JCS would seek presidential approval of these papers at the earliest possible moment, to avoid previous breakdowns in consensus.[82] All the papers should express the views of the JCS, and if they did not, they should be so amended.[83]

The Barrier of a Common Language

Wedemeyer indicated that words like 'current' or 'projected operations' would limit misinterpretation in context and should be used. The JSSC recommended that the decisions of the coming conference be recorded in approximately the same form as 'CCS-199', which differentiated between strategic 'commitments' and strategic 'undertakings'. General Brehon Somervell, head of the Army's Service of Supply, concluded that as long as the definition of 'commitment' remained unclear and inconsistent, difficulties between the JCS and the COS would persist. This anomaly, he added, required immediate resolution if the nation's full resources were to be utilized.[84] Why the usage of these words caused problems is difficult to fathom, because their meanings are not the same; simply stated, 'commitment' is a promise, a guarantee, while 'undertaking' is an endeavor, an enterprise. Accepting these distinctions, it would follow that an agreement could be concluded on usage, regarding future consultations and contracts. If American resources were held hostage to these words, Somervell's concern demanded serious study.

Regarding the negotiations themselves, the principal American objective was to solicit British support for an early cross-Channel operation, for which the JCS had Roosevelt's backing for the first time. Even so, the difficulty of convincing the British of the operation's immediacy required a major change in their Mediterranean strategy. The Americans predicted that the British would respond half-heartedly to an incidental ROUNDUP tied to a German collapse. King, expressing irritation, said, 'The British "limp along" with an attitude of expediency. Nothing will make us sure what operations can be anticipated in 1944, unless there is a firm commitment to do ROUNDUP.'[85]

After a conference at the White House on 12 May that included TRIDENT's major participants, both country's military advisors met the following day. Procedural arrangements remained high on the American agenda, attested by the following proposals: the JCS wanted a small grouping of JPS, JSSC and JLC officers present as advisors, who could quickly assist in solving the problems submitted for discussion.[86]

These were the assistants armed to anticipate and counter every imaginable argument whose briefcases bulged with studies and statistics.[87] Moreover, once the subject of global strategy had been considered in the first two sessions, the Americans requested that the Combined Planners prepare a detailed agenda. In addition, unless an 'agreed decision' was recorded in the meeting's conclusions, no interpretation as such could be read into the minutes. Furthermore, any preliminary reports presented to the president and the prime minister were to be regarded as 'tentative only' and in the final report 'approved' 'existing' and 'projected strategic undertakings' were to be placed in their order of priority. If successful, the attempt to limit the wiles of its competitor was worthwhile, so they thought.[88] Many of the requests were approved, but as the conference continued, business sessions slowed, because the Americans had greatly increased their support staff and the British had followed suit. At most sessions there were at least 20 staff members arrayed behind and on each side of the Chiefs who sat facing each other.[89]

The Strategies Clash Again

The two delegations debated strategic issues for 13 days. Roosevelt and Churchill met the CCS on six occasions at the White House, and the Chiefs usually met jointly or combined three or four times a day at the Federal Reserve Building nearby. The two sides were deeply divided and the meetings were acrimonious. The British stressed the elimination of Italy from the war in 1943, and the Americans underlined the intensification of Pacific operations and the planning for a second front in northwest Europe instead of further Mediterranean incursions. To break the impasse, the COS proposed that each side present a paper describing how it would pursue the war in Europe. The British called their paper, 'Defeat of the Axis Powers in Europe (Elimination of Italy First)'; the Americans: 'Defeat of the Axis Powers in Europe (Concentration of the Largest Possible Force in the United Kingdom)'.

The Americans believed that a cross-Channel invasion of Europe was necessary to an early conclusion of the war with Germany.[90] Brooke read the British paper; similar to that of the Americans, important differences remained: any plan for a cross-Channel invasion was dependent upon the success of the intensified combined bomber offensive, the naval blockade and the Russian offensive. Marshall's reaction was immoderate. He felt that the landing of ground forces in Italy would establish a vacuum in the Mediterranean, in which Britain would demand more and more American means and unqualified support. It would preclude the assembly of sufficient forces in Britain required to execute a successful cross-Channel operation, the war in Europe would be prolonged, and the ultimate defeat of Japan delayed. Marshall said, 'We were now at a cross-roads ... if we were committed to the Mediterranean, except for air alone, it meant a prolonged struggle and one which was not acceptable to the United States.'[91]

When Brooke insisted that ending Mediterranean operations would prolong the war, contending that the Allies did not have the means to land and hold a Channel beachhead in support of the Russians, the strategic rift widened even further. The Conference verged on collapse. On 19 May Marshall set a precedent, amid an unmistakable air of tension, suggesting that the meeting be cleared of all but the Chiefs of Staff, a procedure described as, 'going off the record'. Ismay recalled the circumstances leading up to it: 'The arguments went back and forth, and occasionally got so acrimonious that the junior staffs were bidden to leave the principals to continue the battle in secret session.'[92]

King, for example, who never trusted the British, was most Anglophobic during regular meetings, more conciliatory during 'off the record' ones.[93] 'Going off the record' did not insure an end to deadlock; it was an extreme procedure within a flawed system whose premise was adversarial rather than co-operative. Converting and reducing strategic differences into obligatory agreements, followed by mutual compliance was beyond the scope of the system. The Combined Chiefs, locked in a continual political–psychological struggle, fought to dominate the other. Although Henry Kissinger was writing about the Napoleonic period, a qualified parallel exists between it and the period under discussion:

> As long as the enemy is more powerful than any single member of the coalition, the need for unity outweighs all considerations of individual gain ... But when the enemy has been so weakened that each ally has the power to achieve its ends alone, a coalition is at the mercy of its most determined member.[94]

Military Collective Bargaining

All the pertinent issues relating to military bargaining were rarely settled at once and thorny issues were usually tabled. Records were not kept during 'off the record' meetings, a loss of information that could not be overcome. An agreement was either broken or subverted without penalty, for any reason, real or imagined, if it no longer served the state, which alone remained accountable. Lacking adjudication, disputes were difficult to resolve, and without a sense of goodwill, co-operation during negotiations was transitory.[95] Because of mutual dissatisfaction, both parties were easily chagrined, expectations were dashed and relationships exacerbated. The Anglo–American search for a combined strategic policy was affected by either side's perception of power and images of strength, which were as important as the material factors. British sensitivity increased as their power decreased, an element which could not be overlooked. The Allies behaved as if they were two rival companies, not partners. [96] The struggle in achieving an agreement related to the depth of commitment and the application of political judgment in assessing national interests. Based on his 'mind-set', each negotiator was committed to and protective of his country's welfare, but how this was interpreted affected the negotiations in process.

Each side failed to convince the other, because they bargained for and were locked into fixed opposing positions, for example, the cross-Channel attack versus the Mediterranean. The more the British and Americans had to defend these positions against attack from each other, the more committed and identified they became to them. Lacking was an acceptance of the legitimacy of the argument and recognition of a common interest that others threatened neither side. Difficulty intensified as attempts were made to reconcile future action with past positions, for example, future Mediterranean operations versus increased Pacific activity. Emphasizing positions diffused the underlying concerns of both sides, such as keeping Russia from collapsing. Agreement became less likely, because intransigence increased. American prevention of any operations east of Sicily serves as an example. The usual result was frequently an agreement, compromised and less satisfactory to either side than it could have been. Fractious, recalcitrant behavior like 'dragging one's feet' increased, as meetings lumbered on. Tactics such as this added to the time, risk and costs of reaching agreement. An alternative to position bargaining is the principled negotiation method that focuses on 'basic interests', 'mutually satisfying options' and 'fair standards'. The greater the degree of role obligation demanded of the negotiators, the greater were the constraints on concession-making and the greater the probability of deadlocked outcomes.[97]

'Off the record', in private and without staff, the eight Chiefs had a 'heart to heart' talk that suggested an attempt at forthright conversation, hitherto unattainable. By force of circumstance, what emerged from this closed meeting led to the most important single decision of the conference, as stated in the paper, 'CCS-242/6', authorizing the Allies to launch a major offensive across the English Channel on 1 May 1944 with 29 divisions, an operation originally called ROUNDHAMMER, later changed to OVERLORD, that Churchill had resisted for over a year.[98]

It read:

> CCS have since approved a directive to General Morgan to prepare plans, among other things, for a full scale assault against the Continent in 1944 as early as possible ... The assembly of the strongest possible force ... in constant readiness to re-enter the Continent, as soon as German resistance is weakened to the required extent.[99]

Churchill's Attempts to Modify the Agreement

The paper also stipulated the following: the transfer of seven veteran divisions from the Mediterranean to Britain beginning 1 November 1943, rearming the French, continuation of Mediterranean operations and the bombing of Germany.[100] The concluding agreement reflected a mechanical splitting of the difference between final positions rather than a solution carefully crafted to meet their legitimate interests. Although the agreement was ratified by Roosevelt and Churchill at a White House meeting on 19 May, Churchill had second thoughts two days later. He tried to repudiate at least half the paper, which had omitted an Italian campaign after Sicily and how 29 divisions would be employed between August 1943 and May 1944. With the credibility of the COS at stake, Brooke advised him not to tamper with the agreement's particulars because of the increased American distrust it would engender. Apprised by Brooke and warned by Hopkins, Churchill desisted. Later that month Churchill unilaterally reopened the agreement, and argued that the meaning of 'to conduct operations best calculated to eliminate Italy from the war and to contain the greatest number of German forces'[101] favored his Mediterranean objectives. He implored Eisenhower and Marshall, who, for their own reasons, grudgingly accepted his supposition, that operations after Sicily, against either Corsica, Sardinia or southern Italy, were viable options. Although Brooke's Mediterranean strategy reaffirmed the Casablanca decisions and had overcome American objections, he was sure that the prime minister was unaware of how close to failure they had come at TRIDENT.[102]

At the conclusion of TRIDENT, Brooke proposed more frequent meetings, because an extended time-lapse led to each nation's views becoming increasingly divergent.[103] The Americans concurred. The conferees agreed that Directors of Plans and JP teams should meet with greater frequency and that planning papers affecting combined strategy should be mutually exchanged.[104] Nevertheless, after 16 months as allies, Marshall could still warn the JCS during the Conference:

> We should be quite guarded in what we say and act like a unit ... we must be very careful of casual commitments which might militate against us ... It appeared that the British want to win the war in the Mediterranean, that the Prime Minister had used the word 'little' in regard to Mediterranean operations. What was his definition of 'little'?[105]

Disillusioned, aging and weary, Brooke agreed, admitting that each side's basic convictions remained unaltered.[106] John Kautsky wrote,

> ...that prophecies based on initially false perceptions can produce conditions that really exist (and thus fulfill the prophecy); that men react to symbols by real behavior, be it activity or quiescence. If men define situations as real, they are real in their consequences.[107]

Even if frequent meetings seemed essential, there was little likelihood that any fundamental transactional improvement would occur. Although the Americans were better organized, more aggressive and more realistic at TRIDENT, they won very little from the British at the conference table. Because victory in the Pacific was still dependent upon first defeating Germany, nothing in the agreement stipulated any change in strategy by which Germany's surrender could be accelerated. Moreover, the Americans accepted that portion of 'closing the ring' in which continued Mediterranean operations would lead to an eventual cross-Channel attack. Opportunism corrupted strategy, but within this constraint, logistics, resources and manpower were dealt with adequately at the operational level. At least in the Pacific wastes, controlled as they were by King, there would be no 'limping along'. After the debacle that followed the 1942 Magnet Conference, he and Marshall doubted that the British would strive to make the cross-Channel attack a reality on 1 May 1944.[108] Brooke, operating on will-power alone, manifesting signs of weariness and depression, could record that his Mediterranean strategy remained intact, but at a price.

> ...in the light of the results that ensued the 'compromise' that emerged was almost exactly what I wanted!... King, however, was the unconvertible one, and I knew well that shipping and landing craft would continue to be sucked up into the Pacific irrespective of the requirements for the war in Europe.[109]

Meeting in Algiers

Churchill's lobbying for an invasion of southern Italy continued during meetings with Eisenhower and other high ranking officials[110] in Algiers between 29 May and 3 June.[111] Churchill, trying to overcome American instinctive distrust of his Mediterranean strategy, exerted great pressure on Eisenhower. Churchill's attempts to circumvent the JCS increased American distrust. According to Marshall, the prime minister, impressed with his own ideas, predicted the strategic outcome, brushed aside all questions, and engaged in a monologue that went on for hours. Hopkins, like Marshall, avoided being drawn in.[112] Finally, Churchill, Brooke and Marshall agreed in principle that Eisenhower would base his decision to invade Italy on the German reaction to the Allied invasion of Sicily. Fears among some of the American planners were aroused: the CCS was a non-participant in the negotiating process.[113] Eisenhower emerged as the conservative, cautious realist, a quality he displayed for the remainder of the war. How different from his determined willingness to fight on the Norman beaches in 1942![114]

Stalin's Reaction

Notified of the TRIDENT decision, Stalin castigated both Churchill and Roosevelt on 11 June, warning that the Soviet Union would experience exceptional difficulties by the postponement of the second front until 1944. More to the point, he stated:

> As for the Soviet Government, it cannot align itself with this decision, which, moreover, was adopted without its participation and without any attempt at a joint discussion of this highly important matter and which may gravely affect the subsequent course of the war.[115]

Angered, he withdrew his ambassadors from Britain and the United States. Soon after, Stalin accused Churchill of bad faith, but the troubled prime minister, attempting to mollify him in a lengthy reply, suggested a meeting of the three leaders at Scapa Flow that summer. Churchill did not know that Roosevelt had already fractured the 'special relationship' by excluding him from a proposed a mid-summer meeting with Stalin. When Churchill discovered the plot – it was Harriman who told him – he confronted Roosevelt in a letter on 25 June, in which he wrote:

> You must excuse me expressing myself with all the frankness that our friendship and gravity of the issue warrant. I do not underrate the use that enemy propaganda would make of a meeting between the heads of Soviet Russia and the United States at this juncture with the British Commonwealth and Empire excluded. It would be serious and vexatious, and many would be bewildered and alarmed thereby...[116]

Roosevelt lied to Churchill and wrote:

> I did not suggest to Uncle Joe that we meet alone but he told Davies that he assumed (a) that we would meet alone and (b) that he agreed that we should not bring staffs to what would be a preliminary meeting ... to cover much of the same ground with him as did Eden for you a year ago...[117]

Even if Roosevelt believed that he and Stalin were better suited than Churchill to settle post-war issues, the president failed to consider the letter's impact upon the 'special relationship'. To Roosevelt, Churchill was a man of the past, Stalin a man of the future. Churchill understood from previous experiences with Roosevelt that American attempts to reduce Britain's gold reserves in the US, plots to take over Britain's Middle East oil interests, and a number of other disputes demonstrated that the 'special relationship' was relatively non-existent in the world of power politics.[118] Churchill circulated a War Office paper which read, 'ranging from the establishment of a *Pax Americana*, in substitution for the *Pax Britannica* to a definite American imperialistic policy which aims at the building up of American power and prestige in various parts of the world.'[119]

Instead of the Roosevelt–Stalin Conference, which never materialized, because of Stalin's disinterest, Churchill left for Quebec. Sailing from England aboard the *Queen Mary* to meet Roosevelt in the French-Canadian city along the St. Lawrence River, Churchill recognized that trans-Atlantic distrust persisted. The Quebec QUADRANT meeting was an event to which neither major participant looked forward.

5 QUADRANT: The Quebec Conference

Preparations

Preparations for the forthcoming 1943 QUADRANT Conference were preceded by a series of JCS meetings held between 6 and 10 August in Washington.[1] The mood was sanguine, with Marshall and his colleagues, veterans of two years of allied negotiations, believing that the time was ripe for a final decision on European strategy with the British. Whether the main effort in Europe should be from the Mediterranean or from Britain remained unanswered.[2] Rear Admiral Charles 'Savvy' Cooke, the top American Naval planner, declared that since Eisenhower's staff was drawing up plans to eliminate Italy from the war and to acquire bases in the Po Valley from which to bomb Germany, an answer was essential. As a result of conversations with Eisenhower's representatives, Cooke stressed that the JCS should choose between the two theaters and reach a decision as quickly as possible. According to General Carl Spaatz, Deputy Commander Mediterranean Allied Air Forces (MAAF), Rome's status as a prize of war was more valuable than it being declared an 'Open City', because its surrounding airfields would obviate the need for those farther north in the Po Valley and the land battle required to take them.

Even British seamanship was held up to scrutiny. For example, at TRIDENT the Americans were told that 132 British-controlled Landing Craft Infantry (LCI) and Landing Ship Tank (LST) in the Mediterranean, needed by COSSAC for OVERLORD, could not sail to England after 1 October because some of their number had foundered in heavy winter seas during previous voyages. King took umbrage with the British notion, indicating that TORCH had been mounted on 8 November. He further disparaged British maritime efficiency and experience by insisting their attitude was defeatist. 'Surely some risk must be accepted', he complained, 'the consequences of which could largely be overcome by vigilance and good seamanship.' Feeling that Churchill and Brooke were taking counsel of their fears, King rejected the British notion that before OVERLORD became acceptable, German strength in Normandy shrunk to 12 divisions. He mocked British policy as one that did nothing, and challenged his colleagues to reach a firm decision at QUADRANT regarding OVERLORD, if it were to be forthcoming.[3]

Secretary Stimson's Influence on Negotiations

Stimson, having recently returned from a fact-finding tour of Britain, agreed, concluding that the prime minister and the COS were almost apathetic and apprehensive about BOLERO. He maintained that if OVERLORD were to take place at all, Roosevelt and his military staff had to assume the responsibility of leadership, because the shadows of Passchendaele and Dunkirk hung too heavily over the imaginations of Churchill and his military commanders.[4] Generals Wedemeyer and Kuter felt that if the seven battle-experienced divisions consigned to OVERLORD were shipped from the Mediterranean to Britain in accordance with the TRIDENT agreement, it would reduce British pressure on the JCS for extensive operations in the Central Mediterranean. Eisenhower's chief planner, General Rooks, proposed that even without the seven divisions, he would still have sufficient force to fulfill planned operations in Italy, Sardinia, Corsica, and southern France. The American planners felt that if these divisions were replaced, Churchill and Eden could press for an invasion of the Balkans; this would have a disastrous effect on the main effort from Britain.[5]

Marshall suggested that knowledge of the issues to which the JCS was bound or wherein they could compromise would be helpful.[6] Liaison between the JCS and the President had improved since TRIDENT, and it is entirely possible that Roosevelt's general concurrence with his JCS at this stage was influenced by Stimson's perceptions of the strategic divergencies, one of which was British Mediterranean strategy and its effect upon American wartime and post-war relations with Russia.[7] Roosevelt, Stimson, and the JCS met at the White House on 10 August. The president notified them that Churchill was opposed to an operation against Sardinia, but favored one in the Balkans, even if it were reduced to a supply operation against Eden's advice.[8]

Roosevelt indicated that the British were troubled by increased Russian influence in the region and wanted to establish their presence there as a counter-stroke. However, he discounted British fears, naïvely believing that the Russians were more interested in establishing kinship with their Slavic neighbors than enslaving them. In any event, he thought it unwise to plan military strategy based on a gamble tied to political results, and remained opposed to any Balkan venture.[9]

Regarding OVERLORD, King and the president requested plans to postpone, abandon, or carry it out without British participation. Marshall responded, 'The trouble with the plan would be that it would greatly overlook the availability of 15 British divisions now in Britain. There is no other spot in the world where 15 divisions can be placed in operation without large export and supply problems.'[10] Before the meeting closed, the participants agreed upon or strongly advocated the following:

1. an American commander to lead OVERLORD;
2. continuation of the present OVERLORD build-up;

3. no divergence from the main effort, and no future changes to be made in basic decisions except for minor modifications;
4. land approximately 15 divisions upon the French coast during the opening phases of OVERLORD, with several divisions to follow from Britain soon after;
5. avoid any secondary operations mounted on a 'shoe string'.[11]

Although Marshall admitted to and complained of the lack of shipping and munitions, he miscalculated his reserve of infantry divisions, believing that no serious problem existed. The scarcity of infantry replacements during the fall and winter months of 1944–45, which caused havoc in Europe, forcibly disproved his presumption: the unknown author of an infantry regiment's printed account wrote, 'The group of replacements that had come to us at Remiremont disappeared rapidly and our resources became low. We were weary and tired. Morale was ebbing ... Still we fought on. Rumors persisted, but the relief never came.'[12] Assessing the information given to him by the JCS, the president believed that American ends and means were well integrated.[13]

Proposing an Agenda

Five days before the first QUADRANT meeting, the JCS completed its agenda for the Conference: they would first insist upon acceptance of the TRIDENT agreement relating to the 1 May 1944 cross-Channel landing. Few problems were expected on this account, but the JCS was concerned that the COS faced difficulties viewing OVERLORD as part of a global strategy involving all theaters. Regarding the Mediterranean, the JCS learned that the British were anxious to discuss immediate and specific operations, such as post-HUSKY, and then to fit them into agreements within the overall picture later. The JCS favored a survey of the Europe–African areas first. Whichever proposal was tabled first, Marshall affirmed that CCS agreements were predisposed toward AVALANCHE, the Salerno landing near Naples, after BAYTOWN, the landing in southern Italy was underway. Even though the Americans could be as opportunistic as the British when it suited them, as typified in the projected Italian landings, they were determined to seek firm commitments on all implementations as applied to OVERLORD and Burma operations, because of time constraints.[14]

An exchange of paperwork between the Allied Chiefs revealed that the British's first priority was the elimination of Italy from the war as part of future Mediterranean operations, with defeat of Japan as the second. Whereas, the American counter-proposal required that progress and planning reports for both the Euro–Mediterranean and the Pacific–Asia areas be submitted before a decision was reached on projected operations within them. The British considered the American agenda too comprehensive to deal with.[15]

Both sides sought the best procedure with which to exploit the other during the meetings; this implied that positions had not softened since TRIDENT. The tenor of American pre-QUADRANT meetings indicated that the JCS was still suspicious of British intentions and consistently wary of many of their proposals and plans. To the extent that their prejudice was sweeping, the JCS had difficulty differentiating and assessing the British point of view on a case by case basis.[16]

Negotiating and Psychology

'Intentionality' is the ability to question and evaluate objectively one's motives and purpose, to know what one is doing, through all the phases of planning and negotiating. This could contribute to increased rationality during negotiations,[17] but King rarely behaved in this manner. Being co-operative was more complicated than it seemed. When the two sides disagreed and personalities clashed, the result was usually deadlock. When the British and the Americans viewed the same facts differently, or did not consider the same possibilities, or did not foresee the same consequences, each had only an incomplete knowledge of the problem. Nevertheless, the pooling of their respective perceptions and judgments, however difficult, could offer the best chance of finding a solution valid for them.[18]

When Marshall agreed to planning for Allied operations against Italy, the American argument over British intransigence narrowed to OVERLORD alone. Brooke was not so sure, estimating '...that Marshall could not see beyond the tip of his nose and was maddening.'[19] Although General Rook's evaluation of American force-level sufficiency in the Mediterranean was wildly optimistic, the Americans had much to gain by attacking the Italian mainland in an opportunistic maneuver with the forces at hand. Trying to knock Italy out of the war could deter little from the BOLERO build-up, unless the object of the landings changed.

Both staffs convened QUADRANT on 14 August, and agreed to the continuation of the TRIDENT procedures that included specific references to the recording of decisions, approval of the minutes, reports to the president and the prime minister and the form of the Final Report. They also agreed to a limit of 12 conferees per side, and, as long as one planner was present, the others were not required to attend meetings. Closed sessions were acceptable when needed.[20]

Reports on Strategy and the Air War

Turning aside from matters of protocol, Brooke reported on German–Italian dispositions in Europe. German divisions were 60 percent under strength and German manpower was stretched to the limit. Italian and satellite forces compounded Germany's problems by withdrawing from the Eastern Front. Some Italian divisions of the 30 stationed in the Balkans and southern France had made surrender overtures, which posed manpower replacement problems for Germany. Portal praised the effective use of daylight bombing in POINTBLANK, the continuing British-based Allied air operation by which complete mastery of the air above Germany would be achieved. Thus far, POINTBLANK had been a great success, but the establishment of strong offensive Allied air forces in northern Italy would expose southern Germany and 60 percent of its aircraft production to air attack, forcing the Luftwaffe to deploy half of its fighter force on the Western Front to counter this new threat.[21] Regarding the European air battle, Portal warned, '...If German fighter strength was not checked in the next three months, the battle might be lost, since it was impossible to judge the strength which the German fighter forces might attain by next spring, if our attack is not pressed home.'[22]

Arnold was less optimistic than Portal, and painted a gloomy picture of American air operations over Europe: early estimates, based on the British experience of replacements for men and machines, had proved too low in the case of Eighth AAF operations. The crews were 'war weary' and in short supply, that is, planes outnumbering air crews by two to one (800 to 400). He hoped that by January 1944 this discrepancy could be reversed by achieving a reserve of one air crew each for an aggregate of 1,900 planes. He questioned the maximum use of Britain as a bomber base in the winter months, because of losses due to bad weather [23] and believed that the North Italian air bases would prove valuable in this regard.[24]

CCS meeting 108 convened on 15 August and revealed that the rift and conflict over strategy remained. King believed that the COS had serious doubts as to the possibility of accomplishing OVERLORD. Brooke disagreed, insisting that if the three conditions formulated by Morgan in his paper were addressed and achieved, the COS would support OVERLORD:

1. reduction in German fighter strength,
2. German strength and reinforcement in France and the Low Countries for the first two months must be kept at specified limits, and
3. the problem of beach maintenance must be solved.[25]

Marshall responded as if he had not heard Brooke's statement; seemingly talking at cross-purposes, he questioned whether the required conditions for a successful OVERLORD were solely dependent upon increased strength in the Mediterranean. Only if enemy resistance were weak would he agree to the seizure of Italian territory and the occupation of the northern Italian airfields. Marshall insisted that the seven Mediterranean divisions be shipped to Britain and OVERLORD be given overriding priority, otherwise it would become a subsidiary operation.[26] General Barker, COSSAC's American planner agreed, considering it mere speculation to think that an 'opportunist' operation would be cheaper in lives. He threatened:

> If we relied on this, we are opening a new concept which will weaken our chances of an early victory and render a re-examination of our basic strategy, with a possible readjustment towards the Pacific.[27]
>
> The CCS should now take a decision that OVERLORD ... in order that the success of the operation could be insured. Any departure from this concept must entail a reconsideration of our basic strategy.[28]

The British argued that successful operations in France necessitated a preponderance of force, an essential element to avoid a catastrophe, which could seriously delay ultimate victory. Success depended, not on the absolute strength of the Allied forces available for OVERLORD, but on the overall strength of the Germans. This relative strength could best be achieved by operations in Italy, aimed at containing the maximum German forces there, and by air action from the best possible Italian bases to reduce the German fighter threat. By fighting a weakened army to a standstill in Italy, Hitler could transfer his reserves from Italy to Normandy and threaten the landing. Marshall and Brooke's irreconcilable positions, a question of emphasis, could not have been more clearly drawn. Brooke wrote in his diary after the meeting ended:

> It was a most painful meeting and we settled nothing. I entirely failed to get Marshall to realise the relation between the cross-Channel and Italian Operations, and the repercussions which the one exercises on the other. It is quite impossible to argue with him as he does not begin to understand a strategic problem! He had not even read the plans worked out by Morgan for the cross-Channel operation and consequently was not even in a position to begin to appreciate its difficulties and requirements.[29]

The JCS reassembled on 15 August. Although Leahy expressed concern over the shifting of the seven battle-seasoned divisions without knowledge of the enemy situation, as advocated by the COS, Marshall disagreed. He argued that the seven divisions were not the problem, but British avoidance of TRIDENT was, an agreement they now found unacceptable. Since it would take six months to move those divisions from the Mediterranean to

Britain in preparation for OVERLORD, the COS lack of adherence could delay the strategic timetable.[30]

He thought that the COS were repudiating the TRIDENT agreement, much as Marshall and King had tried to repudiate MAGNET in 1942, suggesting that not only were either side's tactics similar, but there were only so many tactics from which to choose. Each involved permutations of avoidance and denial, in which one ingredient was some form of punishment, for example the withholding of supplies or the freezing of troop movements. The conduct of the war and the basic decisions achieved at prior conferences, all of which took months to accomplish, were at stake, and Marshall refused to become mired in another Mediterranean campaign not envisaged at TRIDENT, regardless of the British logic for doing so.

Consensually, the American position was hardening against the British, as expressed by Admiral Russell Wilson, a member of the elite JSSC. He observed that the British were undermining OVERLORD by adopting a well-tried technique: emasculation. The result, he perceived, would unnecessarily prolong the war in the Atlantic and, consequently, in the Pacific. The Americans reacted by deprecating British strategy, believing that they would not make a decision until they evaluated enemy intentions. Somehow they would create an emergency which would retain the seven divisions in the Mediterranean. Moreover, the British had ignored the effects of Russian successes and those of the bombing offensive, insisting that OVERLORD's success depended solely on creating a favorable situation in Italy.[31]

Wedemeyer took the JCS through a sequence of British positions, from Casablanca onward, that revealed the capricious nuances of their Mediterranean strategy. He described how HUSKY's purpose, according to them, was to open the Mediterranean and cause Italy's collapse. At that time, the COS believed it unnecessary to mount an attack on the Italian mainland, charging that it would fall by air action alone. He was sure that they had equivocated since TRIDENT, arguing that occupation of Italy was necessary, offering the weak excuse that the Germans must be denied the northern Italian airfields. Wedemeyer insisted that it would do the enemy little good, since the Allies had overwhelming air superiority in the area. He indicated that lower-level British officers agreed with the American OVERLORD planners, but due to political considerations and political pressure from above, they had to disagree. 'The British leadership believe we are wrong.'[32] To what extent Wedemeyer's behavior was sycophantic and tendentious is difficult to assess, because his position was influenced by Embick and interlocked with Marshall's, a view now acceptable to the JCS. Wedemeyer offered no solutions but sought substantiation for his prejudice. Marshall affirmed that the OVERLORD plan was based on contingencies, a condition the British needed to understand before acceptance. Polemics aside, it was Kuter who suggested a substantive arrangement for settling the seven division controversy,

> ...that the British would carry out OVERLORD if the proviso was put in 'CCS-303' – that future movements of forces from the Med would be subject to the approval of the CCS. This was about as firm an agreement as could be reached at this time.[33]

Marshall remained consistent to his need for planning, but he was concerned, as he had been over the TORCH decision, that Churchill and Roosevelt expected changes in plans to be made quickly and easily. Having little idea of how disruptive these changes could be, they were unappreciative of the far-reaching results of change. However, if Roosevelt needed an operation that would help him win political re-election in 1944, OVERLORD would be the operation of choice; there was not an operation in the Mediterranean that could match it for sheer drama, scope or decisive results.[34]

POINTBLANK conversations continued on 16 August. Best JIC air bombardment estimates revealed that unless unrelenting pressure was maintained to insure victory in the autumn, Germany, by a conservation of its strength and by the development of new air defence measures, might be in an unassailable position by spring.[35] Great emphasis had been placed on air bombardment before the war as the economical and direct means of destroying an enemy's ability to continue fighting, but Roosevelt, like Portal, had lost faith in it.[36] Marshall and his adherents recognized that only OVERLORD, assisted by air, could defeat Germany, although he had diverted half of the available manpower to the AAF and weakened the Army.

Playing their Pacific threat card *ad nauseam*, the Americans warned that if OVERLORD were reduced to a subsidiary operation, they could redirect their efforts elsewhere.[37] Therefore, Marshall sought acceptance of the TRIDENT proposals without British qualifications and reservations. The JCS introduced a new word, 'indirection' to underline COS intractability, that is, the British approach to OVERLORD was by indirection; attacking the enemy via Italy was by indirection, or a possible movement into southern France through the north of Italy and the Alps, discounted by the JCS as slow and ineffective.[38] Marshall recounted how Churchill felt differently now toward OVERLORD, proclaiming at dinner the night before, that every effort should be made to further it. Although Marshall proposed that the prime minister's inhibiting conditions remained unchanged, that of bolstering forces in Italy at OVERLORD's expense, Churchill responded, 'Give us time.' Sudden shifts in Churchill's plans had resulted in convoys being diverted and 60,000 troops added to Eisenhower's forces, shifts that the JCS would stand no longer, no further circumlocution, no further 'sucking in'; the hand to mouth handling of logistics must end. As Marshall saw it, Germany's only hope was either to divide, delay or play for an adjusted peace, but the Americans were going on the offensive.[39]

Seeking to soften the American position with qualifiers, Brooke evoked a strong JCS response. His 'qualifiers' were seen as a British excuse to press for further Mediterranean operations or as a defence against being accused of breaking faith with earlier agreements. Aware that past British 'agreements in principle' ended up being little more than debating devices, Marshall and his colleagues pressed for a final showdown.[40] Although the president supported OVERLORD, the JCS, prior to his arrival, realized that after three days of intense debate, a compromise was developing in which the 'overriding priority' for the operation would be lessened.[41]

Halfway through the CCS morning meeting on the 19th the arguing between Marshall and Brooke became so heated that he asked to go 'off the record' in an attempt to reconcile the Anglo–American differences. The room was cleared of the 60-odd administrative officers, an indication that the staff limits recommended at the beginning of the conference had been ignored. Brooke wrote in his diary,

> Our talk was pretty frank. I opened by telling them that the root of the matter was that we were not trusting one another. They doubted our real intentions to put our full hearts into the cross-Channel operations next spring, and we had not full confidence that they would not in future insist on our carrying out previous agreements irrespective of changed strategic conditions.[42]

According to the Americans, the British failed to realize the unprecedented complexity involved in properly arming and equipping forces that had to be carried thousands of miles to the theaters of war. Improvisation, though perhaps an attractive approach, could not take the place of timetables.

Before the meeting began, Mountbatten had approached Brooke for permission to perform an experiment concerning 'Pykrete', a material formed from a frozen mixture of diluted pulp and water for possible use in the constuction of floating seadomes or giant aircraft carriers. Code-named HABBAKUK, Brooke, who considered it a folly, shouted, 'The hell with HABAKKUK, we are about to have the most difficult time with our American friends and shall not have time for your ice carriers.'[43] However, when the session adjourned, Brooke with Marshall's agreement, allowed Mountbatten to perform his experiment. With the Combined Chiefs gathered behind him; Mountbatten fired. The first bullet shattered the ice, the second rebounded off the 'Pykrete' and buzzed angrily around their legs. Brooke told the following story:

> It will be remembered that when the original meeting had become too heated we had cleared the room of all the attending staff. They were waiting in an adjoining room and when the revolver shots were heard, the wag of the party shouted: 'Good Heavens, they have started shooting now!'[44]

Perhaps the above vignette is apocryphal, but Churchill, Arnold, Leahy and King have elaborated upon it, reflecting the need to relieve difficult negotiations with a dash of levity. Adding to the humor and sense of unreality of the episode was their willingness to continue HABAKKUK's research, development and construction.[45]

The Results of QUADRANT

Operation ANVIL, as part of Operation OVERLORD, was originally conceived during the Conference and included in the Chiefs of Staff's 'Final Report' of 24 August 1943. The CCS directed Eisenhower, serving as Supreme Allied Commander in the Mediterranean, to submit an outline plan for a possible operation against southern France.[46] Eisenhower's October report lacked enthusiasm, because limited resources precluded the launch of a full-scale attack. Because of a shortage of landing craft, the initial assault was limited to one division, considered as a feint only. Even concerted operations in Italy, it suggested, might prove more valuable to OVERLORD than ANVIL itself.[47] Facing British opposition, Morgan disagreed, asserting that OVERLORD and ANVIL must take place simultaneously if two of the German mobile reserve divisions, stationed in southern France, were to be tied down by formations under Allied Force Headquarters (AFHQ) control. He opposed Eisenhower's recommendation that the operation should be considered only as one of several possibilities.[48] At the first plenary session on 19 August, the CCS presented the results of five days of continuous discussion to the president and prime minister: The CCS stipulated:

> OVERLORD – target date, 1 May 1944, to land in France and strike at the heart of Germany and destroy her forces. Between OVERLORD and Mediterranean operations, the sharing of scarce resources to be distributed and employed to insure the former's success.
>
> Consideration of a northern Norway landing, (Operation JUPITER), only if OVERLORD is rendered impossible. Unremitting pressure on the German forces in Italy. Offensive operations against southern France (to include the use of trained and equipped French forces) should be undertaken

to establish a lodgement in the Toulon–Marseilles area and to exploit northward in order to create a diversion in connection with Overlord – Air-nourished guerrilla warfare in southern France. Balkan operations limited to supply, special operations and bombing of strategic objectives.[49]

The Landing Craft Problem

Churchill and Roosevelt accepted the paper with reservations.[50] During the second plenary session on the 23rd, the prime minister, favoring the OVERLORD concept for 1944, but fearful of excessive casualties, requested that a rule be applied, as prepared by Morgan, that if there were more than 12 mobile German divisions in France at the intended moment of the Allied landing, the landing would be canceled. He also insisted that the assault force, including landing craft, be increased by 25 percent and Allied fighter superiority be achieved before the landing. The perennial ocean-going landing craft problem persisted, the shortages of which limited all prospective operations, including the passage to Italy. Disagreeing over landing craft procurement, the British desired a definite allocation per month or a percentage of monthly construction, while the Americans wanted to tie them to specific operations. The Americans, whose Navy controlled landing craft production and distribution, refused to give the British Navy a 'blank-check', particularly when it was using some of them for net protection at Scapa Flow.[51] Even though 204 Landing Craft Tank (LCT) and Landing Craft Infantry (LCI) were to be deployed against Germany by December 1943[52], no oversight bilateral committee existed. The existence of one would have reduced the incentive for deception and manipulation and insured proper apportionment. Concurrently, the inevitable Italian collapse, accelerated by the surrender of Sicily on 17 August, lured Allied forces toward Italy, certainly as far as Churchill suggested, beyond Rome to the Ancona–Pisa line and the northern airfields, beyond those in the Florence region.[53]

Brooke's Deliberations

Brooke felt both sides had failed to arrive at the best strategy, but grew philosophical, concluding that when working with allies, compromises with all their evils became inevitable.[54] Compromises, however, need not be evil. They are not laws unto themselves. Most agreements are based on compromise, but when one side or another is forced to compromise to avoid stalemate, the result can be less than even minimal expectations. Unfortunately, almost all Allied agreements could be broken with impunity, against which the aggrieved party would retaliate. During the two-month period between TRIDENT and QUADRANT, the COS, their intentions dubious, unilaterally ordered the seven divisions reassigned to Britain to 'stand-fast', thus breaking the TRIDENT agreement. Brooke's desultory mood increased. Personally, he felt '...flat and depressed, weary of battling against difficulties, differences of opinion, stubbornness, stupidity, pettiness and pig-headedness.'[55] By contrast, the Americans were satisfied with QUADRANT's results: they were mastering the art of military diplomacy, Roosevelt supported Marshall now, the Mediterranean was becoming more aligned with OVERLORD as the major operation (in conjunction with the bomber offensive), and the COS disavowed interest in the Balkans. Marshall felt closer to his goal of fighting a war with a minimum of loss, expense and time, as British power and influence were waning. As a result, Brooke would be denied the most coveted command of the war, OVERLORD. With his role unchanged, Brooke was faced with making the most of British assets; henceforth, he would negotiate on the merits of a specific issue, pitting a greater role for strategic principles against the raw physical and economic power of the US. In so doing, Brooke had succeeded in keeping the bomber offensive intact and operations in the Mediterranean alive with the forces allocated at TRIDENT. The CCS agreed that available resources would be distributed and employed between OVERLORD and Mediterranean operations to ensure OVERLORD's success.[56] If planning at Casablanca represented the beginning of coalition's offensive phase in the war against Germany, and TRIDENT the halfway mark, QUADRANT was the beginning of the end, even though negotiations at Quebec fell short of the final showdown desired by Marshall.[57]

JCS Formulation of Policy on Assumptions

The sort of misinterpretation and assumptions that led to confusion in combined negotiations were clearly demonstrated by the JCS in Meeting 109: General Whitely reported that it was Eisenhower's intention prior to QUADRANT to hit the Germans whenever and wherever possible. According to King and Rooks, Eisenhower had never received final CCS approval of AVALANCHE, the invasion of Italy. The secretary concurred. General Handy (Marshall's Chief of the Operations Planning Division) believed that AVALANCHE would be mounted on 9 September. Arnold indicated that he didn't think Eisenhower needed any further directives.[58] One senior British officer wrote of Anglo–American confusion and misperception this way:

> Some Americans are curiously liable to suspect that they are going to be 'outsmarted' by the subtle British – perhaps because we sometimes do such

stupid things that they cannot take them at face value but suspect them of being part of some 'dark design'.[59]

While the JCS searched for an answer, Eisenhower's Chief of Staff, General Walter B. Smith successfully concluded Italian armistice negotiations at Casibile, Sicily, the results of which would be announced simultaneously with carrying out AVALANCHE, on 9 September.

6 TEHRAN: The Second Front, the French Resistance and the French Army

OVERLORD and ANVIL, projected amphibious landings for 1944, were considered as inter-dependent parts of the same operation, the hammer and the anvil that would crush the German Armies in western Europe. They were also a part of the tangled allied political–military web in which Roosevelt and Churchill participated. Stalin demanded a second front, while Churchill demurred and viewed increased Anglo–American Mediterranean activity as a means of countering Russian advances into central Europe. Churchill was convinced that the OVERLORD strategy, while satisfying a political expedient, could result in defeat.[1] Roosevelt, however, remained unwilling to accept any delay or postponement beyond May 1944 to fulfill his second front promise to Stalin.

At the Tehran EUREKA Conference of November 1943, Stalin's unexpected enthusiasm for a landing in southern France pushed the timing of OVERLORD ahead at the expense of the Italian campaign and exacerbated existing Anglo–American strategic difficulties. The second front concept, immediately accepted by Roosevelt and reluctantly endorsed by Churchill, was characterized by Stalin as a giant 'pincer' composed of simultaneous landings in Normandy (OVERLORD) and Provençe (ANVIL), with ANVIL assigned the subordinate role.[2] The debarkation points of the 'pincer' would be 500 miles apart and were, consequently, more like two separate fronts. Marshal Voroshilov of Russia reduced the technical problems of the landings to those of a 'river crossing', but Marshall disagreed and warned, 'The difference between a river crossing, however wide, and a landing from the ocean is that the failure of a river crossing is a reverse while the failure of a landing operation from the sea is a catastrophe.'[3]

Tactical and logistical failures during the Italian winter and spring campaigns of 1943–44, for example, the transfer preparations of seven divisions to Britain after the Sicilian campaign, the Rapido River fiasco and the attritional battles at Monte Cassino and Anzio, precluded a cross-Channel attack on the prescribed date.[4] ANVIL, the adjunct, was also delayed, its purpose and landing site repeatedly contested. At times, the operation verged on being canceled entirely.[5]

Toward a EUREKA Agreement

At a pre-EUREKA meeting on 11 November, the COS, supported by Eisenhower, proposed that it was vital to maintain the momentum in Italy without exhausting the allied armies.[6] Unfortunately it did; from January to May 1944, on Anzio alone, the allies lost 7,000 troops killed, 36,000 wounded or missing and another 44,000 hospitalized for various non-battle injuries and illness out of a total of 125,000 men. The infantry suffered 80 percent of the casualties and officer losses exceeded 100 percent.[7] In an *aide-mémoire*, the COS stated,

> ...We must not regard OVERLORD on a fixed date as the pivot of our whole strategy on which all else turns ... With the Germans in their present plight ... we should stretch the German forces to the utmost by threatening as many of their vital interests and areas as possible and, holding them thus, we should attack wherever we can do so in superior force.[8]

Marshall's Mediterranean position was well known, but he consented to defer further arguments until Russian needs were assessed at Tehran.[9] What the British sought was a postponement of OVERLORD for one to two months, the time assumed for the allied armies in Italy to reach the Pisa–Rimini line north of Rome.[10] There, allied forces could attack toward Trieste, Austria, the Balkans or southern France.

Conceding nothing to their two partners, the British knew that if this tactical move succeeded, it would improve the chances of OVERLORD's launching, and Rome's capture would be a crowning public relations success. By contrast, Stalin favored going onto the defensive in Italy, deferring the capture of Rome. He concentrated on the landing in southern France, and catching his allies by surprise, brushed aside any suggestion of operations in the Balkans.[11] Stalin boldly proposed that divisions in Italy be moved to facilitate ANVIL and endorsed Marshall's idea that ANVIL precede OVERLORD by two or three weeks. Moreover, Stalin, who considered France to be the weakest spot on the entire German front, insisted that once Rome fell all available forces in Italy be sent to fuse with OVERLORD. Stalin declared that his armies would synchronize their attacks to coincide with those of the invasion forces and submitted that OVERLORD and ANVIL be launched no later than 31 May. OVERLORD, Stalin asserted, ought to be a maximum effort, and ANVIL a two-divisional one.[12]

Churchill, no longer the dominant partner, fought on unsuccessfully with undiminished vigor for questionable eastern Mediterranean operations ACCOLADE and HARDIHOOD alone. Eisenhower and Wilson (General Henry Maitland Wilson then C-in-C Middle East), meeting on 11 October 1943 at La Marsa, Tunis, agreed to ACCOLADE's postponement after due consideration.[13] Moreover, to further the success of the French landings, the allies proposed that all future plans for operations in the eastern Mediterranean should be suspended, with major resources and assault shipping allocated to the two French assaults or to the campaign in Italy. The conferees recognized that the very existence and magnitude of OVERLORD and ANVIL were dependent upon the availability of landing craft and shipping.[14]

The Americans favored ANVIL for various reasons:

1. Roosevelt's promise to Stalin.
2. After Operation TORCH, the Americans had diverted precious equipment from their own units to reorganise and rearm the French Army.
3. American planners believed that the reconstituted French divisions could play an integral role in the new front in southern France.
4. The operation was essential to protect OVERLORD's southern flank once German resistance in Normandy collapsed.
5. By joining ANVIL to OVERLORD enemy formations to the south and west of the Loire River would be effectively trapped, thus allowing for greater French participation in their country's liberation.[15]

Once ANVIL and OVERLORD joined forces, the greatest concentration of troops would form on a line between Switzerland and the North Sea, advance against the whole length of the Rhine, break into the heart of Germany, and meet the Red Army advancing from the East.[16] The ANVIL plan of 1943 may have been instrumental in Eisenhower's controversial choice of a 'broad' over a 'narrow' front concept in the fall of 1944, a choice that General Bernard Montgomery strongly disputed. The CCS closed the conference with an unequivocal statement of intent: 'OVERLORD and ANVIL are the supreme operations for 1944. They must be carried out during May 1944. Nothing must be undertaken in any other part of the world which hazards the success of these two operations.'[17] By supporting OVERLORD and ANVIL, the allies agreed that,

> Within the limits of available means and without prejudice to major operations, patriot forces everywhere within enemy occupied territory in Europe, should be furnished supplies to enable them to conduct sabotage, propaganda, intelligence and guerrilla warfare.[18]

Creation of SOE

When Churchill became prime minister in 1940, he directed his government to explore ways of disrupting the Nazi occupation of Europe. After further investigation, between July and October, Special Operations Executive (SOE), approved by the COS and administered by Hugh Dalton, the Minister of Economic Warfare (MEW) was formed to conduct 'irregular warfare'.[19] Nothing in the inter-war years necessitated the establishment of either a British irregular warfare agency or a French chain of resistance, because neither government remotely contemplated the alacrity of the French defeat in June 1940 and its aftermath. In late August 1939, the French C-in-C, General Maurice Gamelin, expressed the view, prevalent on both sides of the Channel, that, 'Hitler will collapse the day war is declared on Germany ... the German Army will be forced to march on Berlin to suppress the trouble that will immediately break out.'[20]

When France collapsed instead, time was needed to absorb the shock of being driven from the continent, to redirect British strategy, to assess the demands of clandestine warfare and to build the appropriate structures through which German-occupied Europe would be penetrated and attacked. Unfortunately time with which to find, train and direct the agents, as part of an overall strategy, was in short supply. Lord Selborne (who replaced Dalton) later summarized the position facing Britain. 'Underground warfare was an unknown art in England in 1940; there were no text-books for newcomers, no old hands to initiate them into the experiences of the last war; lessons had to be learned in the hard school of practice.'[21] At its inception, SOE was described as 'no more than a hopeful improvisation devised in a really desperate situation.'[22]

The Reorganization of Secret British Agencies

On 27 May, secondary sections of the British War Office and Secret Service were consolidated and ultimately led to the formation of SOE. Established to maintain contact with resistance groups in France, SOE circuits consisted of an organizer, his lieutenant and a wireless operator who were infiltrated into France to train, supply and direct saboteurs recruited locally. The Resistance in France represented a loose organization acting against the German occupation in 1940 that engaged in sabotage, espionage, and propaganda; early Resistance was almost entirely a matter of secret initiatives by individuals and small groups consisting of a minute percentage of the French population. Linked together with like-minded political friends, they sometimes acted alone against the enemy, according to their own personal beliefs.[23]

In addition to the non-Gaullist F-Section, a Gaullist RF-Section was established to co-operate with de Gaulle's *Bureau Central de Renseignements et d'Action [Militaire]* (BCRA). Under London's direction, both were to assist the French Resistance in operations against specific enemy targets chosen by the COS.[24] General Colin Gubbins, an early participant and later the leader of SOE, stated: 'Thus from the very moment of the fall of France and the commencement of total warfare against Germany, trained British officers and others were parachuted into occupied territories to start the organization of resistance.'[25] Since 'Republican' France no longer existed, Dalton and the SOE tried to subvert the German occupation of Europe, under Churchill's supervision.[26]

However, a fundamental consideration to the success of an undertaking of this magnitude was the state and condition of the resistance elements following the crushing defeat of France. Expectantly, SOE agents, initially drawn from the three military branches, from public schools and universities, the City and from industry, were trained in clandestine operations.[27] Whether acting singly or through networks, they represented an anti-Fascist 'fifth column'; using various methods of subversion within the defeated countries and with arms supplied by Britain. Planned was the disruption of the German hegemony by fomenting economic discontent and indigenous revolt, such as industrial and military sabotage, labor agitation, strikes, propaganda, terrorist acts against traitors and German leaders, boycotts and riots.[28] However, Dalton's view was that a left-wing political revolution by the industrial working classes lacked the practical precision needed to assist Britain in fighting the Germans. In addition, London-based 'Governments in Exile', fearing retaliation and reprisals, opposed violent resistance, including assassination. Both views combined to limit prospective SOE activity in Occupied Europe.

'For the first two years of its existence, SOE was dependent upon the Secret Intelligence Service (SIS) for its personnel, technical assistance and communications.'[29] The COS, acting on the 1942 recommendations of the JIC, directed that SIS be given priority over SOE in most of the western European countries. With few planes and meager arms, SOE had little chance of seeing action.[30] Although Churchill wanted to aid the conquered people, subvert the occupying power, and to land an army of liberation,[31] he believed that unlike the Great War, the Second World War would be decided by an economic and psychological struggle rather than by one of attrition. The Future Operations Planning Section (FOPS) of the JPS reported on 16 June 1941 that even with full American help, 'we cannot hope to defeat the existing German Army in the field and so open the road to Germany and victory.'[32] In the War Office, doubts prevailed against the British soldier's ability to defeat his German adversary.[33]

SOE was expected to play an ever-increasing role in European subversion and revolt. The original concept of partisan and guerrilla activity, as viewed by Dalton and integral to SOE's brief, was exchanged for indigenous secret armies and paramilitary organizations in support of an invasion.[34] The Resistance, which had begun subversive activities almost at the signing of the Franco–German armistice, had to be nourished, supplied and protected, if its morale were to be supported. In late 1942, two important changes affected France: a complete German occupation and the beginning of a London partnership between the American Office of Strategic Service (OSS) and SOE. The dissolution of the two French zones demanded that the politically disparate Resistance movements, in many respects operating independently and disconnected from each other, needed to be unified. Only one organization, the indigenous *Francs Tireurs et Partisans* (FTP), representing the Communist *Front National*, had operated across both zones. In the Occupied Zone, five major Resistance movements were active: *Ceux de la Libération*, *Ceux de la Résistance*, *Défense de la France*, *Libération-Nord* and *Organisation Civile et Militaire*. Resistance groups in southern France under such headings as Emmanuel d'Astier de la Vigerie's *Libération* and Henri Frenay's *Combat* merged. These two organizations and the FTP united in March 1943 and established the *Mouvements Unis de la Résistance* (MUR); the new umbrella organization recognized de Gaulle as head of the French Committee of National Liberation (FCNL). In May 1943, Jean Moulin, de Gaulle's Resistance representative, who had worked tirelessly to establish the MUR, subsequently succeeded in forging the *Conseil National de la Résistance* (CNR), an all-encompassing Resistance organization composed of *resistants* from various backgrounds and professions, pledged to evict the enemy from France. On 27 October 1942, Churchill and de Gaulle considered establishing an organization in France that would prepare the French people for a national revolt to conform with an Anglo–American invasion. Britain approved of the idea as long as SOE remained its responsible agency allowed to contact Resistance organizers in France regardless of their political persuasion. Complications abounded: the FTP, which stróde its own Communist and military path, was suspicious of the military Resistance groups, such as the *Armée Secrète* (AS), de Gaulle's military wing, or the now defunct 100,000-strong Vichy Armistice Army, from which many soldiers formed a clandestine fraternity known as the 'Organisation de Resistance de l'Armée' (ORA).[35] The FTP preferred the leadership and guidance of the Communist Party or the CNR within France, rather than the FCNL in Algiers, although both councils had declared de Gaulle as the sole leader of the French Resistance.[36] Contacts had been established early in the war between the Resistance in France and the BCRA, which tried to organize and co-ordinate clandestine activities against the Germans from London.

Contacts Between and the Proposed Merger of OSS and SOE

Sympathetic to Britain's plight, a small group of American secret agents, controlled from London, not Washington, assigned to the embassy in Vichy, operated throughout France during 1940–41. While avoiding direct contact between themselves and SOE agents in the field, the Americans sent intelligence estimates to their controllers in London who shared them with the British. Since consultation and added co-operation between OSS and SOE was sought, Col. William J. Donovan of OSS and Sir Charles Hambro of SOE signed an agreement to this effect, negotiated in London on 24 June 1942.[37] Until 1943, SO operations were controlled by the European Theater US Army (ETOUSA), but on 11 November Special Operations Branch (SO) joined SOE under the control of the Chief of Staff of the Supreme Commander (COSSAC).[38] Even if assimilation appeared to be taken for granted in practice by both organizations, experiences in North Africa, Washington and London revealed that Allied personnel were not as co-operative as they might have been:

> In general SOE–OSS relations were a microcosm of the sense of historic antagonism which continued to exist along with the spirit of co-operation generated by the war so amply demonstrated in Anglo–American discussions about the future role of the British Empire in world affairs.[39]

Sir Robin Brook, who as liaison with OSS was responsible for western Europe SOE operations, concluded that co-operation at the operational level was tempered by friendship and mutual respect.[40] When Eisenhower assumed command of SHAEF, which also served as the command structure for Allied ground forces in Europe, in January 1944, he inherited the problem of employing and controlling the French Resistance during the liberation of France.

Allied Planning and the French Resistance

Even in late 1943, COSSAC had expressed concern that if a French general strike or an uprising were going to take place at all and succeed, it had to be done on a national scale, as part of Allied strategy.[41] Attempting to resolve the twin problems of resistance and civil affairs, Eisenhower, pressed for time and relying on COSSAC, requested and received from Roosevelt permission to deal informally with the FNCL, in the person of de Gaulle's military attaché, General François d'Astier de la Vigerie, Emmanuel's brother. Eisenhower, realizing that Resistance co-operation was necessary, tried to resolve the muddle by agreeing to rearm the Resistance with SHAEF assets, placing senior

French officers on his staff as advisors and choosing General d'Astier of the FCNL responsible for all questions pertaining to resistance action in France. Eisenhower also sought to utilize French divisions for the military occupation of France and in the coming battles on her territory, rather than assigning some Anglo–American divisions for occupational duty.[42]

Two separate North African meetings, one between John J. McCloy, Assistant Secretary of State for War, and Henri Frenay and another between Churchill and Emmanuel d'Astier in January 1944, resulted in the same conclusion: that if the Allies were to obtain any benefit from the French Resistance, the entire operation had to be co-ordinated with the Normandy invasion.[43] As soon as Churchill returned to London on 27 January 1944, he convened a meeting attended by Lord Selborne, General E. E. Mockler-Ferryman, head of SOE and other important French and British representatives. Churchill hoped to force his ideas upon these men whom he could dominate, rather than risk open controversy with the Americans.[44]

Although the bombing of Germany was Churchill's ultimate priority, he insisted that enough planes be diverted from Bomber Command to supply SOE-supported Maquis in southern France, 20,000 of whom, between Geneva and Grenoble, were insufficiently armed. By intensifying rearmament in the southeast, he might succeed in having ANVIL canceled. Even though he refused to consider augmented assistance to other regions of France, except for the northwest, his decision upset air drops to such an extent in other areas, including Yugoslavia, that he was forced to relent, albeit reluctantly. Avoiding any mention of the 27 January meeting, in a letter to Roosevelt, he described Emmanuel d'Astier de la Vigerie as the 'Scarlet Pimpernel' type, intrepid and resourceful.[45] Concurrently, McCloy's summation of his meeting with Frenay, in which he wrote that, 'They [French Resistance] ought to be taken out of the OSS level and put on the basis of staff planning, and it should be done at once', was now in the hands of the JCS. They asked Eisenhower how his SHAEF Headquarters was related to the French Resistance.[46] He turned to SOE for an answer, not knowing that Churchill had already ordered a course of action for it and the Maquis. Eisenhower replied: 'We have had contact in the past and are now continuing contact with and assisting French resistance groups through the French Committee of Action. Under my general supervision and direction is SOE/SO with whom we are working.'[47]

By 7 March 1944, Eisenhower changed the SOE/SO designation to Special Force Headquarters (SFHQ), and on the 23rd, he designated SFHQ as the co-ordinating authority connected with the organization of resistance groups in support of OVERLORD.[48] Eisenhower cabled Washington: '...There are highly important functions necessary to the success of the projected military operations which no agencies other than OSS are prepared to fulfill.'[49]

Accounting for most foreseeable contingencies, such as an enemy withdrawal or an unconditional surrender, SHAEF had various instructions filed with the Resistance through SFHQ. These possibilities smacked of earlier British phantasies, that is, that Anglo–American air bombardment and naval blockade would so erode German morale and fighting power that an Allied invasion would become unnecessary.

SOE and OSS in North Africa had operated independently and co-operatively at the working level throughout the Mediterranean since November 1942. The SOE base, code-named MASSINGHAM, was headquartered near Algiers. One month before, Donovan and George Taylor of SOE met in Washington and decided that a common OSS/SOE establishment should be created. SOE Washington cabled SOE London with the agreed recommendations. Unfortunately, the notification was never circulated; concurrently, at a similar top-level staff meeting in London, those in attendance came to the opposite conclusion. Donovan was furious, feeling he had been double-crossed by SOE. The melee ended with SOE and OSS aborting the agreement and establishing two independent bureaus, with an attendant loss of efficiency after the TORCH landings.[50]

At an Allied Force Headquarters meeting in January 1943, attended by Lt. Colonel Douglas Dodds-Parker, MASSINGHAM's newly appointed commander, Maj. General Colin Gubbins, executive director of SOE, Donovan, and Lt. Colonel William Eddy, head of OSS-Algiers, Eisenhower, AFHQ's commander, urged those present to work even closer together.[51] This appeal for added co-operation was based on a CCS directive of December 1943, requiring Eisenhower to consolidate the two groups within a new single organization called Special Operations Mediterranean (SOM); the OSS tacitly declined to participate, regardless of his sense of urgency.[52] SOE/SO integration was finally accomplished in Algiers on 21 April, after a year's delay. Approved by SHAEF and in operation on 23 May, two weeks before the Normandy invasion, the newly created Special Projects Operations Center (SPOC), was detailed to organize resistance groups in southern France in support of OVERLORD and in preparation for ANVIL.[53] By 21 May 1944, Supreme Allied Commander/Mediterranean relinquished control of resistance groups in southern France, organized as part of SHAEF's strategic component.

Formation of the French Resistance

The Germans defined a 'terrorist(s)' as any person or group acting against the state. Sometimes men, openly evading the German imposed mandatory forced labor service, the *Service du Travail Obligatoire* (STO) in early

1943, joined small groups of guerrillas, Les Maquis. A 1943 SHAEF survey revealed that the bombing offensive offered a better investment than the Resistance whose returns were limited.[54] For most of 1943–44, SHAEF viewed any future Resistance accomplishment as a bonus.[55] Gervase Cowell, current SOE Advisor, stated:

> It would be in one sense correct, if brutal, to say that COSSAC plans did not take the Resistance into consideration, insofar as they did not include their possible contribution in their calculations, but viewed it as a potential bonus. In another sense, since the plans made by SOE to co-ordinate the activities of the Resistance groups with those of the orthodox invading armies were all approved by SHAEF, the activities of the Resistance did form part of the overall planning...[56]

SOE/SO and later SFHQ and SPOC realized that the Resistance required arms and supplies, if they were going to subvert the Germans and assist in the invasion. Before Allied air-drops increased the following year, the Maquis was ill-equipped to fight and poorly trained. Although air-drops were the most practicable method, SOE was constrained by a lack of air transport otherwise needed for the bomber offensive. In 1942 and 1943 only 40 aircraft were available; in 1944, air-drops to the Balkans were 13 times greater than those to France.[57] Therefore, the demand for air support always outstripped the supply. However, Dodds-Parker recalled, '...that by June 1944, it was estimated that in response to radio messages on the BBC or Algiers Radio, hundreds of reception-committees could be alerted to receive a drop the same night in France alone.'[58]

Nevertheless, on 15 June 1944, SHAEF warned General Pierre Koenig, head of the *État Major des Forces Françaises de l'Intérieur* (EMFFI), 'that the FFI should avoid open clashes with the enemy in which his superior weight in equipment would give him an undue advantage.'[59] Previous pitched battles in the Jura and Alpes-Maritimes had led to disastrous results. Sabotage, by comparison was an excellent weapon and more cost-effective than either pitched battles or aerial bombing. The simple act of interchanging destination cards between railway goods-wagons wrought havoc and led to excessive time delays.[60] When de Gaulle thanked Churchill for British support, the JCS interpreted de Gaulle's remark as criticism of US participation in supplying arms to the Resistance. They cabled Eisenhower on 19 April:

> We are informed by the State Department that the matter of arming resistance groups has become an important issue politically. With the French there is a widely held opinion that everything being done in this field is done by the British, and that America, for political reasons, is against

> arming the Resistance. We desire that, insofar as it is consistent with the requirements of military operations, you take such action as lies within your authority to bring about an equalization of effort between American and Great Britain in supplying and delivering equipment to resistant groups.[61]

Eisenhower complied, conferred with Koenig and assigned 25 more aircraft to Special Operations over the protests of Air Marshal Sir Arthur Tedder, 'who doubting the value of the Resistance movement, considered the increase unjustified.'[62]

In 1940, Dalton romanticized that SOE's first task was to mobilize and ignite left-wing opinion on the Continent into a revolutionary blaze that would force the enemy to flee. When the task was found to be beyond the scope of SOE, the British transformed it from action service to an allied service involved with training, arming and employing paramilitary forces in Britain and France, in support of OVERLORD. Earlier, Hitler's invasion of Russia unleashed an upsurge of anti-Fascist feeling throughout France, most pronounced amongst professionally-trained Communist groups, hitherto unavailable to SOE.[63]

Those originally 'specially employed' by SOE had entered occupied Europe disguised as civilians, but as D-day approached, much of their work and that of others was accomplished in a variety of allied military uniforms.[64] COSSAC changed its perception of the Resistance from an information-gathering service to a combat organization, integrated with the OVERLORD and ANVIL operations.[65] However, CCS instructions stipulated that the French, whose security was weak, were not to be involved in any detailed planning for OVERLORD. According to M. R. D. Foot, French wireless codes were easily broken by German Intelligence.[66]

During the spring and fall of 1942, plans were at SOE's London headquarters to train three-man teams called Jedburghs to assist the Resistance.[67] To be parachuted into France, 'these uniformed teams acted as focal units from D-day onward for contact, communication and control between themselves, the Resistance and the invading troops.'[68] By 1944, there were approximately 137,000 Maquis in France, awaiting Jedburghs delivered instructions from the Supreme Commander.

Although the Maquis were initially deficient in stores and money, air-drops increased once air supremacy over western Europe was achieved in the spring of 1944. Operation 'CARPETBAGGER' introduced massive daylight air supply missions to the Maquis who became customer-members in business with the Jedburghs.[69] During June, July and August 1944 82 Jedburgh teams were dropped into France. SOE established 'safe houses' and reception committees in enemy-held France earlier for these incoming Jedburghs. The first Jedburgh team, called 'Hugh', dropped blind (without a reception committee) near Chateauroux, a town 100 kilometers southeast of Tours, during the early hours of 6 June; two other teams followed three days later.

With the invasion imminent, Eisenhower agreed to a tripartite administrative structure known as the EMFFI, which was established within SFHQ and commanded by Koenig, de Gaulle's representative. Although the change-over occurred on 6 June, the first fully integrated section was not in operation until 2 August, much too late to have assisted the Normandy landings.[70] Koenig had the authority to veto any SHAEF contemplated Resistance action, but SFHQ never intended to relinquish power and control of financial, aircraft, communications and distribution resources that it held in practical fact to him.[71] Gubbins offered his reaction to an aide, 'The taking over of French Resistance by Koenig has led to a first class battle here lasting six weeks. I have got most of my own way through sheer force of logic of events, but I feel that Koenig will make an awful mess of the whole thing.'[72] However, the June and July SFHQ Reports disclosed that

> Results of FFI activities ... generally with OG, SAS and Jedburgh assistance greater than expected, despite lack of arms. Potentialities if arms supplied more fully, would be immense ... Brittany forces crystallizing round 400 uniformed SAS troops of 4th French Parachute Bn. and Jedburgh teams. In Brittany, on 1 July there were 30,500 resistance troops, of whom 5,000 were armed. Resistance to be built up to 77,000 men and Field Headquarters ... by the end of July to create a military diversion. Brittany resistance aided advancing Allies by attacking moving columns, attacking isolated groups, protecting bridges from destruction, etc. Also mopped up behind Allied thrusts and kept Lines of Communication open as Allies advanced into Peninsula in August....[73]

To finance the Resistance in relation to OVERLORD, SOE, as the principal British procurer of foreign funds, purchased 700 million francs worth of French currency on the black markets of Europe and Asia. The difference between the official and 'black market's' rates of exchange saved the British government almost a million pounds sterling per month. Since January 1944, SOE secretly obtained for the Bank of England well over 1.7 million pounds sterling worth of foreign currencies including 445,000 French francs in notes of small denominations.[74] SOE had also acted as paymaster for the British Treasury, by turning over sums of up to 100 million francs per month to the FCNL, who apportioned it among the Resistance in France, based on unit participation.[75] Weapons were not the only supplies that were air-dropped. Each Jedburgh officer jumping into France carried 100,000 francs in an army-issued money belt, while the W/T operator carried 50,000. During September 1943, Colonel Roger Heslop, 'Xavier', the leader of SOE's MARKSMAN circuit, landed in eastern France with 500,000 francs for his personal use, although he was requested to keep an account of expenses.[76] OG paratroopers were issued French Louis d'Ors, valuable gold coins if a bribe were necessary.[77] OSS Berne headquarters distributed 4 million French francs per month to those French regions adjacent to Switzerland. During the period 29 March 1943 to 20 November 1944, Berne's total disbursement reached 66 million French francs.[78] By 9 June, 5.5 billion francs were in circulation with the Allied armies in France,[79] but agents in the field signaled their complaints, regardless of the totals: 'Must receive 5 million francs to feed men send soonest' or 'Destroyed 8 railway bridges, 3 trains, 14 engines, 3 observation posts, made 40 prisoners. You must send us arms, ammunition, explosives. We can not fight with our bare hands.'[80]

Anglo–American antipathy towards de Gaulle and French security measures hampered and delayed tying the Resistance to OVERLORD planning. The OSS War Diary states: 'No French officer was ever taken into confidence and given the slightest bit of advance information on the date selected for the opening of the second front. Prior to D-day, Koenig was completely bypassed by SHAEF.'[81] Excluded by political and military prejudice, French general officers were not considered part of the Allied team. Eisenhower said as much at a meeting with press correspondents on 31 August 1944:

> Relations with French generals were not easy: they had not grown up as members of this team. They were liable to suffer from an inferiority complex after events of 1940. It has not been easy to get them doing things, the way if we turned to a British or American Commander and asked him to do so and so; we have to use a little strong-arm method.[82]

W. H. B. Mack who served as British Foreign Office Political Liaison Officer with Eisenhower observed at a COS meeting that the Chiefs disliked de Gaulle intensely and vetoed his return to Britain from Algiers on D-2.[83] Roosevelt's pursuance of Vichy policy and his choice of Giraud excluded de Gaulle and his chosen generals from the center of policy and planning. In spite of Churchill's ambivalence towards de Gaulle, he remained loyal to him, as illustrated by a willingness to share the date of the TORCH landings, a decision that Roosevelt immediately vetoed. SHAEF Directive of 23 March 1944 to SFHQ, which prohibited the disclosure of military intentions, aimed to keep de Gaulle in the dark, although the other Allied governments (in exile) were banned as well. French representatives were included in SOE/SO planning for the infiltration of Jedburghs and French patriots on and after D-day, but the exact date was not revealed.[84] By 31 May 1944, Churchill insisted that de Gaulle be told of OVERLORD, in spite of COS feelings to the contrary. Churchill invited de Gaulle, then in Algiers, to come to London to broadcast a radio message to the French nation that called for the Resistance to unify in support of the critical D-day period. With Eisenhower's concurrence, Churchill briefed de Gaulle on 4 June concerning the invasion plans, believing that security was safe at this late date. As a precautionary measure, de Gaulle and his Chief of Staff were sworn to secrecy.[85] The prime minister discovered on 5 June that de Gaulle not only refused to broadcast, but he would not allow French liaison officers to accompany the invasion force. Cadogan recorded Churchill's reaction at a Cabinet meeting:

> We endured the usual passionate anti-de Gaulle harangue from the PM. On this subject, we get away from politics and diplomacy and even common sense. It's a girls school. Roosevelt, PM, and, it must be admitted de Gaulle, all behave like girls approaching the age of puberty. Nothing to be done.[86]

John Bross, an OSS officer stationed in London, concluded that the British objected to French participation in Allied planning, because of their poor security and fractious political in-fighting. For these reasons, the British were strongly opposed to organizing the Resistance on a national basis and wanted it decentralized.[87] Lord Selborne reported to Churchill that Gaullist groups in France were playing for political stakes at the expense of military action. The unrestrained temptation to over-centralize and expanded Gestapo activity led to increased Resistance casualties.[88] Even if de Gaulle were considered reliable, some FCNL representatives were not. Since it was impossible to know who among the French could be trusted, no one would be trusted, including de Gaulle.[89] As a last resort, French officials insisted on the right to by-pass SHAEF and to negotiate directly with the US and British governments, in lieu of CCS representation. They were refused any special rights or admission to the CCS.

Jean Moulin: Security and his Arrest

Jean Moulin, President of the CNR, considered to be the most impressive figure in the whole French Resistance, had returned to France, in part, to improve Resistance security. He had planned to reorganize it along classical cellular lines to minimize the risks of capture or penetration, 'no one cell to know another; only the leader to know the identity of his superior and propaganda services to be separated from para-military groups.'[90] Before these security measures were applied, Moulin was captured in Lyon and tortured to death by the Germans in June 1943. Moulin's seizure and demise was part of a ferocious German counterattack on French Resistance groups during that year: many F and RF circuits were attacked, penetrated and smashed, their leaders either killed or in hiding.[91] As a result of over-centralization, a group of senior French Secret Army officials meeting in Switzerland in June were exposed to the Gestapo. When the visiting French officials returned to France, they were arrested by the Germans who seized many important incriminating documents.[92] By contrast, the Communist FTP, whose members numbered 100,000, suffered fewer casualties, because it was decentralized. Proposed was a Maquis Plan to alleviate the over-centralized Resistance command by establishing self-contained elite forces parachuted into appropriate sub-regions of France. Under Eisenhower's command, but attached to the various district Maquis chiefs, they would eliminate the need for an overall central Resistance Headquarters. Once these military missions were established, the general direction of the Resistance movement would be based outside of France entirely.[93] The institution of the Maquis Plan represented both the beginning of the paramilitary movement and the first inclusion of the French on any basis of equality with the Americans and British.[94]

Co-ordinated Military and Resistance Action in Normandy

SHAEF's 'color-coded' action messages were transmitted by the BBC from London on 5 June to the various Resistance networks, revealing that the invasion and insurrection were imminent. A string of action messages, based on one of the following plans: rail, transport, power, telecommunication, fuel and ammunition storage and sabotage, set the Resistance in motion on missions throughout France. Guerrilla actions taken against German Army formations and headquarters and defence against German acts of destruction and demolition were also included as Resistance objectives.[95]

SPOC and ANVIL

To insure maximum assistance to ANVIL, the organization and direction of the Resistance in southern France developed in two phases under SPOC control. The first phase of 15 July was to provide equipment for major Maquis missions in all the regions of south and central France: 2,136 tons of stores were dropped in July from Britain and Algiers. On 1 August, two weeks before ANVIL, the second phase developed with the expansion of these Maquis regions into 3 main areas: the Rhone with 25,000 armed men and the Massif Central and the Pyrenees with 12,00 each. One additional 'color-coded' action message, assigned the Resistance in southern France to protect the port facilities at Marseilles, Toulon and Sête. Other events followed: 500 men were parachuted in to assist in the heavy fighting that broke out on either side of the Rhone river; the Spanish frontier was closed to escaping German troops and the large towns of Limoges, Chateauroux and Poitiers were liberated; public utilities were seized and the enemy withdrawal disrupted. 20,000 German troops were taken prisoner between 11–13 September. Resistance accomplishments in support of ANVIL were the equivalent of four or five divisions, according to Gen. Alexander Patch, the American task force commander.[96]

Within the first week of OVERLORD, 960 railway demolitions out of a planned 1,055 had been carried out. On D+1, 26 trunk lines were unusable, including the main lines between St. Lô, Avranches, Cherbourg and Caen, due to Resistance activity in the north. There were 300 rail cuts confirmed between 6 and 27 June. Enemy reinforcements were delayed between 48 and 72 hours, while the 2nd SS Panzer Division was delayed 12 days trying to reach Normandy from southwest France. The two main railway lines along the Rhone were closed to German divisions trying to reach the battle area from southern France for most of the crucial D-day period. With much of the telecommunication network sabotaged by Resistance groups, the Germans were forced to use wireless communications, allowing for easy intercepts by Allied tactical Intelligence. June diversionary Resistance activities in central and south-eastern France absorbed the attention of 16,000 German soldiers and the 11th Panzer Division.[97] American General Omar Bradley, Commander of 12th US Army Group, notified SHAEF that he had received excellent co-operation from Resistance forces. The Resistance made a spectacular contribution to the liberation of Paris in which 30,000 to 50,000 patriots participated in a *levée en masse*. Armed with whatever weapons they could assemble, they fought through the streets, seeking to destroy Germans and collaborators on whatever terms.[98] After the Normandy invasion, virtual civil war mixed with the liberation of France. It was a period of rough frontier justice in which some criminal elements took advantage of the situation and pursued ends of purely personal gain or revenge. Some went on a rampage of murder and looting, others peremptorily settled old scores, but these escapades were few and quickly stopped. Direct executions by the Resistance mingled with all sorts of obscure settling of scores. Reporter Paul Abrahams, in his article on European resistance in 12 November's *Financial Times* sensationalizes the random killings by a few guerrillas and distorts and minimizes the overall contribution made by the Resistance in France.[99] He fails to realize that in most countries the bulk of the population takes the line of least resistance, avoiding disruption to its daily life whenever possible, while the small percentage of activists, placing their lives at risk, fight to drive out the enemy occupier. Of the French adult population 2 percent fought in the Resistance. Some two million persons, or around 10 percent of the adult population took an even lesser risk. The overwhelming majority, approximately 44 million Frenchmen, did nothing to eliminate German oppression by fire and sword.[100]

Eisenhower, who believed that the Resistance had surrounded the Germans with a terrible atmosphere of danger and hatred that ate into the confidence of their leaders and the courage of their soldiers,[101] wrote to Gubbins in May 1945,

> While no final assessment of the operation value of resistance action has yet been completed, I consider that the disruption of enemy rail communications, the harassing of German road moves and the continual and increasing strain placed on German war economy ... by the organized forces of Resistance, played a very considerable part in our complete and final victory.[102]

Evidence from many quarters, including the unsolicited testimonials of high-ranking German prisoners of war, indicates that the Resistance contributed to Germany's defeat in the West.[103] However, it is difficult to measure the exact contribution and effectiveness of the Resistance, because operational records were not kept. Additionally, strategic deception, in which the Resistance guided by SOE, played an important part, succeeded in hoodwinking the Germans in believing that the chosen invasion site was the Pas de Calais and not Normandy. Pre-D-day diversions, further afield, included false action radio messages, an increased tempo of air-dropped supplies and stepped-up guerrilla attacks, which were used to thwart and confuse the enemy, as part of two deception plans, BODYGUARD and FORTITUDE. As a result, in March 1944, the Germans increased their garrison of first-class troops in Denmark from four to eight divisions, and Hitler defended Norway with more divisions than necessary. He feared the military presence of General Andrew Thorne, GOC Scottish Command, a former British military attaché in Berlin during the thirties,[104] who had impressed the Fuhrer with his military skill and knowledge.[105] Believing that the British Fourth Army under Thorne might invade Norway, Hitler deflected about 50 U-boats from the Atlantic convoy routes and stationed them along the Norwegian coast. As a consequence, the British released a large number of escort vessels from convoy and support duties to protect the Normandy landings from submarine attack.[106] Integral to these deception plans, the Resistance contributed to the lodgement, breakout and pursuit of the Allied armies beyond the expectations of the Anglo–Americans, the results far exceeding the expectations of the military.[107]

Preoccupied with fighting the war in a conventional manner, the Allied military hierarchy devoted little time to the Resistance and clandestine warfare. The bombing of Germany was an Allied strategic cornerstone that demanded the combined utilization of two limited resources, intelligent, well-trained personnel and sophisticated technology. These shortages in personnel, aircraft and supplies imposed tight restrictions on irregular warfare. Moreover, poor security within the French political–military system and German infiltration and destruction of many Resistance networks hampered SFHQ and Resistance efforts. At best, successful execution was seen as an adjunct to the great land battles in northwest France. Much more could have been accomplished if the major participants had selectively admitted the French into their deliberations. Few men addressed the issues of trust and co-operation, however delayed, with the candor of Eisenhower in a statement to de Gaulle:

> I shall need your support in France ... I can not tell you on what theoretical basis my government will instruct me to deal with you! But above principles, there are actions. I would like to tell you that, where action is concerned, I shall recognize no other authority in France but yours.[108]

Arming the French

As American wartime production increased between 1941 and 1943, the US extended Lend-Lease, in principle and with modifications to the Gaullists. This removed an enormous burden from Britain's financial concerns. The November 1942 invasion of North Africa demanded that the question of American large-scale and rapid rearmament assistance to the French be addressed. Prior to that time, Free French Forces operated under the control of the British who assumed the responsibility for their maintenance, training and supply. This practice was formalized by a CCS directive of 24 March 1942 in which the Free French Forces remained within the orbit of British provisions and training.[109] De Gaulle's two infantry divisions, which had fought with the British Eighth Army, were augmented by thousands of poorly clad volunteers from the French African Army that had subsisted under the Franco–German armistice of 1940.

De Gaulle's Need for American Material

At the mercy of the US for war material,[110] de Gaulle, in the Spring of 1942, wishing to implement a rearmament program in preparation for the eventual return of French forces to metropolitan France, decided to seek increased American aid for the project. This included not only the re-equipping of existing French forces, but of those additional forces expected to be recruited.[111] He believed that a revitalized modern army would restore the prestige and national pride of the French. However, Marshall refused de Gaulle's proposals for an increase in direct US aid, not only because armament was needed elsewhere, but also because increased French demands for material were considered unwarranted.[112]

Churchill's and Roosevelt's personal dislike of de Gaulle intruded at the military level and hampered the French Army's rearmament and training that depended upon Allied goodwill and commitment. Churchill expressed his concerns in a letter to Roosevelt on 18 June 1943, but evaded the president's recommendation to break with the French leader directly:

> It is imperative that the French Army in North West Africa should be in loyal and trustworthy hands especially on the eve of the great operations which impend. I agree with you that no confidence can be placed in de Gaulle's friendship for the Allies ... and I myself could not be responsible ... if our bases and lines of communication in North Africa were disturbed or endangered through the existence of a French Army under potentially hostile control ... I am glad therefore to learn the clear instructions you have given General Eisenhower not to 'Permit de Gaulle to direct himself or to control through partisans of any committee the African French Army, either in the field of supplies, training or operations.'[113]

At a secret meeting of 23 October 1943, Roosevelt's military emissary in North Africa, General Mark Clark, pledged assistance to the 137,000-strong French North African Army, providing, of course, that it would join the war on the Allied side. Agreement was reached between Clark and French Admiral Jean Darlan on 22 November, two weeks after TORCH. Augmenting the French forces were 60,000 secretly trained colonial militia, previously unknown to Clark, and 103,000 men mobilized the same day. If the infrastructures of West and North Africa had been more efficient, the total would have gone beyond the 300,000 available effectives.[114]

The Anfa Plan of 1943

During the Casablanca Conference, Roosevelt and his protégé, French General and Commander in Chief, Henri Giraud, conferred and formulated a set of principles, known as the Anfa Plan, pertaining to French rearmament. This included the delivery of enough material for three armored divisions and eight motorized divisions as well as an air force. In return, France would furnish 165,000 tons of shipping to the inter-allied pool. Since Roosevelt disliked de Gaulle, the president excluded both Churchill and de Gaulle from the rearmament decision-making process. Upon discovery, the prime minister objected. Henceforth, French rearmament became subject to the military priorities and decisions of the CCS and not to the Americans alone.[115] Rearming a French Army created additional problems between these three Allies that related to the allocation of global shipping, one of a number of scarce resources. Churchill expressed his apprehension, 'The commanders have been told they must cut their requirements to the bone.'[116] His COS agreed, feeling that the combination of limited shipping and an increased allocation of scarce military supplies to the French would prejudice operations such as HUSKY.[117] The Americans, however, interpreted the shortages of tonnage and escort facilities as limiting factors soon to be overcome.[118] The British insisted that French rearmament was not required to implement agreed strategy and could not be justified militarily. A 12 March CCS meeting became deadlocked over the crisis,[119] but by 18 May it concluded that, 'The rearming and re-equipping of the Free French Forces in North Africa should be proceeded with as rapidly as the availability of shipping and equipping will allow, but as a secondary commitment to the requirement of British and American forces in various theaters.'[120] The French were dissatisfied, because the agreed pace of rearmament and training relative to the 24 percent casualties they suffered in Tunisia would slow the creation of a modern army.[121]

Apportioning Scarce Supplies

In the light of world-wide strategy expressed in the practical terms of shipping, armament and production schedules, did the Americans consider Anfa an 'agreement in principle', much as the British perceived SLEDGEHAMMER in 1942? Were the French insisting, just as the Americans did during SLEDGEHAMMER, that it was a firm commitment? Would either side's interpretation result in an irreconcilable conflict? How these questions were treated, follows.

When the president wrote the words, '*oũi, en principe*' in the margin of the original document, his statement in French was more binding than 'yes in principle', subsequently used in the official text.[122] However straightforward some statements may seem, their implications can vary from language to language. These semantic differences once again contributed to misunderstandings among the allies.

Although supply shipments were underway, the current allocation of 25,000 tons per convoy was not enough to reach the 11-division target set by the Anfa Plan. The Americans attributed this shortfall to the shipping demands of the Tunisian campaign, but according to Giraud, they were not pushing the plan vigorously enough. Eisenhower warned that if French uneasiness over rearmament was not dealt with on the political level immediately, 'I have here to face the insinuation that we are not straightforward, that we are long on promises and short on performances. This impression must be dispelled before the situation deteriorates.'[123] To assuage French fears, Roosevelt informed Robert D. Murphy, his political representative in North Africa:

> You can tell them [the French in North Africa] that at no time did I or General Marshall promise equipment for the French divisions at any given date. What was agreed on was the principle of rearming them to be done as soon as we found it practicable from a shipping point of view … The French must remain calm and sensible.[124]

The French Military Scoreboard

Giraud attended a special meeting of the CCS on 8 July 1943, seeking to exchange archaic Franco–German weapons, issued under the 1940 Armistice agreement, for modern ones. Although handicapped, ten French divisions fought in the five-month-long Tunisian battle, in which they suffered 15,000 casualties, out of a total of approximately 75,000. Twenty per cent had been killed, many of them officers. Moreover, Giraud indicated that besides limited replacements, scarce resources and the heavy wastage of clothing and equipment had left his remaining troops in rags. Discontent and damaged morale among the men were evident, and he urged that an initial installment of clothing and equipment for 100,000 men be delivered immediately. Assessing combat effectiveness, Giraud reported that certain units of the French Army, supplied with modern American equipment, had clearly benefited and were now capable of undertaking active service in Europe, particularly in France. In exchange for this material, the French offered a secure North African base that included ports, airfields and communication facilities.[125]

Promises Made, Deliveries Delayed

To demonstrate good faith, Marshall tried to replace Roosevelt's 'agreement in principle' with a firm offer: American depots would supply the French with the necessary material by delaying the activation and supply of a number of American divisions in 1943. Marshall observed that he was committed to equip 11 or 12 French, unless the matter was dropped soon.[126] Political implications overshadowed the military aspects; although cost-effectiveness favored the Americans activating their own divisions, they faced the arduous process of converting a tattered foreign army into a modern one. French military leaders were difficult and sometimes unrealistic in their demands, but these were typical complications of coalition warfare. Lack of a common language and culture separated the protagonists and provoked misunderstandings. Resolution of the differences in customs, dietary habits and clothing sizes added to the pressing problems of allied shipping, of port, storage and distribution facilities and the lack of trained personnel to handle this infrastructure with efficiency. For the Americans, French rearmament was an inconvenience driven by politics, over which they equivocated for three months. Nevertheless, one benefit of having France supply manpower meant fewer Americans in combat and less disruption to the American civilian work-force.

Many of the participants were dissatisfied with the time and direction rearmament was taking, some were openly distrustful: Eisenhower was stymied by Roosevelt's indecisiveness; Murphy reported that the French thought they were being 'hoodwinked'; Giraud complained that there was opposition to rearmament, if not deception; Roosevelt advised that an 'agreement in principle' did not involve detailed commitments and Marshall agreed, implying that Giraud had knowingly misrepresented the facts, an opinion which distorted reality.[127] King believed that de Gaulle was constantly increasing his prestige and would certainly take advantage of these 11 divisions to further strengthen his political position and Leahy thought that de Gaulle planned to use 9 divisions to enhance his reputation in France. If de Gaulle got into France, with these well-equipped divisions, Leahy ruminated, he could readily take charge of the government by force.[128] The president understood that Eisenhower, who wanted these French divisions combat-ready, thought that 60 days was all that was needed to determine whether they were going to prove worthwhile. If they did not, Eisenhower could opt out of the agreement by simply providing the French with discarded

American equipment left behind in North Africa, and Marshall concluded, if that be so, the Americans would not ship any new equipment to the French but simply supply them with existing equipment already on site.[129] Concurrently, Jean Monnet, a French financial expert approved by the British and American officials, flew to Algiers to brief Eisenhower and Giraud on the rearmament case, as seen from Washington, in an attempt to dissipate their doubts.[130]

Colonel Bessell's Assessment

During this running controversy, Colonel William Bessell of the OPD considered the possible effects of empowering new French or American divisions on the American manpower situation and on overall allied efficiency. Reporting to the JCS, he and his committee observed that the US was not only the 'arsenal of democracy', but was also a source of untapped manpower reserves. American continental military facilities could train up to 60 divisions a year and keep almost 11 million men in uniform indefinitely, but skilled civilian manpower was not easy to replace. If the war became a slow attritional process, he doubted if the American public would accept any unnecessary prolongation. Because of time constraints, 11 projected French divisions was the limit, but he urged their maximum use once raised.[131]

Marshall blundered when he reduced the Victory Program military manpower ceiling by 25 percent and assigned half of the 7.5 million men in uniform to the Air Corps. Would French troops make up the shortfall? From 1943 onward, combat-ready troops were always in short supply, because the JWPC, unduly optimistic, failed to appreciate or emphasize their value. Army planners even considered cutting back the Army's personnel needs as the German Army seemed on the verge of collapse during the late summer of 1944.[132] The outcome of these combined miscalculations are best described in a series of fall and winter attritional frontier battles in northwest Europe comparable to those of the Italian campaign.[133]

Problems in Rearmament and Training the French

During the same meeting, General Rooks, Assistant CoS (AFHQ) expressed his doubts about French combat ability; he believed that the French divisions which had fought in Tunisia, composed mostly of poorly trained African troops with a small proportion of white officers, had not used their American equipment efficiently; therefore, combat-effectiveness and organizational cohesion suffered.[134] Among these troops, serious shortages of trained technicians prevailed and the replacement of combat losses would have to wait until the liberation of Europe. Arthur Funk, serving as a young American naval lieutenant in Casablanca, stated 'that many of the French quartermaster personnel lacked an English language facility and mechanical ability to assemble crated equipment in timely fashion. Most of the accompanying instructions were written in English.'[135] Until the unification of the *Armée d'Afrique* with the Gaullists after TORCH, Free French military operations were more symbolic than real.

It was not only logistics that complicated French rearmament; conflicts arose when the French decided to concentrate on combat units alone, because support units were traditionally despised in the French Army. It relegated supply duties to the Americans who insisted on a balance between combat and support units, matching their own structure.[136] Either the French accepted the US Army's organizational techniques or suffer the consequences – take it or leave it, but French senior officers felt it to be unheroic to raise supply companies at the expense of combat formations. Even with American insistence, it took the French Army most of the war to develop a true appreciation of the balance between logistical and operational concerns. The conflict between a decentralized French system and a highly centralized American one was modified but never resolved. Moreover, the Americans insisted that the doctrine of combined-arms task organization be applied, replacing a French system of separate commanders for each individual arm within each division. ANVIL's time constraints demanded that the French be trained quickly.[137]

Variations in French and American Leadership

Compared to American commanders who would complain to higher authorities if supplies were delayed, French commanders remained traditionally passive. However Giraud did complain when the Americans narrowly interpreted and breached a section of the Anfa Plan: their substitutions of modern equipment for obsolescent weaponry, such as the M-3 gun for the 74-mm and the M1903 rifle for the M1, that affected French combat efficiency. Lt. General Wilhelm D. Styer, COS, Army Service Forces denied Giraud's claim on 4 November 1943, insisting that the assignment of a few substitutions had not handicapped French units in any appreciable way and was still 'equipment of the most modern kind.'[138]

The French Training Section

American assistance in the French training program was specifically geared to technical instruction alone under the rubric of the US Fifth Army's French

Training Section (FTC). After consultation with Giraud, Marshall, on 18 April 1943, approved a two- to six-month training cycle with American material, in order for individual units to reach combat-effectiveness and technical efficiency.[139] Conceived by the Americans and approved by the French, the FTC establishment of divisional schools to which students were assigned, became the most successful method of training. American instructors collaborated with their French colleagues to train each division's cadre in the most efficient manner known. French members of the FTC co-operated with various schools in the US and in North Africa in order to train thousands of French personnel to become military specialists. If a problem existed, it was not the implementation of the course-work, but the questionable proficiency of English among some of the students.[140]

By October 1943, not only were seven divisions receiving technical training from American personnel, but five of these divisions were designated for amphibious training as well. Although the training program had reached a satisfactory level, progress had been impeded by the lack of officer supervision, equipment and training aids. Sometimes the French failed to take advantage of American offers and by the end of October training of service units still lagged behind schedule. Courses in regimental signal communications and chemical warfare suffered, because of poor co-ordination or flagging interest. To improve the level of training commensurate with battle conditions, instructors accompanied infantry divisions into combat and reported their findings upon returning to North Africa.

Throughout the war, French commanders were acutely conscious of their manpower limitations. Addressing this problem, three training centers were established during mid-May 1944 in Italy to serve the *Corps Expéditionnaire Français* (CEF) to meet its combat replacement and skilled manpower requirements. When the French Expeditionary Force grew to five divisions, the Americans turned over an American training camp in North Africa to it, capable of housing 8,000 to 10,000 men. However, General Patch, C-in-C of the US Seventh Army, assumed the general direction of CEF training ten days before the ANVIL landing, because technical training remained insufficient. On 10 September, almost one month after ANVIL's launch, Patch recommended that the French take responsibility for and control over the training of their personnel. When British General Sir Henry Maitland Wilson became SACMED, three FTS training centers operated in southern France. By late October, as the battles moved northward, the training of French troops under American guidance in North Africa ended.

Political ramifications had delayed the creation and implementation of a French rearmament program. The administrational structures needed to rearm and train the French had been established in ragged fashion and lagged behind demand. However, most of the supply and training problems were finally overcome in time for the French participation in ANVIL. When the war ended, approximately 700,000 French men were deployed, 11 divisions and 300 supporting units served; all of the supporting units and eight of the divisions had received the latest American equipment, which represented over three million measured tons. Ever bound to the Americans for logistical support, French divisions proved highly efficient in combat during the Italian campaign. By early 1944, the French Army was ready to join its Allies in the invasion of the European continent and the liberation of its homeland, 'winning American confidence and overcoming British skepticism' in the process.[141] In spite of the political differences at the higher levels that plagued rearmament, the French First Army set an enviable battle record during the final phases of the war. Creating a French Army in North Africa enabled three quarters of a million American men to remain working in industry rather than serving in the military. As civilians, they not only contributed to the defeat of the Axis, but they were well placed to satisfy the insatiable post-war demand for consumer goods and tools needed for reconstruction.

When de Gaulle declared the FCNL to be the Provisional Government of France, he demanded that the French Corps fighting in Italy under General Juin and the ten French divisions mounted in North Africa under General de Lattre de Tassigny play a leading role in the liberation of southern France. Having these forces at his disposal, de Gaulle was poised to liberate the French populace with a modern army. Psychologically and emotionally it was a matter of self-respect and national prestige. On the Anglo–American side, the benefits of arming the French proved to outweigh the disadvantages.

7 ANVIL, OVERLORD and the Italian Campaign

Before the Tehran (EUREKA) Conference, Churchill requested a summit meeting in Cairo (SEXTANT I) to resolve and co-ordinate Anglo–American strategic policy before meeting the Russians. Because of disastrous British ventures in the eastern Mediterranean, which were proving highly prejudicial to a deteriorating Italian campaign, Churchill sought a modification of the QUADRANT agreement, that addressed the transfer to Britain of seven Mediterranean-based divisions and 60 LSTs scheduled from November 1943.[1] The attritional battles south of Rome, in which 11 ill-prepared and under-manned Allied divisions encountered 19 experienced and well-positioned German divisions, foreshadowed a long arduous winter campaign and had aroused his concern. To relieve growing anxiety over the front's tactical imbalance, Churchill and the COS sought to redirect the transfer of those men and craft, designated for the cross-Channel attack, into the Italian campaign.[2] Churchill petitioned Roosevelt, despite the president's resistance, and questioned the practicality of the relevant QUADRANT decisions. Churchill's willingness to negotiate more openly represented a change from the artful positioning of the MODICUM and SYMBOL meetings. Roosevelt entertained Churchill's entreaties related to the following issues: increased American support for British efforts in the eastern Mediterranean, Operations ACCOLADE and HARDIHOOD,[3] and the merger of the two Mediterranean commands into one.

However, Roosevelt, preoccupied with the possibility of a personal meeting with China's Generalissimo Chiang Kai-Shek in Cairo, considered the QUADRANT agreement as settled. Both he and the JCS were alarmed and irritated at Churchill who sought to re-negotiate parts of the agreement, as if he were again abandoning OVERLORD in preference for an intensified Mediterranean policy.[4] Although the Americans remained focused on a May OVERLORD, they were not indifferent to the problems raised by Churchill regarding the attritional warfare unfolding under appalling weather conditions and shortages on the Italian peninsula. The British wanted to raise the level of the Italian campaign, the Americans fought to preserve the sanctity of OVERLORD.

According to John Winant, American Ambassador to Britain, the British believed that the psychological moment for launching OVERLORD could not be fixed months in advance. Moreover, they feared that the QUADRANT agreement took precedence over subsequent changes in the military situation.

He concluded that the principal difference of opinion between the two parties was simply one of timing.[5] Unknown to Winant was the Russian expectation of an executed OVERLORD at the earliest possible moment.[6] Contrary to British thought, the Americans, fighting a two-ocean war, considered logistics as the primary factor for creating such an opportunity. Unfortunately, Churchill and Brooke aroused American suspicions again by advocating further British operations in the Dodecanese, a group of islands off the Turkish coast.[7] Brooke complained in his diary entry of 1 November,

> If only I had sufficient force of character to swing those American Chiefs of Staff and make them see daylight, how different the war might be. We should have been in a position to force the Dardanelles by the capture of Crete and Rhodes. We should have had the whole of the Balkans ablaze by now, and the war might be finished in 1943! [8]

Although Roosevelt agreed to meet Churchill on 22 November in Cairo, he carefully avoided meeting him privately. 'Roosevelt was an artist in avoiding discussion of issues he did not want to discuss. On the other hand he was affable enough to make Churchill reasonably optimistic.'[9] By avoiding a decision on future strategy prior to EUREKA, Roosevelt dashed Churchill's hopes for further Mediterranean action. Brooke hoped to present a united Anglo–American strategic policy to Stalin at Tehran, the opposite of what Roosevelt intended. If the president got his way, they would go to Tehran without a common plan.

Cairo: SEXTANT I

The participants at the Cairo Conference of 22–26 November tried to cram too much work into too little time, exhausting the participants before they traveled to Tehran. Churchill's attitude did not help. Brooding over the near-disaster at Salerno, he was convinced that a planned invasion of France would fail. When he discovered that 25 percent of the landing craft assigned to strengthen OVERLORD were to be transferred elsewhere, he exploded. Hopkins considered Churchill's behavior unsuitable.[10] Brooke thought that Churchill's petulance covered a wish to form a purely British theater in the Mediterranean on which all the battle laurels would fall.[11]

According to John Eisenhower, son of the General, SEXTANT I was laden with acrimony for several reasons: an accumulation of unpleasant decisions deferred from previous conferences, leaving basic disagreements unresolved, the loss of British partnership dominance, the concern over the meeting with Stalin and the presence of Chiang and his wife in Cairo.[12] CCS meetings were lengthy, overcrowded and their participants frequently bad tempered.

Structural problems surfaced when Marshall petitioned the COS that approximately 50 officers in the American party would attend, to which General Handy took exception. He considered the number insufficient to fulfill the needs of the American representatives.[13] Briefcases in which important secret papers were stuffed, were called 'albatrosses', because they were chained to their owners until they arrived safely in Cairo.[14]

The Conference registered two tripartite plenary sessions, five CCS, five COS, and five JCS meetings, each body meeting separately, plus numerous informal military and political meetings and working luncheons, some attended by Chiang's military representatives. Nine of the items on the agenda pertained to Southeast Asia and four related to OVERLORD/ Mediterranean.

The JCS considered the British proposals in 'CCS-409', which recommended shifting the war effort in Europe to the Mediterranean with a subsequent delay of OVERLORD for perhaps two months. If the delay were acceptable, the other proposals made by the COS presented no particular difficulty, but if the delay was unacceptable to the JCS, the problem appeared insoluble. King believed, that due to the slow progress in Italy, the British had a valid request, but certain issues: advance to the Po, Trieste and southern France needed further clarification by Eisenhower. It was a question of landing craft production, availability and distribution.[15]

The CCS met for the last time in Cairo on 26 November at one of the most crucial meetings of the whole conference. Before adjourning, the JCS, anxious that the Russians at Tehran might advocate a Balkan–Mediterranean policy or a Turkish entry into the war in preference to OVERLORD, persuaded the COS to submit to private consultations on the issue before agreeing to a joint Anglo–American position. Brooke approved of the American suggestion of a unified Mediterranean command, but rejected an overall commander for Germany and an overall strategic bombing commander based in Washington, to which AOC Bomber Command Harris would never accede. Conciliatory in mood, the Americans accepted a limited postponement of OVERLORD.[16]

Eisenhower, as AFHQ Commander, supported an all-out winter offensive in Italy and a build-up of Allied forces capable of moving east or west beyond the Po. Owing to the shortage of landing craft, he considered a cancelation of ANVIL, but if additional means were available, he recommended limited operations in the eastern Mediterranean and the Balkans, garnering support from his British colleagues.[17] Marshall understood that Eisenhower, like all theater commanders, fought for his own corner and said, 'that the JCS tentatively accepted the British proposals implied in the capture of the Rimini–Pisa line and the capture of Rhodes, but that further discussion would wait until the CCS returned to Cairo from Tehran.'[18]

Eastern Mediterranean versus Far Eastern Operations

The real quarrel began, not over OVERLORD, but over the relative merits of operations in the eastern Mediterranean versus those in the Far East. At a dinner attended by Churchill and the COS, Marshall, who remained adamant regarding further operations in the eastern Mediterranean, was unshaken by the prime minister's bombast. Marshall described the following scene to his biographer, Forrest Pogue:

> Churchill was red hot and all the British were against me. It got hotter and hotter. Churchill stood before me, his hands clutching his lapels and declared, 'His Majesty's Government can not have its troops staying idle. Muskets must flame'. I responded sharply, 'God forbid if I should try to dictate, but not one American soldier is going to die on that Goddamned beach.'[19]

The extent of American flexibility on OVERLORD was tied to the British approving BUCCANEER, the Andaman Islands operation in the Far East, which would have precluded an amphibious attack on Rhodes. When Brooke suggested that BUCCANEER be canceled and the freed landing craft deployed to the Aegean, Marshall reacted severely. A heated argument developed that Brooke called, 'the father and mother of a row.'[20] King became so angry with Brooke's arrogance regarding shipping resources, that he almost climbed over the table to get at him.[21] Because of Roosevelt's secret commitment to Chiang regarding BUCCANEER, the operation was not negotiable.

Because of these disagreements and the increased emotional content expressed, the conference room was cleared of staff, and the major participants went 'off the record'. In so doing, the 'off the record' portion was not officially transcribed, thereby eliminating any possibility of later scrutiny. Disputes arose from causes no deeper than the different shades of meaning given to some simple word, for example, British 'demand' versus American 'request'. Although the British conferees sometimes outwardly demonstrated light-heartedness, behind their outward aplomb, they held their position to a man. Because the war had gone on much too long, British planners were more dispassionate toward high-level war preparations than their American counterparts. Basing operations on mathematical calculations, having had extensive experience with a variety of military actions, the British realized that cost-effectiveness remained a primary consideration in any proposed operation.[22] Therefore, they considered their clash with the Americans over strategy a personal matter and abhorred any interference from Stalin.

The Tehran EUREKA Agreement

Five days later, the Americans returned from Tehran with a binding agreement, based on Soviet strategic preferences comparable to their own. It was as if the Americans had written the agreement themselves: operations in the Eastern Mediterranean, the Aegean and the Dodecanese were made obsolete in the three days of 28–30 November. OVERLORD and ANVIL were assigned to replace them, considered by Stalin as a single, indivisible military undertaking.[23] Both were planned to coincide with a Soviet summer offensive and expanded Allied operations in Italy. Moreover, Stalin insisted that a supreme OVERLORD commander be named quickly. Forced to leave Cairo without a decision on combined plans for Europe in 1944, Churchill opted to argue against the overall American plan in front of the Russians.[24] An angry Churchill, who, feeling excluded, discounted and disappointed by Roosevelt's naïve but successful attempts to curry favor with the Russian leader, could only comply.

Cairo: SEXTANT II

The Americans had departed for Tehran in a despondent mood, believing that Stalin wanted an Allied operation near his own front, in the Eastern Mediterranean. When he favored the American view instead, the British were astounded. They said ANVIL could not be done because of limited resources, but when American plans, hastily drawn, demonstrated it could, they lost the argument.[25] Returning to Cairo on 2 December, the exhausted travellers found themselves locked in debate for the next five days, but the American contingent was elated with the gains made at Tehran. One major issue, Operation BUCCANEER, and three subsidiary issues – the Italian campaign, ANVIL and Aegean operations demanded resolution. When the Americans announced that policy-making at SEXTANT II had to be completed within the week, they offered no apologies, but Churchill expressed his apprehension over an early separation. Moreover, he asked Roosevelt to abandon BUCCANEER, because of the landing craft shortage in the Mediterranean. BUCCANEER seemed doomed when Mountbatten requested a threefold increase in manpower and material. Roosevelt hesitated, his Chiefs divided. Both sides remained deadlocked; to break the impasse, the British recommended a smaller operation, but the president vetoed that, even though the British were supplying most of the forces. Suddenly, Roosevelt capitulated and canceled BUCCANEER, because both it and OVERLORD could not be mounted on the required scale.[26] The British had prevailed, but BUCCANEER remained one of the bitterest strategic arguments of the war. At the third plenary session on 4 December, Churchill called on Brooke to express his views.[27]

> This Conference has been most unsatisfactory. Usually at all these meetings we discussed matters till we arrived at a policy which we put forth to the Prime Minister and the President for approval and amendment. And that we subsequently examined whether ways and means admitted of this policy being carried out. Finally putting on paper for approval which formed our policy for the future conduct of the war. This time such a procedure had been impossible.[28]

Nevertheless, the British military hierarchy remained dominant in the Mediterranean. Wilson assumed supreme command of a unified Mediterranean Theater on 24 December 1943, General Sir Harold Alexander was appointed C-in-C Italy and Admiral Sir Andrew Cunningham, Naval C-in-C Mediterranean. Eisenhower transferred to OVERLORD as Supreme Commander Allied Expeditionary Force (SCAEF). Under the agreement 68 landing craft would remain in the Mediterranean until January 1944 as part of projected operations in Italy. In addition, Aegean operations were left to the discretion of SCAEF, and finally, OVERLORD was postponed from 1 May to 1 June.[29] Prior to adjournment, Brooke recommended that each COS should study how best to reduce the enormous work-load of future conferences, warning that they would undoubtedly have to occur at shorter intervals. Yet nine months were to pass before the Allies convened at Second Quebec (OCTAGON) in September 1944. The conferees were exhausted and had had enough of each other.[30] On 31 December 1943, the US Secretariat and the COS recommended a formula to the CCS that would improve procedures at future conferences, in recognition of the negotiating debacle at SEXTANT.[31]

The Cairo and Tehran meetings were tripartite summits whose results represented a form of coalition warfare based upon an alliance of distinct parties combining to fight a common foe, but not united enough in their efforts to form a co-ordinated strategy. The Second World War was a coalition *entente cordiale* and not a Grand Alliance. Policies between the two alliances differed to the extent that Stalin could only influence but not co-ordinate, resulting in costly, separate, disjointed military offensives.[32] Moreover, as Churchill's influence with Roosevelt waned after 1943, the president responded to Churchill's two-page letters either by cable or through a surrogate that sometimes failed to address many important military questions, weakening the relationship further.[33] This turnabout may have been partly due to Roosevelt's declining health, diagnosed after Tehran as hypertension, hypertensive heart disease and congestive heart failure.[34]

The ANVIL versus the Italian/Balkan Debate

The decision on the timing, preparation and size for both French operations was unavoidable, because of the May guarantee. Reporting to the CCS on 17 January 1944, Eisenhower weighed the requirements of OVERLORD, increased from three to five divisions, against the feasibility of a simultaneous three-divisional ANVIL. Generals Montgomery, Smith and Morgan considered the plan to mount both operations simultaneously unworkable, due to the landing craft shortage. If ANVIL could not be eliminated entirely, they suggested, reduce it to a one-divisional threat.[35] Eisenhower refused, insisting that not only would ANVIL be effective, it would satisfy Roosevelt's commitment to the Russians and the financing of a French Army.[36] He and Marshall realized that if ANVIL were canceled, the French forces assigned to it would stagnate or fall prey to some British scheme.

Eisenhower recommended and the CCS agreed to postpone OVERLORD beyond 1 June in order to keep ANVIL alive. While the COS debated ANVIL's cancelation in early January, Portal and Cunningham recommended that it support OVERLORD as a two-divisional diversion. Churchill doubted that, and on 4 February, he concluded that OVERLORD and ANVIL were not strategically entwined as perceived by Stalin.[37] Churchill's attitude reflected the worsening of the Italian campaign and the Allied failure at Anzio. Brooke concurred, writing, 'We had a long COS meeting about the wire to send the American COS to convince them that with the turn operations have taken in the Mediterranean, the only thing to do is to go on fighting the war in Italy and giving up any idea of a weak landing in southern France.'[38] Marshall disagreed, and in a strongly-worded statement underlined ANVIL's role as an instrument for reducing the enemy build-up against the OVERLORD lodgement during the critical period of Allied consolidation and expansion. He added that adequate resources would be found to provide for an expanded assault lift for both amphibious operations, but noted that the transfer of French troops from the Mediterranean to Normandy was impractical, because of shipping shortages. Although he agreed to extend the assault target date from 31 May to 2 June, the extention would not affect SCAEF's preparations. Allied defeats at Cassino and Anzio, as the Italian campaign deteriorated further, upset allied logistical and tactical timetables. Marshall considered the theater

> ...a vacuum demanding our time and resources in a region which never will be decisive militarily ... and the partial diversion of our strategic bombing effort against the Reich in support of surface operations.
>
> ...Although it is agreed that the campaign in Italy has not developed according to expectation, it is not agreed that this situation affords a sound basis on which to intensify the Italian campaign at the expense of ANVIL...
>
> Therefore, we consider that on balance, the results to be achieved by slow and costly progress north in Italy as compared to a stabilized strategy combined with ANVIL in support of OVERLORD, weigh heavily in favor of the latter.[39]

Roosevelt and Churchill proposed that Marshall and the COS meet in either London or Washington to settle the matter.[40] Brooke agreed, but Marshall demurred because of pressing Pacific concerns; instead, he authorized Eisenhower to represent the JCS in the forthcoming negotiations.[41] Marshall considered Eisenhower's ability to work with the British remarkable, because, according to Stephen Ambrose, 'Many American officers found their British Opposite numbers to be insufferable not only in their arrogance but their timidity about striking the enemy.' Neither Marshall nor Eisenhower was immune to similar feelings, but Eisenhower was able to keep them well hidden and reserved for his diary. To those around him, he always projected a spirit of allied cooperation and partnership. The COS agreed, provided that in the event of disagreement, the question would be referred back to the CCS.[42]

If OVERLORD were to be the decisive battle of the war, Marshall's behavior is open to question. Whatever his intentions, by designating Eisenhower as his intermediary, Marshall removed himself from direct involvement. 'Marshall only picked officers who were confident in the outcome of the actions they were undertaking',[43] and Eisenhower was his man.

BOLERO's massive American build-up of men and material was nearing completion in preparation for OVERLORD. John Charmley labeled the build-up an 'invasion' that desecrated Britain and caused pain and suffering to the inhabitants: rape, pregnancy, extra-marital affairs, and illegitimate babies.[44] Angry at Churchill, considering the American horde of invaders a consequence of selling out to Roosevelt, Charmley's view is too narrow, his tone strident. David Reynolds and Graham Smith have individually described the American invasion and occupation in a more reasonable light. To British women, GIs represented the glamor, fun and excitement that Hollywood promised.[45] The GIs made themselves at home, played darts, politely drank the weak warm beer at the pub, and shared their rich full day's rations with the locals. When fraternization turned to fornication, when Army negro segregation and white GI prejudice collided and exploded over British women, the authorities in both armies grew alarmed. Of the three million American servicemen stationed in Britain, 130,000 were black, nineteen were hanged and 70,000 married their 'war brides'.[46]

On 4 January, Generals Bernard Montgomery, C-in-C 21st Army Group, Walter B. Smith, Eisenhower's COS and Admiral Bertram Ramsay C-in-C Allied Naval Expeditionary Force (ANCFX), met in London and agreed to a diversionary role for ANVIL.[47] By approving ANVIL, they hoped to please Eisenhower, who, in turn, hoped to please Marshall, all at severe cost to OVERLORD. Brooke intervened and stopped the foolishness, at least on the British side, remarking sarcastically, 'What a way to run a war!'[48] Marshall expected Eisenhower to accomplish the conflicting Herculean problems facing him, not only as the newly appointed Supreme Commander, but also as the agent for the JCS. Eisenhower, recalled to Washington, missed important preliminary Anglo–American staff talks that, in his absence, were complicated and needlessly prolonged. Upon returning, one of Eisenhower's messages read, 'Late developments in Italy create the possibility that the necessary forces required cannot be disentangled in time to mount a strong ANVIL.'[49] Marshall accused him of *localitis*, a pejorative term indicting Eisenhower for succumbing to the British point of view. Eisenhower denied the charge. No one was more loyal to Marshall than Eisenhower, but Marshall's unwillingness to negotiate directly led to this and further complications.[50]

Negotiations by Proxy

Two meetings convened on 21 February 1944; a JCS morning meeting and a JCS-Presidential afternoon meeting, the same subject dominated both meetings: the need for a simultaneous ANVIL.[51] Marshall's failure to negotiate with the COS in London became apparent. At the earlier meeting, Marshall explored the impasse that had developed between the COS and the JCS in connection with OVERLORD–ANVIL. To break it, he proposed two alternatives for consideration: if the Allies failed to reach Rome by 1 April, they ought to defer to ANVIL and release approximately 40 percent of its landing craft to OVERLORD – or fight a defensive war in Italy and make their main Mediterranean offensive through southern France. However, he was sure Montgomery and Churchill would disagree.

Marshall urged that a telegram be sent to Eisenhower in response to 'COS(W) 1156', the British directive which urged complete abandonment of ANVIL, and to request his in-depth report of the negotiations in process. Marshall was prepared to defend him for the delay, but the COS had circumvented the Supreme Commander rather than risk a clear-cut break with the JCS. Eisenhower had to either reach an agreement quickly, or failing that, prepare a carefully stated rebuttal for his Washington superiors. Acknowledging Eisenhower was under great pressure, they dispatched a message to him, 'CM-OUT 8770' that closed with, 'and the JCS will support your decision subject of course to the approval of the president.' King wanted to settle the ANVIL question in Washington, rather than risk compromising Eisenhower's position any further. He added that the president should be informed of the deadlock in view of the commitments made at Cairo and Tehran. Agreeing, The JCS proposed to formulate a definite program for action, rather than merely describing the present OVERLORD–ANVIL impasse to Roosevelt.[52]

COS Proposals to Break the Deadlock

Via cable, the COS requested that ANVIL be canceled, asked for an immediate response, and invited the JCS to come to London for talks. Moreover, the COS gave first priority to the deteriorating Italian campaign, insisting that sufficient resources were lacking to mount ANVIL, destroy the German forces in Italy and accumulate the means to carry out a re-enforced five divisional OVERLORD. Since Eisenhower maintained that landing craft were available for both operations, the JCS strongly opposed ANVIL's cancelation. At the afternoon White House meeting, the president agreed, noting that failing to mount ANVIL would displease the Russians. However, if ANVIL could not be mounted, the JCS insisted that its divisions be transferred to OVERLORD.[53]

Roosevelt approved of the message sent to Eisenhower, but cautioned SCAEF that the US would not abandon ANVIL in the light of previously broken promises to Russia. He moralized, that having done so in the past, it had better not do so again.[54] While the president conceded that 'Eisenhower was badly pushed and placed in a difficult position as the JCS representative,' he did nothing.[55]

Before the meeting ended, the president told of a British proposal to send a joint expeditionary force into Yugoslavia led by an American. Marshall said, 'that it would be very bad indeed and probably (would) result in a new war.' The President assured the JCS that Yugoslavia was not an option, because he and the American public wanted to get the Army out of Europe as quickly as possible, telling Churchill as much. In an aside, Roosevelt observed that the British were selling US Lend-Lease tires through a commercial company at exorbitant prices.[56] No discussion followed, but the purpose of the President's 'British-bashing' remained in doubt. If these accusations were bandied about, they would do little to improve the immediate negotiating climate.

Eisenhower's Search for Compromise

Eisenhower was co-operative and realistic. He searched for a compromise between Marshall's insistence to mount ANVIL and Brooke's desire to cancel it. On 19 February, the COS and 21st Army Group Planners attacked and rejected a plan Eisenhower proposed, because it sacrificed separate assault lifts for special forces and eliminated that ready combination of assault and reserve forces on the same ship.[57] The American planners had made a fundamental error that bedeviled calculations for months to come; having failed to consult with either COSSAC or British GHQ Home Forces, they concluded that an LST's capacity was 30 tanks, the figure for stowage in transit. When loading tanks for an assault landing, the true figure was 25.[58] Minimum OVERLORD assault loading requirements were nearly satisfied but fell short by tantalizingly small percentages, that is 0.07 percent for men and 0.05 percent for motor vehicles.[59] Eisenhower realized that only by weakening OVERLORD could he mount a simultaneous ANVIL; and both were held hostage by events in Italy.

Competition from Anzio

At the end of December, Churchill, convalescing from pneumonia at Marrakech, discussed future Italian operations with his Mediterranean Commanders, Wilson and Alexander. With Brooke in London, Churchill, as Minister of Defence, exercised his 'military talents' on these appointees with a free hand. When Churchill's doctor and confidant suggested that Hitler not only directed the policy, but even planned the details of war, Churchill responded, 'Yes, that's just what I do.'[60] He pressed for a landing at Anzio and the capture of Rome, before the Allies undertook OVERLORD and ANVIL. Churchill, Wilson and Alexander concluded that a two-divisional assault, supported by elements of infantry, airborne troops, and armor should be sufficient to achieve their objectives. Unfortunately, Churchill failed to seriously consider the enemy's will to resist, or his strategic reaction after the landing. On 3 January, with the landing three weeks away, Allied commanders defined Anzio (Operation SHINGLE), as a high-risk venture, but none were willing to argue against the Churchill's enthusiasm.[61] The decision-making process unraveled, because the implications of decisions at each level were not pursued downward for study. General John P. Lucas, who would lead VI Corps' assault, attended a meeting on 9 January, at General Alexander's Italian headquarters. He wrote:

> I felt like a lamb being led to slaughter but felt entitled to one bleat so I registered a protest against the target date as it gave me too little time for rehearsal. I was ruled down ... The real reasons can not be military...[62]

SHINGLE would be executed, but with far less means than originally planned. Although the demands of the Italian campaign overrode ANVIL's needs, allied preoccupation with ANVIL gave little assurance that SHINGLE would succeed. If SHINGLE failed, strategy and policy would suffer. Hitler reacted promptly to the slow pace of the Allied advance in Italy and of assault shipping departing the Mediterranean for the UK. He issued a formal directive on 4 October 1943, noting that not only would his forces resist and fight for central Italy, but possibly go on the offensive. He concluded that the Allies planned to seize Rome and then attack southern France or the Balkans.[63] Hitler's prescience was borne out by Wilson's summation of the central Italian campaign, in which SACMED made the error of assuming that German and British intentions for Rome were identical: 'The political effects of the capture of Rome would, in my opinion, be as important as the military consequences. The prestige of possession of the Italian capital, like Stalingrad, was equally important to the enemy as ourselves...'[64] French General Alphonse Juin, Commander of the French Expeditionary Force during the battles for central Italy, commented on the high price paid for a politically-driven campaign:

> Once again we have run into one of the stumbling blocks of coalition warfare: the Allies cannot come to an agreement and co-ordinate their efforts. Questions of prestige are shaping events, each one wanting to make the entry in to Rome. History will not fail to pass severe sentence.[65]

Even with the benefit of ULTRA intercepts,[66] the insufficiencies of Anzio, like Salerno before it, reminded Eisenhower that without military dominance at the sharp end, the invading OVERLORD forces could be driven into the sea or suffer from a similar stalemate.[67] A post-war indictment read:

> The 43,000 casualties suffered on Anzio were the result not of compelling military logic but by frivolous political forces and a tragic series of faulty assumptions. Specifically, the landings lacked a single clear objective; the turning movement was too shallow and the most glaring defect was the inadequate size of the landing force.[68]

The popular historian, Alistair Horne, in his biography of Montgomery ignored Churchill's responsibility for Anzio and its demands for landing craft. Needed to supply and reinforce the six divisions pinned to the beachhead, ANVIL would go without. Horne blames the Americans for producing destroyer-escorts and escort carriers in 1942–43, urgently needed in the Battle of the Atlantic, rather than producing enough landing craft.[69] Adding to the shortage, were Britain's design and production difficulties that severely hampered the landing craft program in 1943. Unfortunately, American shipyard conversion to landing craft came too late to offset the shortage in

1944.[70] King's tight control over the release and distribution of landing craft [71] and Montgomery and Eisenhower's demands for a reinforced five-divisional OVERLORD added to the problem. Marshall's warning to the president revealed, 'that more shipping than is now in sight is essential if the national war effort is not to be neutralized to a serious extent.'[72] Both Horne and Nigel Hamilton erred by writing that landing craft were sent from Britain to the Mediterranean rather than the other way round, perpetuating a belief that the Americans were not only intransigent, but strategically naïve.[73]

On the 19 February Eisenhower and the COS agreed that Italy required immediate attention: ANVIL would revert to its original scale, while planning continued, and 20 British LSTs (Landing Ship Tank) and 21 British LSIs (Landing Ship Infantry), in exchange for 6 US AKAs (Attack transports) would sail from the Mediterranean to Britain, on 20 March.[74]

SHAEF recommended that OVERLORD be strengthened and ANVIL reduced to a threat. It suggested that the land opposition to OVERLORD was 'unlikely' to be less, and in the early stages might 'exceed', what the COSSAC Plan had allowed. There was no evidence that any reduction of ANVIL would lead to substantial changes in enemy dispositions. British Intelligence emphasized on 24 February, that if the plan of tying down German formations in Italy were to succeed, Hitler had to be deceived about Allied intentions and resources in the Mediterranean. If it failed, German formations would transfer to Normandy to augment the forces already there. The JIC evaluations indicated that the enemy 'appeared' nervous about a threat to southern France, but suggested an assault in the Adriatic on the Istrian Peninsula, immediately after OVERLORD, would offer greater assistance than ANVIL.[75]

The onerous conditions in Italy prompted Montgomery to reverse his position, and on 21 February he wrote the following petition to Eisenhower: 'I recommend very strongly that we now throw the whole weight of our opinion onto the scales against ANVIL. Let us have two really good major campaigns, one in Italy and one in OVERLORD.'[76] After a month of discussions, Eisenhower, acceding to Montgomery's recommendations which echoed those of his superiors, responded, 'OVERLORD would have no real support from the Mediterranean. This bothers me.'[77]

Conferring on 18 February in Italy, Wilson and Alexander agreed that either a one-divisional assault in the spring or a two-divisional assault later against southern France was dead.[78] Marshall and Eisenhower sought compromise by:

1. suggesting that the reallocation of assault shipping should take effect in April;
2. by planning ANVIL as a two-divisional assault composed of 88 LSTs, 90 LCIs, 60 LCTs and 8 LSIs;

3. reviewing its feasibility on 20 March.

All of the principals agreed on 24 February that if ANVIL were impracticable after the review, anything above a one-division lift would be withdrawn from the Mediterranean and assigned to OVERLORD. The Italian campaign was granted overriding priority over all existing and future operations in the Mediterranean and given first call on all military resources in the theater.[79] Eisenhower canceled ANVIL on 21 March.[80] At one stroke, by waiting until Rome was captured, the Americans threw ANVIL away, the operation conceived to siphon German reserves from OVERLORD. Without its 'anvil', the 'hammer' was compromised, the JCS claiming that the Germans had gained the strategic initiative by default. They disagreed with the COS that the capture of Rome was worth the heavy engagement in Italy and reasoned that 'After the bridgehead and the main front have been joined, there will remain, in our opinion, no further military objectives in Italy which justify the time-consuming and costly effort to attain them.'[81] Even with America's phenomenal production capacity, a *sine qua non* of coalition dominance, it failed to achieve the actual power needed to force British compliance.[82]

The Proposed Transfer of Pacific Landing Craft

Fearful of feeding the Italian campaign's insatiable appetitie, the JCS opposed a continuation of the Italian campaign beyond Rome and amphibious operations near the Po Valley and Istria. Marshall agreed to ANVIL's postponement, but refused to its cancelation. If the COS would accept a two-divisional ANVIL, mounted on 10 July in support of OVERLORD, he would transfer 26 LSTs and 40 LCI(L) from the Pacific to the Mediterranean.[83] King concurred and the COS accepted the American proposal, assuming that when the strategic situation was reviewed in June, the additional landing craft would be used in a non-specific Mediterranean operation offering the most benefit to OVERLORD.[84] The British assumption was in direct opposition to the JCS who had consigned the Pacific landing craft to ANVIL only. On 29 March, Dill warned the COS that the JCS was not receptive to any deviations. To the JCS, ANVIL was the July support operation for OVERLORD [85] and protesting the British view, cabled,

> ...that the delayed ANVIL will be vigorously pressed and that it is the firm intention to mount this operation in support of OVERLORD with the target date indicated. The USCOS are firm in their conviction that a decision must be taken to launch ANVIL on a specific date. They consider

it is clearly evident that the operation will not be launched unless such a decision is taken...[86]

As the debate continued Brooke criticized his JSM staff in Washington, feeling that it functioned as nothing more than a post office delivering messages from London.[87] Dissatisfied, Brooke shrugged off the possibility of traveling to Washington, and like Marshall, refused to grasp the nettle. By avoiding direct confrontation, he mismanaged and prolonged the negotiations.

An Alternative to ANVIL

Speculating on the consequences of a canceled ANVIL, General Roberts of the OPD wrote a memo to his superior, Handy:

> We get into political difficulties with the French; Overlord will lose at least ten fighting divisions. Our service forces continue to support the western Mediterranean. Our divisions and French divisions will be committed to a costly, unremunerative inching advance in Italy. The people of both the United States and France may or may not take this indefinitely and once committed to Italy, we have our forces pointed towards southeastern Europe and will have the greatest difficulty in preventing their use for occupation forces in Austria, Hungary and southern Germany.[88]

Roberts' argument in support of a southern France landing as the sole alternative not only increased American Anglophobia, but disregarded the possibility of a drive into northern Italy by a combination of all existing and newly created Allied divisions. For example, if ANVIL had been canceled, its seven divisions, released from a ten-week amphibious training schedule, could have carried the May DIADEM offensive beyond the Franco–Italian border. Allied fighting power, already dominating sea and air, would have increased by a 5:1 ratio; more than enough to further damage the already weakened German Tenth and Fourteenth Armies. Roberts' assessment, in support of Marshall's prejudice, that a land move into France from Italy was too slow, may have questioned Alexander's generalship, which, like Montgomery's, failed at the breakout and pursuit phase of a battle.[89] In theory, if the German Army, faced with unremitting pressure, had collapsed on both the Norman and Italian fronts in July, rather than September, the Allies would have gained two more months of fine fighting weather, time enough to effect a linkage on the Franco–German border for the advance into Germany in 1944.[90] Only Churchill had considered a land attack on southern

France from Italy as a possibility, but he weakened his case when he placed it on par with a move into Istria, thus raising opposition.[91]

The Istrian Alternative

In March and April 1944, the Allies were bogged down south of Rome, and any consideration of reaching the Pisa–Rimini axis was still in the future. What strategy to pursue after that was mere speculation. Alexander, supported by many of the military principals in the Mediterranean, including Wilson and General Mark Clark (Commander, Fifth Army), considered a plan, Operation ARMPIT, to break through the Apennines and carry the Ljubljana gap, through which the main road and railway runs from Italy into northern Yugoslavia. Vienna lay at the end of this 250 mile narrow road network, an objective of great political and psychological value.[92] Istrian landings were opposed by Admiral H. Kent Hewitt, commander of the US Eighth Fleet in the Mediterranean and US General Jacob L. Devers, Wilson's theater deputy. One survey of the region revealed that, '...besides occasional anchorages and a few tiny beaches, nowhere is it suitable for the classical, broad scale, textbook style of landing.'[93] Alexander, his COS, Lt. General Sir John Harding, Allied Armies Italy (AAI), who had devised a plan that would fulfill Churchill's dream of a British advance on Vienna, either minimized or ignored the experience of the Italian campaign in which it had taken their troops over a year of fighting to reach northern Italy. Lt. General Sir Sidney Kirkman, GOC British 13th Corps, did not: fighting along the Gothic Line was severe, 'Central Europe as a goal was political and military moonshine',[94] and Alexander's June cables to London, stating that his armies were ready to assault the Apennines and the Alps, were 'pipe dreams'.[95] However, two weeks after the Normandy landings, Eisenhower cabled Marshall, 'It is my belief that the prime minister and his Chiefs of Staff are honestly convinced that greater results in support of OVERLORD would be achieved by a drive toward Trieste rather than to mount ANVIL.'[96]

Discounting the frightful winter weather and poor Istrian infrastructure, it was doubtful that a force of more than six divisions could have been sustained through the Ljubljana Gap to invade the Danube Valley; moreover, the railroad tunnels through the gap were vulnerable to destruction by German demolition experts.[97] Alexander closely questioned Lt. Colonel Peter Wilkinson of SOE in March 1944 concerning the feasibility of an Istrian landing. He replied, 'that it contained formidable technical difficulties and great risks.'[98] Roosevelt agreed, and in a letter to Churchill, wrote that an operation through the Gap was unacceptable, because it did not support OVERLORD.[99]

Until July 1944, the German General Staff, OKW, believed that the Allies planned a large-scale amphibious attack in the Gulf of Venice, the objective being Austria and southern Germany.[100] An amphibious threat in the northern Adriatic would force the Germans to divert troops from Normandy, but landing in the Balkans would have limited Allied concentration in western Europe and probably lengthened the war by several months.[101]

British Misperceptions

The COS, having accepted the American legacy of landing craft, misread the terms of the will: 66 Pacific landing craft in exchange for ANVIL. Stung by the British rejection, the Americans refused to squander additional resources for an indeterminate operation in the Mediterranean. The British had failed to make the connection between an American public demanding a swift German defeat and their clamor for an intensification of operations in the Pacific. King's burgeoning naval power there would not be sacrificed for an ambiguous ANVIL. The JSM advised the COS that Wilson be notified to proceed, plan, and prepare vigorously for a 10 July ANVIL, while maintaining flexibility.[102] Marshall believed that Churchill had agreed to ANVIL at Tehran, but the prime minister insisted that the strategic situation had changed vastly since then, and that Rome could not be sacrificed today for an ANVIL tomorrow.[103]

American Productive Might

During 1943, American shipyards built more than 19,000 assault craft of which two or three types were British. King, who assumed control over all landing craft, allocated the meager sum of only 1,000 of this number for use in Europe. The maximum capacity of British shipyards was about 350 a month, which produced a total of 4,000 by May 1944. Even with the addition of the American 1,000, a total of 5,000 specialist ships could only lift three OVERLORD divisions.[104] In mid-summer 1943 landing craft programs were increased significantly. Certain shipyards were converted, carbon and alloy steel reallocated, 2,200 medium Army trucks were canceled, skilled manpower was reassigned, and GM diesel engine manufacturing facilities were expanded, the most critical component of all.[105] The Evansville, Indiana Shipyard, a 30-month-old gigantic facility created on the site of a municipal dump along the Ohio River, met the government's frantic call for stepped-up production by producing 20 LSTs in April–May 1944. Known as 'The World's Champion LST Builder', its 19,000 shipyard workers set all kinds of production records.[106]

Momentary Compromise in Anger's Wake

Feelings remained tense in London and Washington. At a rare and urgently called Saturday CCS meeting, Dill found Marshall obdurate and remained unwilling to withdraw landing craft from the Pacific to assist a weak course of action in Italy.[107] Moreover, he planned to reappraise further American resource allocations to the Mediterranean.[108] Brooke wrote, 'History will never forgive them for bargaining equipment against strategy and for trying to blackmail us ... by holding the pistol of withdrawing craft at our heads.'[109] Cunningham wrote that, 'the Americans had consented ungraciously to abandon ANVIL.'[110] Without the extra landing craft, ANVIL, in support of OVERLORD was dead, regardless of Anglo–American strategic differences. The COS proposed a compromise to break the deadlock in the form of a directive to Wilson, which in summary, stipulated that actions against the Germans in the Mediterranean offered OVERLORD the greatest possible assistance, particularly by an early all-out offensive in Italy, and that a threat against southern France and the seizure of any opportunity, there or elsewhere, would be most beneficial.[111] The JCS agreed, but not before two of their amendments were inserted: all offensive action in Italy would be discontinued when the mission was accomplished, and ANVIL would be given a high priority. Although Dill considered the agreement flawed, he recommended that the COS accept it.[112] He wrote, 'No formula can be a substitute for honest agreement.'[113]

Wilson, Eisenhower and the COS planned to meet in London to consider the future of forces in the Mediterranean made redundant by Italian operations. According to the JCS if ANVIL were revived and agreed upon, King would allocate a month's production of landing craft for the operation. The COS contemplated a possible landing, mounted from North African ports, along either the southern or western coasts of France three weeks after OVERLORD.[114] The JCS was notified that the results and final proposals of the conference would be made immediately available. The tension of many weeks quickly subsided and the atmosphere brightened perceptively in Washington.[115]

American Joint Staff Planners, ordered to study and submit recommendations on 'CCS-561', felt only a landing, the landing west of the Rhone River was worthy of the extra Pacific landing craft proposed by King. It was doubtful whether a landing in western France could have succeeded, because of certain disadvantages: a long ocean journey, sole dependence upon carrier-based air-cover, prey to the U-boat menace in the Atlantic, a poor supply situation and increased distances from Mediterranean bases.[116]

Operational Considerations and a Balkan Adventure

The results of the Wilson/Eisenhower meeting were contained in 'CCS-561/2' and implied how intertwined were operations DIADEM, ANVIL and OVERLORD. Since Eisenhower depended upon the seizure of a deep-water port and a breakout from the Norman lodgement area, he could not release landing craft and airborne units to the Mediterranean before that occurred. Once the operations in Italy and France succeeded, Wilson recommended any of three locations for an amphibious assault: Sète, west of the Rhone, the Gulf of Genoa and Civitavecchia, 40 miles north of Rome. By 7 June it seemed clear to Wilson that he could prepare for an amphibious landing against southern France by 15 August.[117] Although some French and American units were already engaged in amphibious training, Wilson continued to emphasize operations in Italy, a drive to Vienna and an Adriatic amphibious operation in September, which echoed the argument of the COS.[118]

Prior to flying to Europe on 8 June to visit the Norman beaches, the JCS won approval on 26 May for a closed session to be held at the conclusion of every regular CCS meeting. No reasons were given for this change, and, as usual, no records of these sessions were to be kept, but the arrangement might have had something to do with the COS stalling on ANVIL.[119] Eisenhower warned Marshall in late June that,

> ...I have the further impression that although the British Chiefs of Staff may make one more effort to convince you of the value of the Trieste move, they will not permit an impasse to arise, and will, consequently, agree to ANVIL. I feel that their idea would be to keep intact the tactical ground and air staff that has been functioning so well in Italy. They would then frankly recognize the Italian area as a secondary one and turn over the troops there to General Clark or other qualified officer.[120]

On 10 June, four days after OVERLORD, the COS took exception to Wilson's French assessment and postponed the choice of the landing site, until the battles raging in France and Italy were decided. The COS believed that ANVIL, like any other operation, depended upon a most careful balance of strategic factors: it was false to assume that it was the only alternative, nor could the intrusion of unforeseen events be excluded from eliminating ANVIL and deeming it inappropriate within the larger European picture by 15 August.[121]

On 19 June, Wilson notified Eisenhower that landings in western France were too difficult; Instead, he recommended that the Allies advance eastward beyond the Po, through the Ljubljana Gap and into the Danube Plain, possibly supported by a September amphibious operation at the head of the Adriatic.[122]

The ANVIL controversy flared once again when Eisenhower's forces suffered logistically from a severe Channel storm that lasted from 19–24 June and jeopardized the timetable of an attack on Caen by the 21st Army Group. The attack was postponed for a week and demonstrated the need for the additional port that ANVIL could provide.[123] At a 16 June meeting in Naples between Marshall and Wilson, the Field Marshal reversed himself and opposed any limitation on DIADEM's successful advance. Rejecting Marshall's recommendation to seize a major French port, (Cherbourg had not been captured), Wilson instead proposed ANVIL's cancelation in exchange for his Italian/Balkan alternative. Eisenhower, in receipt of Wilson's cable, appreciated his wish to pursue the DIADEM offensive, but remained committed to ANVIL and opposed a thrust toward Vienna.[124] Eisenhower cabled Marshall, 'AFHQ apparently fails to appreciate that achievement of a successful bridgehead in France does not of itself imply success in operation OVERLORD as a whole ... that it will be in urgent need of any assistance possible from elsewhere for sometime to come.'[125] The two ports under consideration were Marseilles and Bordeaux. Marseilles, if cleared quickly, was much better suited to handle large-scale replacements than Bordeaux, which, although closer to the battle area, had constricted beaches.

The JSM, authorized to send a copy of Wilson's cable to Eisenhower to the COS and the JCS, did not receive its copy until 27 June.[126] The delay led to further misunderstanding. In the meantime, the JCS received Eisenhower's report, which included a summary of Wilson's comments, four days before the JSM copy arrived. Eisenhower reported Wilson's Italian and Balkan recommendations as opposed to his own strong preference for ANVIL, but noted that Wilson was prepared to carry out ANVIL, if the decision were made.[127] The JCS quickly accepted Eisenhower's proposals, rejected Wilson's and ordered him to launch a three-divisional ANVIL against southern France by 15 August.[128] The JCS stated:

> We are convinced that the best use to which we can put our resources in the Mediterranean is to launch an ANVIL at the earliest possible date. This is the only operation which: will provide early and maximum support for OVERLORD, provide for an additional major port required by SCAEF and will put the French forces into the battle for their homeland ... The resources to be employed in ANVIL will be predominately US and French. We do not believe that extensive and long preparation to achieve perfection of arrangements is necessary or justifiable.[129]

The Disagreements Intensify

The COS reacted with a firm rejection of ANVIL and insisted that Wilson continue DIADEM, while mounting a threat against southern France.[130] Not knowing that the COS had not seen Wilson's report, the JCS was dumbfounded. Consequently, the JCS considered the British proposal an abrogation of the agreement reached in London and a reversion to the old argument of ANVIL versus Italy. While the JCS had succumbed to this argument two months before, they refused to do so again. The Americans insisted that effective employment of large forces in the Mediterranean and those awaiting transportation from the US be initiated at the earliest possible date.[131] In unequivocal terms, the JSC cabled the COS:

> ANVIL will be launched at the earliest possible date. You will use every effort to meet a target date of 1 August. You will prepare for the operation on the basis of approximately a 3 division assault an airborne lift for the equivalent of 1 division and a build-up to at least 10 divisions as quickly as the resources made available to you will permit, having in mind in your preparations the steady reduction in German capacity to resist and the vital importance of prompt support of the OVERLORD operation.
>
> You will use all available Mediterranean resources not required for ANVIL to carry out your present directive with regard to operations in Italy...[132]

On the 26 June, the British Chiefs defied the Americans and turned ANVIL down. They pressed for the destruction of all German forces in Italy, citing, 'Any compromising of the prospects of the destruction of the enemy armies in Italy as this critical phase in the war, without a compensation in the early destruction of equal forces elsewhere, would be wrong.'[133] They warned that Eisenhower's demands for additional Allied Mediterranean forces be met by shipments to the Breton and Norman ports closest to the battle area.[134] The Americans signaled the next day,

> The proposal of the British Chiefs of Staff to abandon ANVIL and to concentrate on a campaign in Italy is unacceptable. The fact that the British and US Chiefs of Staff are apparently in complete disagreement in this matter at this particular moment when time is pressing presents a most deplorable situation. We wish you to know now, immediately, that we do not accept the statements in your answer in general with relation to the campaign in Italy as sound and as in keeping with the early termination of the war.[135]

Negotiations stalled, the JCS concluded that no reason existed to continue the discussions and cabled: 'The wording of the directive we have proposed in "CCS-603" give sufficient latitude to the commanders concerned, both as to resources and target date. We ask that it be sent to Wilson immediately.'[136]

The JSM had become alarmed at the sharpness of the American response. To soften the impact of the American reply, the Mission sent a private message to London explaining the reasons for the American reaction, as described above. The JCS was adamant that ANVIL must not be reduced to a threat in favor of a major campaign beyond the Pisa–Rimini line. In view of the hardened American attitude, the JSM suggested that the COS should either agree to ANVIL with good grace or make a straightforward confession that the fundamental issue had not been clarified in London and must now be aired and resolved.[137]

A Pivotal ULTRA Intercept

JSM efforts to ease matters appeared futile. The American reply, described as 'rude' by Brooke and 'rather tough' by Cunningham, only served to get British backs up. Believing their strategy correct, the COS agreed on 28 June, to stand fast.[138] New ULTRA intercepts supported the British position and revealed that the Germans were prepared to fight for northern Italy, south of the Apennines in order to prevent a breakthrough into the Po Valley, the loss of which would have severe military and political consequences. Moreover, Churchill and Brooke's positions were substantiated: nothing would be gained by a landing in the south of France which was not already ensured by the Italian campaign, that ANVIL would impair the possibility of destroying Kesselring's forces. If cryptographic difficulties had not delayed the delivery of the intercepts, the Americans might have opted for a quick and overwhelming victory in Italy and an end to the war in 1944.[139] They deemed it 'unthinkable for want of patient discussion to risk taking a false step at this critical period of the war.'[140] Side-stepping the COS appeal and dismissing German intentions, the Americans chose to defeat the Germans in Normandy, rather than to destroy them in Italy.[141]

As the Washington 29 June negotiations ended in deadlock, the JCS stood firm against the points stressed by the JSM.[142] Cunningham recorded: 'It was decided that though militarily we were quite unshaken in our views, since the Americans appear to be so set that we had better agree to carry out ANVIL. I feel myself that taking the long view we shall gain by this seeming surrender.'[143] The divergent Anglo–American military positions were best expressed in a flurry of letters, which included charts and lengthy staff-constructed supporting documents. These were exchanged between 28 June and 1 July, in which a pleading Churchill was thwarted by an unyielding Roosevelt.

Churchill to Roosevelt:

> The Deadlock between our Chiefs of Staff raises most serious issues. I most earnestly beg you to examine this matter in detail for yourself. I think the tone of the US Chiefs of Staff is arbitrary and, certainly, I see no prospect of agreement on the present lines.[144]

Roosevelt to Churchill:

> It seems to me that nothing can be worse at this time than a deadlock in the Combined Staffs as to our future course of action … You and I must prevent this. ANVIL, mounted at the earliest possible date, is the only operation which will give OVERLORD the material and immediate support.[145]

Churchill persisted:

> We are deeply grieved by your telegram. The splitting up of the campaign in the Mediterranean into two operations neither of which can do anything decisive, is the first major strategic and political error for which we two have to be responsible…
>
> …I fear a costly stalemate for you … What can I do Mr. President when we are to see the integral life of this (Italian) campaign drained off into the Rhone Valley in the belief that it will in several months carry effective help to Eisenhower so far away in the north?
>
> If you still press upon us the directive of your Chiefs of Staff to withdraw so many of your forces from the Italian campaign, His Majesty's Government, on the advice of our Chiefs of Staff, must enter a solemn protest. It is with the greatest sorrow that I write to you in this sense.[146]

Roosevelt was obdurate, but replied,

> I appreciate deeply the clear exposition of your feelings and views on this decision. My Chiefs of Staff and I have given the deepest consideration to this problem and to points you have raised. We are still convinced that the right course of action is to launch ANVIL at the earliest possible date. I do not believe we should delay further in giving General Wilson a directive … Will you ask your Chiefs to dispatch it to General Wilson at once.[147]

COS Attempts at Conciliation versus Churchill's Anger

According to Brooke, Churchill, Wilson and Alexander had ruined Allied chances of destroying German forces in Italy in 1944 by introducing the

Balkan alternative. He also noted that the some of the president's reasons for choosing ANVIL were more political than military. Roosevelt advised Churchill that he would not have survived politically if OVERLORD had suffered the slightest setback if large forces had been diverted to the Balkans.[148] Brooke dissuaded Churchill from sending another letter to Roosevelt, in which the prime minister stated that he would do anything 'to end this deadlock except become responsible for an absolutely perverse strategy.' If Roosevelt desired, he continued, 'I would come at once across the ocean to Bermuda, or Quebec, or, if you like, Washington, given good weather and a fast aeroplane.' Brooke believed Churchill was spoiling for a fight, one that would lead to a fatal rupture with Roosevelt. Churchill felt that he had every right to expect some consideration from his friend, since their joint ventures had 'dazzled the world'. Feeling petulant, Churchill expressed his resentment on 1 July, certain that by meeting Roosevelt, as he so frequently proposed, they would have settled matters.[149] 'All right', Brooke wrote of the current Anglo–American relationship in his diary, 'If you insist on being damned fools, we shall be damned fools with you, and we shall see that we perform the role of damned fools damned well.'[150]

The CCS directed Wilson on 2 July to launch a three-divisional ANVIL as soon as possible with a target date of 15 August.[151] Cunningham observed that Churchill could 'never give way gracefully'. 'He must always be right and if forced to give way gets vindictive and tries by almost any means to get his own back.'[152] Churchill was furious and wanted to impress upon the Americans how ill-treated the British felt.[153] Visiting London at the time, Harold Macmillan, who knew little of the protracted negotiations, decided that

> in my view of the heavy contribution of American forces to the European campaign and the general situation, we should have to give in if Eisenhower and Marshall insist upon ANVIL. We can fight up to a point, we can leave on record for history to judge the reasoned statement of our views, and the historian will also see that the Americans have never answered any argument, never attempted to discuss or debate the points, but have merely given a flat negative and a somewhat Shylock-like insistence upon what they conceive to be their bargain.[154]

John Winant, American Ambassador to Britain, who was familiar with the exchange of messages, sent one of his own to the president at Hyde Park, in which he said that, 'I wanted you to know how deeply the prime minister has felt the differences that have ended in his accepting your decision. I have never seen him as badly shaken. He believed completely in the program he was supporting...'[155] So convinced of the perversity of American strategy was Churchill that in his outrage he considered resigning.[156] Cognizant of his loss of power within the coalition, Churchill maintained his view in an exhortation to the COS,

> ...Let them take their seven divisions ... Let them monopolise all the landing craft they can reach. But let us at least have a chance to launch a decisive strategic stroke with what is entirely British and under British command ... I am not going to give way about this for anybody. Alexander is to have his campaign ... if we take everything lying down, there will be no end to what will be put upon us.[157]

Unlike Churchill, the COS sent a position statement to Washington on 12 July. It stated that the JCS should have no doubt whatsoever about the British attitude towards Mediterranean operations. Both His Majesty's Government and the COS emphatically declared that ANVIL was not the correct strategy; but having accepted ANVIL, the British intended to do their utmost for it to succeed.[158] By retreating before the Americans on this issue, they were not trying to gain their point by delaying tactics.

The JSM decided to omit these remarks from a forthcoming COS message, feeling they would only prolong the agony. Dissatisfied, the COS demanded their words be transmitted to the JCS. The JSM concluded that it had three options open to it: to put forward an additional paper, explain the matter, or present it as an item for discussion in a closed session at the next CCS meeting.[159] Admiral Sir Percy Noble cabled the COS that he was quite willing to speak to Marshall; the COS replied that they wanted their remarks placed on the record at a CCS closed session.[160] Noble agreed and on 28 July, wishing to avoid further controversy, he explained that COS remarks were merely a statement of fact and should not be construed, in any way, as an attempt to reopen the debate. The CCS took note of the statement and thought that the long, contentious debate over ANVIL had ended.[161]

Breakout in Normandy and Churchill's Machinations

On 27 July 1944, Churchill requested that ANVIL be renamed DRAGOON; chosen to deceive the Germans, it also stood for the contempt he felt for the operation. 'Done', he later wrote, 'in case the enemy had learned the meaning of the original code word.'[162] Cherbourg fell on 29 June and the first cargo ships arrived on 16 July. During the last week of the month, American forces finally broke through the German lines, poured out of the Normandy bridgehead and opened the way for Patton's Third Army to sweep into the heart of France. By contrast, Wilson informed London that Alexander, after taking Florence, had called off his Italian offensive for three weeks, due to the loss of American and French troops transferred from DIADEM to

DRAGOON. Moreover, Allied air power in Italy would be reduced in order to provide the necessary air cover for the same operation.[163] Although Marshall said, '…we will do our utmost to support Wilson in the two battles he has to fight in southern France and Italy',[164] it did not square with COS apprehensions. These concerns faded for the moment, when Churchill announced to the COS that on 4 August Eisenhower had decided to cancel DRAGOON and re-route its divisions to Brittany. The prime minister intimated that Eisenhower had wired the president. Churchill, disregarding the advice of his staff who felt he was circumventing the JCS, cabled the president, 'I beg you will reconsider the possibility of switching DRAGOON into the main and vital theater where it can immediately play its part…'[165] Churchill insisted on COS support when he sent a similar cable to the JCS. On the 6 August Brooke discovered, to his consternation, that the alleged Eisenhower cable had never been sent and DRAGOON's status remained unchanged. Whoever double-crossed whom, Churchill had again damaged his relationship with the Americans.[166] For Churchill, DRAGOON was the last straw, an act of sheer folly; he mused, 'If only those ten divisions could have been landed in the Balkans.'[167]

Unyielding, Churchill pursued his argument with Eisenhower at a 5 August meeting in Portsmouth. Eisenhower's naval aide, Captain Harry Butcher, described Churchill as someone obsessed with shifting DRAGOON to the Brittany ports. In the face of Eisenhower's emphatic but patient opposition, he persisted over a 15-day period.[168] Although, it was Eisenhower's longest argument of the war with Churchill, both he and the JCS firmly agreed that DRAGOON would not be canceled.[169] Churchill appealed to Hopkins, his sounding board and confidant during much of the war, for assistance,[170] and wrote on 6 August,

> I am grieved to find that even splendid victories and widening opportunities do not bring us together on strategy … The ten divisions now mounted for DRAGOON could be switched into St. Nazaire … If we are forced to make a heavy attack from the sea on the well fortified Riviera coast … we start 500 miles away from the main battlefield instead of almost upon it at St. Nazaire … If you feel able to embroil yourself in these matters, I should be glad if you would bring my views before him (Marshall)…[171]

Hopkins warned Churchill on 7 August that Roosevelt would reject his proposal. When Roosevelt replied the following day, he denied Churchill's appeal and supported Eisenhower, stating, '…it is my considered opinion that DRAGOON should be launched as planned at the earliest practicable date and I have full confidence that it will be successful…'[172]

Resolute, with time running against him, Churchill invited Eisenhower to 10 Downing Street on 9 August to discuss an alternative to DRAGOON: continue loading the ships, set sail through the Straits of Gibraltar and enter France at Bordeaux. For Churchill to entertain the idea of abandoning a carefully planned operation, shift it 1,600 miles on the eve of its execution, alter the balance of the whole campaign in western Europe and abandon a strategy having the appearance of finality, seemed like a complete abdication of responsibility.[173] Astonishingly, the British Chiefs of Staff supported Churchill in his folly. When Churchill threatened to resign, Eisenhower, who knew Churchill well, realized he was bluffing. Nevertheless, he could not understand why Churchill, obviously agitated and despondent, attached such importance to DRAGOON.[174] On 10 August, five days before DRAGOON's implementation, the CCS informed Eisenhower that with the Brittany diversion dead, he was to proceed with ANVIL/DRAGOON as originally planned.[175] Churchill's frustration and prolonged preoccupation with this one campaign illustrated his inability to direct strategy and influence Roosevelt, his grudging admission of American domination of the coalition, his fear of the Russian threat, his uncertainty regarding the fighting spirit of the British soldier and his concern over Britain's emerging manpower crisis.[176]

ANVIL's Metamorphosis

Planning for ANVIL had gone through many stages, since its beginning on 19 December 1943, when AFHQ asked Patton's Seventh Army Headquarters planning staff to consider drawing up plans for an amphibious operation which would involve American and French forces. The scale of the assault, increased from three to ten divisions, required the acquisition of the port of Marseilles and the seizure of the naval base at Toulon.[177]

On 28 February 1944, General Alexander Patch, a veteran of the Pacific 1942 Guadalcanal campaign, became the US Seventh Army commander designated to lead ANVIL. Debate raged over ANVIL's future. Was it to be abandoned, postponed, diminished or expanded? General Jacob Devers at AFHQ insisted that planning continue, Patch asked for a firm target date. In early spring, experienced French officers were added to the planning staff and French Resistance fighters supplied tactical intelligence information in support of the landings.[178]

In late May, de Gaulle chose General Jean de Lattre de Tassigny to command ANVIL's French contingent. By 15 July SACMED ordered American General Lucian Truscott's VI Corps in Italy to release the 45th, 3rd and 36th Infantry Divisions, two French divisions and certain auxiliary troops to Seventh Army. Finally an agreement was reached: ANVIL would take place on 45 miles of coastline between Cannes and Cavalaire, east of Toulon not later than 30 August.[179] The attack began when Paratroopers and Special Force units landed on the night of 14 August, D-1. On D-Day, 15 August 1944, after nine months of Anglo–American wrangling, the ANVIL invasion force, having embarked from various Mediterranean sea ports and air fields, converged on the French coast. Set in motion were 1,300 ships, 4,000 planes, and 250,000 men. Visibility was four miles, hazy and improving with a gentle shifting wind and negligible sea.[180] The landing proceeded on schedule against light opposition. Pre-H Hour bombing and gunfire were extremely effective and very little naval gunfire was required later.[181] After the airborne landings, the assaulting infantry cracked the beach defences and no Allied aircraft were reported lost.[182] Wilson cabled his superiors that the operation was a major tactical success:

> Secret operation DRAGOON slight opposition only encountered by 36th Division landing on beaches either side of Agay road. Isle Port Crus captured. Pre 12 hour gunfire reported very effective. No air attacks up to noon. Two small enemy ships sunk during initial assault.[183]

The first infantry divisions ashore were followed by similar elements of the American Seventh and French First Armies. In little more than a month 380,000 troops crossed the beaches. Movement was swift. French forces took Toulon in 11 days instead of the predicted 20; Marseilles fell in 13 days rather than 45, even though Hitler designated both ports as fortresses. Seventh Army's Task Force Butler and elements of the 36th 'Texas' Division drove 190 miles in seven days to liberate Grenoble in the French Alps on 22 August.[184] Eisenhower wrote to Marshall in late summer, 'Every day I thank my stars that I held out for ANVIL in the face of almost overwhelming pressure.'[185] The retreating German Nineteenth Army was battered and almost trapped at Montelimar. The landing, the liberation of southern France, the advance northward astride the Rhone valley that trapped 79,000 Germans, and large amounts of equipment were captured or destroyed.[186] On 12 September Seventh Army patrols made contact with Patton's Third at several points near Dijon and Autun, thereby sealing the fate of thousands more German troops.[187] On 15 September Eisenhower assumed operational control of Devers' newly constituted 6th Army Group, under which were gathered the American Seventh and French First Armies. In less than one month, not the three that Churchill had gloomily predicted, these Franco-American Armies had surged northward 400 miles from the Mediterranean.[188] 'The lines of communication at the end of the first 45 days were twice as long as the plans for the operation had estimated.'[189] Considered by Liddell Hart as an operation that went according to plan, but not according to timetable, ANVIL came ten weeks too late to help OVERLORD.

Eisenhower claimed in *Crusade in Europe*, that 'There was no development of that period which added more decisively to our advantages or aided us more in accomplishing the final and complete defeat of the German forces than did this secondary attack coming up from the Rhone Valley.'[190] His post-war view does not support American military doctrine, that of inflicting a massive defeat upon the German Army. Only four under-strength German divisions, composed of a high proportion of ethnic Germans from eastern Europe, over-age native Germans and impressed Poles, Russians and Czechs, were stationed south of the Loire and in Provence.[191] Five divisions had already headed north to participate in the Normandy battles of June and July. Those left behind were incapable of defending against ANVIL.

Thus ANVIL's professed objective, to keep German reserves occupied in the south and away from OVERLORD, failed. Moreover, ANVIL's ground forces were given the role of protecting Eisenhower's southern flank in August when air power, having functioned in this role since the Normandy breakout, could have continued to do so. On 17 August, Ultra intercepts demonstrated that Hitler's response to ANVIL was not reinforcement but evacuation; ULTRA had unmistakably indicated that a southern France invasion would accomplish no more than threatening to do so.[192] A threat no longer, ANVIL sounded the alarm for the German Nineteenth Army to begin a hasty but well co-ordinated retreat northward. ANVIL's timing served the Nineteenth, whose retreat coincided perfectly with the German forces retreating headlong from Normandy, well. Both enemy remnants hastily organized a line in defence of the upper Rhine in September. If ANVIL had simply threatened the Nineteenth, it would have been cut off by the OVERLORD forces advancing eastward.[193] Instead, ANVIL was part of Eisenhower's broad-front strategy and reflected the American Army's preference for moving directly forward behind overwhelming firepower and massive resources, rather than by feint, exploitation and maneuver.[194] ANVIL's strategic shortcomings were overshadowed by the arrival of the Franco–American Armies whose presence inspired the French people to join in their liberation.

8 Conclusions

During the inter-war period, Britain and the US suffered from an unwillingness or an inability to provide for timely protection against potential enemies – even when threatened with increased levels of military aggression by Japan, Russia, and Germany. How to be safe and solvent remained an immutable question. While an unknowing, distracted or apathetic public relied on its government for protection, the government expected the public to take up arms if and when war came. A composite and mutual failure between the government and the governed resulted in neither Britain nor the US being prepared for Hitler's onslaught in late 1939. If the main purpose of the State is self-perpetuation, both countries defaulted: the House of Representatives, in August 1941, extended the Selective Service Act by just one vote, 203 to 202, denying the events in Europe. The introduction of British manpower conscription was an outcome of Lend-Lease negotiations. The aftermath of the First World War and economic mismanagement leading to the Great Depression were contributing factors that slowed attempts at establishing a suitable national defence. Concurrently, belief-systems that included appeasement and isolationism inhibited the rearmament needed to fight an unlimited war. At odds with a commitment in theory to universal military obligation was an aversion in practice to compulsory national service. In part, the deprivation of the Great Depression added to US military inductees being in generally poor health, and one in five was functionally illiterate.[1] The same could be said in Britain.

Britain, handicapped by limited manpower and scarce materials, realized that money alone could not increase its meager resources. Fighting for her survival in 1940, Britain, having exhausted her ability to buy supplies on a cash-and-carry basis, and facing bankruptcy, was forced to appeal to the US to defer payment. During 1940 and part of 1941, hamstrung by the American public's isolationist mood, Roosevelt's sympathetic words were not matched by deeds, while the American business community exploited Britain's crisis and seized the opportunity for economic gain. If this opprobrium were not enough, the beleaguered country had to satisfy the equivalent of a notional American means test: a testament of its will to fight before supplies would flow. This senseless condition manifest of the 'double-bind' defines loss as the only outcome. And yet, if Roosevelt's enactment of Lend-Lease was a compelling act and if Churchill's need for a special relationship was a brush with phantasy, they followed from Churchill's sense of 'realpolitik'. Early American supplies of antiquated weaponry and dilapidated destroyers were no match against Hitler's modern equivalent. Many in Congress failed to realize that Britain was fighting for both countries. Disappointed, but not deterred, facing an appalling reality, Churchill created and perpetuated the mythic connections of a 'special relation' in which he accommodated but did not appease Roosevelt. Rather than 'go it alone' or sue for peace, Churchill, by binding Britain to America, sought provision for the post-war generation to remain free. Henceforth, the strands binding the two countries would oscillate, become thicker, more tangled and more secure.[2] 'Unlike Chamberlain and his colleagues, Churchill managed to grasp the connection between policy and military power.'[3]

Roosevelt's lethargic behavior reflected the American political scene, to which he was finely attuned, and did little to educate the public concerning the magnitude of the German threat or the consequences of a British defeat. Whether Roosevelt was pragmatic or misinformed, he played Britain off against his wish to remain in office, in spite of his professed sympathies. He gambled for these high stakes and won.

Moreover, equally as maddening to Churchill was Roosevelt's exaggerated preoccupation with American western hemispheric security that had little in common with the war raging in Europe. Anxious about the possible German seizure of strategic Caribbean islands, Atlantic outposts and parts of South America, followed by an invasion of the US through Mexico or the Gulf and Atlantic coasts, Roosevelt remained indecisive. Churchill's crystal-clear hope, his major strategic objective was to bring the US into the war on Britain's side. Although Churchill warned against waiting too long, because the British people could not hold out forever and courage alone was not enough, Roosevelt refused to stir. His political actions had delayed total American mobilization and jeopardized Britain's sovereignty, but Germany's 1941 invasion of the Soviet Union offered some relief to Britain's survival, but not a solution. The enemy act of aggression Roosevelt hoped to provoke in order to justify an American declaration of war, came not from the Germans, but from the Japanese at Pearl Harbor. Until then, Roosevelt had refused to hazard the risks of domestic and international confrontation that accompanied bold and aggressive leadership.

Lend-Lease to Russia developed slowly because the British and American Chiefs predicted her imminent defeat. When that failed to occur, Roosevelt resolved to give Russia all possible aid to keep her fighting. By 1942, the president realized that the Russians were killing more Germans and destroying more equipment than the western Allies put together. Later that year, a massive concentration of 226 divisions, totaling more than six million men, faced each other on the Eastern Front.[4] Even if 25 allied divisions were able to advance on and take Vienna in April 1945, it seems doubtful that an allied military presence there would have had any lasting geographical or political impact on the advancing Red Army and its commissars.

The parliamentary system was better equipped to mobilize the British nation for war than its American counterpart. As prime minister, Churchill represented a coalition government – an instrument of the people and the expression of its combined political will. Civilian responsibility characterized by the decision-making power of the War Cabinet, willing to improve the functioning of the war economy quickly, related to a committee system that had deep roots in British constitutional practice. Establishing and disbanding committees as needed contributed to Britain reaching a level of economic mobilization in a 'command economy' unmatched by the US. If the British complained that American strategy was sometimes politically driven, they were correct. The presidential elective process remained in force during the war and to remain in office, Roosevelt had to win re-election. In power, he had to out-maneuver his political rivals and overcome varying degrees of Congressional dissent, if his policies were to be accepted or enacted into law. Even for a healthy man in peacetime, this would have been an arduous process.

Unlike Britain, America saw itself to be an unhurried slumbering giant that once awakened could accomplish anything including winning the war. Unlike its British counterpart, American industry and labor failed to co-operate as willingly or with the same sense of urgency in 1940–41. Not only did industry demand ironclad guarantees before it increased production, it also insisted that the government accept cost- plus fixed-fee contracts. The emerging defence program suffered from waste, favoritism and lack of direction, with government agencies doing business with larger rather than smaller companies. Roosevelt created government offices to cope with industrial expansion, but administrative oversight was not enough, because these agencies lacked the authority to decide major policy questions. Cost overruns, misuse of manpower, pricing violations, poor resource allocation, excessive corporate profits, divisive industrial action were not brought under control until 1943.[5]

Even with the proliferation of inefficient government agencies and Roosevelt's loose-handling of the economy, American industry and labor produced an overwhelming total of 300,000 aircraft and 51 million tons of merchant shipping, besides a variety of essential military products. This underlines what Geoffrey Crowther wrote in 1940, '...if a country has more well-trained men that its enemies, more equipment and more raw materials to replenish its stocks and feed its people, even the most appalling financial bungles can hardly prevent it from winning the war.'[6] The advent of Lend-Lease aid (an 'Act to Promote the Defence of the United States') and the establishment of various Combined Boards enabled Britain to gain access to America's colossal productive and technological resources, at a price. Britain had tied her supply position to American foreign policy; and fixed her dependence upon the US.

In April 1941, plans were set to establish British and American nucleus military missions in both Allied capitals. As representatives of their respective COS, they were intended to collaborate in the formulation of military plans and policies, once the US entered the war. Subsequently, the British–American military committee (CCS), created at the ARCADIA Conference, was changed to and established in Washington only. The American equivalent of the JSM was struck from the agreement and never established in London. Hence, Washington became pre-eminent in combined planning and only the JSM would meet regularly with the JCS in the American capital. This arrangement had unfortunate consequences: Americans officers lost the opportunity of becoming familiar with prominent COS figures and their customs and practices in London. Learning to 'speak the same language', an invaluable aid to a negotiating process, was lost. Roosevelt's abolishment of the American mission did not abolish many of Brooke's suspicions regarding American duplicity after SEXTANT II.

Within the official histories, as elsewhere, emphasis has been placed on co-operation rather than division between the the major participants. These descriptions run contrary to their own personal accounts and diminish the effect of the 'special relationship'. The Chiefs created the thrust, direction and 'big picture' of the war, leaving it to the working planners to formulate their concepts. If a planning section failed to support its chief's strategy, as was the case in proposing a Sardinian operation over a Sicilian one, Brooke insisted Sicily be the operation of choice.[7] The Chiefs faced the complexity of fighting a global war, learning that operations and logistics were inextricably entwined. Separate from the civilian industrial work force, for every soldier at the front, eight others toiled in support. Chiefs of Staff decisions were left for subordinates to implement; how these men succeeded, along the whole chain of command, in war zones separated by thousands of miles, can be measured by the time it took to defeat the enemy: five years. Marshall and Brooke had chosen known and qualified subordinates to do the job; some failed and were replaced; others failed and were not.

One contributing factor to the length of the conflict may have been a level of self-deception in American strategic thought. Such commanding figures as Marshall and Stimson espoused the traditional American doctrine of Grant's mass concentration of men and material at the vital point in order to destroy the enemy. Applying the theory was another matter, and when the attempt was made, territorial advance seemed more important. However ambitious early American plans were, that is, SLEDGEHAMMER, it would

be another 18 months after December 1941, before the US could field a trained, albeit an inexperienced army. Not at TORCH, but only on the third Mediterranean amphibious operation did they collide with the full force of the German Army, with initial dire results. By 1943, massed concentration was eroded by the scuttling of the preconceived 200 divisional American Army reduced to 80 divisions, with approximately half of its 7.7 million men assigned to Air Corps; and by the year's end, the US was still deploying more men against Japan than against Germany. 'Germany-first' was a misnomer, and although victory through air power alone was modified and de-emphasized, the ground forces lacked the talent and intellect needed to defeat the Germans quickly in the imagined final encounter. The manpower and logistical crisis in the fall of 1944 eliminated any serious attempts, regardless of effort, to employ and fulfill American doctrine. The Eisenhower/Montgomery controversy of whether to attack Germany on a narrow or broad front was not a military argument, but a political one, a test of American power and will within the coalition. At the front, pressure for individual US infantry replacements increased exponentially and fathers with children were drafted for the first time. These shortages eliminated any possibility of ending the war by Christmas 1944.

In theory, the US Army's plan for converting civilians into soldiers at the end of a 17-week basic training course was designed to supply an army in the field with unlimited combat replacements. Small group cohesion and leadership, required to survive for even a day on the battlefield would be learned 'on the job'. If the costly loss of life during a series of battles in northwest Europe and Italy are any indication, it suggests that the Allied generals did not properly serve their combat soldiers. British and American generals suffered from conservatism and unimaginative caution, and for the most part, they lacked the ability to achieve operational success consistently, were inferior to the Germans in leadership and were predisposed to conduct careful campaigns with limited objectives. The US First Army, relying on infantry tactics rather than combined arms, whose successes were offset by a lack of flexible exploitation, buried more dead than any other American Army.[8] If any doubts pervaded Marshall's thoughts regarding the American soldier's ability to defeat the German in combat, they was not apparent. Certainly not in the way that it disturbed Churchill and cast doubts upon the tenacity of the British combat soldier. Time after time he found the Army inadequate, better organized for fighting a colonial war insuring imperial pacification than smashing the Germans. Using the Alam el Halfa and the Normandy battles as examples, much of the British staff and tactical leadership failed to believe in initiative and flexibility insofar as their application was instinctive and automatic.[9]

The Anglo–American service chiefs who fought the war were at the top of their profession. In Marshall and Brooke were found the most outstanding soldiers of their generation. However, as soldiers, they were chosen to lead for other reasons than their negotiating skills. In conference, Brooke's demeanor irritated Marshall and King. On the other hand, it was Dill, more than any other, who demonstrated skills that usually led to compromise and agreement when none seemed to exist. He understood and could interpret the American position, got along exceedingly well with Marshall, and saved many negotiations from collapse.

The 'indirect approach' in the Mediterranean served as the only area for the effective use of British arms. Reality not theory intruded: to fight the Italians in North Africa rather than the Germans in northern France was within British capabilities. To the Germans, North Africa was a side-show, to the British it was their main operational theater where Hitler could be attacked at his weakest link. The Americans, eager to appropriate Britain's dwindling resources to further their own definition of 'Germany-first', discounted the art of the possible. They failed to appreciate the value of attacking through the Mediterranean, as an intermediate step, albeit diversionary, toward Germany's destruction. Even though Roosevelt approved of TORCH and the Casablanca Agreement, Marshall repeatedly disavowed further offensive action in the Mediterranean. He, King and Wedemeyer failed to assess Britain's strategy on its merits. And rather than defend their own strategic concepts, they remained preoccupied with deflecting Brooke's recommendations.

Both John Grigg and Keith Sainsbury believed that a Normandy beachhead was possible in 1943, if the Anglo–Americans agreed to forgo the opening up the Mediterranean for shipping and the benefits of Italy's collapse. Missing is the lack of amphibious technology needed for success. One year earlier, a cross-Channel landing in 1942 would have been even more problematic: a small beachhead frontage, too few men and little reserve against a well fortified and aggressive enemy. If a Normandy landing had succeeded in 1943, the potential for the beachhead becoming another Anzio was high, because of German Army and Air Force capabilities. Of primary concern to the British was the relative speeds of build-up between the Allies and the Germans, and until 1944, the enemy could bring overwhelming strength to bear against any landing. In sum, the amphibious technology, the additional allied manpower reserve and the elimination of the enemy air force had not happened in 1943.

There are a number of 'ifs' on which to speculate: what if Tunisia had been taken at Christmas 1942 rather than the following May? What if the Allies had by-passed Sicily in 1943, had stayed clear of Italian entanglements and island hopped from Sardinia to Corsica, then to southern France? What if ANVIL had remained a threat in 1944 and the intact 15th Army Group (AAI), during September of that year, had broken through the Gothic line in northern Italy with the coast road to France open?[10]

Did ANVIL live up to its planners' expectations? To answer, one must ask: 'What plan is being considered?' Originally, ANVIL was conceived as a simultaneous operation to OVERLORD, it then became a feint only, and re-emerged, in its final form, as a three-divisional assault. Tactically, it was a successful, professional and superbly executed amphibious operation. Strategically it failed, because it was non-synchronous with OVERLORD, no longer its anvil. 'The actual landing in southern France only encouraged Hitler to withdraw its substantial garrison back to reinforce the main [Norman] front, whereas if a feint had been employed, there was more chance of trapping them after the Normandy breakout.'[11] ANVIL established Eisenhower's broad front policy, a sign of his military conservatism. ULTRA decrypts revealed that Hitler's response to ANVIL was not reinforcement, but evacuation. ULTRA had unmistakably pointed to this conclusion, and indicated that the Germans considered the southern France invasion as nothing more than a threat.[12]

The strategic debate changed to one of logistics with the inclusion of Marseilles and Toulon. As seaports they served their designated purpose: six divisions passed through them in October and December 1944,[13] and by the end of the war almost a million troops disembarked, the equivalent of 45 divisions. Monthly supplies reached 30 to 40 percent of Eisenhower's needs, and over four million long tons of cargo were unloaded.[14] The introduction of American-armed French forces as part of ANVIL was more political and psychological than strategic, and the Italian campaign suffered when French troops under Juin were withdrawn. If ANVIL had been abandoned, Eisenhower planned to have those French forces enter France through Normandy.

The growing flow of US manpower and supplies to France assured the triumph of Marshall's concept of a concentrated, decisive war, an objective reinforced by the addition of the 'unconditional surrender formula'.[15] Britain had no choice but to follow. The ANVIL debate defined the fundamental differences between British and American thinking. The US with its vast resources could afford head-on colliding power-drives applying the 'direct approach'. The British, using allies to make up for her lack of resources and depending upon an economy of effort to succeed, relied on the 'indirect approach'.This kind of warfare had to be flexible and opportunist.[16]

Therefore, Brooke and the British did not gull and out-maneuver Marshall and the Americans; the American reaction to conference negotiating results was a symptom not a cause, maintained by the JCS's accumulative perceptions of the British. Historically, Anglophobia and anti-colonialism pervaded sections of the American public and the civilian–military leadership. Moreover, American military planners believed that Britain's national policy and strategy considered the defence of her empire to be incompatible with American interests, a policy that could influence and infect the US, resulting in a disastrous subordination of American forces, strategy, and interests to those of a foreign power.[17] To the extent that London's perceptions of Britain and the Empire, as part of an inter-dependent global system dependent upon Middle Eastern oil, among other things, dictated a defensive and dispersed strategy, that was true. It did not mean, however, that Britain sought to subvert the US or bend its will, any more than American Western Hemispheric defence could corrupt Britain's strategy and concerns.

Unfortunately for British interests, Embick, Chairman and Army representative on the JSSC was hostile to Britain throughout the war. By 1942 and early 1943, his committee and the S & P of the US Army's General Staff studied the political aspects of the British Mediterranean strategy. To reiterate, S & P was primarily responsible for strategic thinking and war planning within the Army and for liaison work with the other military services and the State Department. JSSC and S & P concluded that British strategy was militarily unsound, politically inspired and contrary to American interests.

Separate from what motivated American behavior, during an interview in 1948, Major General Ian Jacob, Assistant Secretary to the War Cabinet, agreed in principle with Liddell Hart's suggestion that,

> if we had not been driven by American confidence and enthusiasm we would never have dared to make the cross-Channel assault ... if the Americans had not been restrained by the British determination to guard against every mishap and to plan and prepare to the last detail the assault would almost certainly have been a ghastly failure.[18]

The American military leadership's fixed beliefs and prejudice poisoned and jeopardized inter-allied negotiations. To argue the relative merits of different strategic view points is to be expected; to argue strategy as a means of subverting one's coalition partner is not. To suggest that British strategy was used to gain unfair advantage for secret purposes, at American expense, resulting in control of places and events, smacks of fraud and deception, by which all other issues pale. By contrast, the Americans may have regarded OVERLORD and ANVIL as symbols of the neutralization of British Mediterranean strategy and the end of Britain's alleged secret intentions in the Mediterranean. The British had no secret master plan, but their disdainful demeanor did little to assuage American fears and suspicions. For the good of the coalition, Churchill's military advisors ought to have moderated his importunate Balkan suggestions. Grudging concessions on each side were made for the sake of coalition accord, but the suspicions of intention by either group were amply justified. If there really was a special relationship between Britain and America, it was of contention and argument.[19]

The coalition prevailed, because the external threat, with all its variations, was greater than its internal discord and dissent. Its citizen armies, whose many officers performed as middle and upper-middle management within the various integrated headquarters, knew little of the prejudiced and competitive nature of the major participants ranged above them. These younger officers, and the men they led complied, co-operated, and worked to end the war as quickly as possible.

Although Allied grand strategy suffered at the hands of the Anglo–American leadership, and the use of hidden agendas and subterfuge impeded its implementation, the coalition can be explained as a representation of the human condition. Fraught with uncertainty and imperfections, it was also effective and competent to the extent that, on balance, policies such as 'Germany-first' prevailed over 'Japan-first'. The combined boards and staffs, established to manage all aspects of the war, performed well, satisfying the needs and translating the complexities of global warfare into successful operations. The system was good enough – just.

Notes

INTRODUCTION

1 G. Weinberg, *World in the Balance: Behind the Scenes in World War II*, (Hanover, NH, 1981), p. xi.
2 F. Pogue Interview with Gen. G. Marshall, 15 Jan. 1957, in *Ordeal and Hope*, (New York: 1966), pp. 76–9; H. Wynter (ed.), *The Higher Strategic Decisions of the War*, I & II, (London, 1945), pp. 15, 16, 112.
3 G. Craig, 'The Political Leader As Strategist', P. Paret, (ed.) *Makers of Modern Strategy*, (Oxford, 1990), pp. 502–3.
4 Gen. Sir W. Jackson to Author, *Some Thoughts on British Strategic Thinking*, 23 Jan. 1991.
5 R. Weigley, *The American Way of War*, (Bloomington, 1973), pp. 328–9.
6 J. Ehrman, *Grand Strategy*, vol. V, (London, 1956), p. xvi.
7 Maj. Gen. J. Deane, *The Strange Alliance*, (New York, 1947), pp. 319–20.
8 JCS Office of the Chairman, *Basic National Defence Doctrine*, Washington, 24 July 1990, (Department of Defence, Joint Pub 0–1), pp. III–35.
9 Lt. Col. W. Silkett, 'Alliance and Coalition Warfare', *Parameters*, XXIII, 2, (Summer 1993), pp. 74–85.
10 W. Clark, *Less Than Kin*, (London, 1957), p. 1.
11 T. Wilson, *The First Summit: Roosevelt and Churchill At Placentia Bay, 1941*, pp. 152–62, (Lawrence, KA, 1991); C. Thorne, *Allies of a Kind*, (London, 1978), pp. 101–5, 273–7.
12 Sir B. Liddell Hart (ed.), *The Rommel Papers*, (London, 1984) p. 369.
13 Winston Churchill defined the term 'special relationship' in 1940, as the friendship that developed between him and President Roosevelt. A romantic by nature, Churchill used it to gain the President's assistance for Britain's war effort. Robert E. Sherwood, American author and one of President Roosevelt's speech-writers, called it a 'common-law alliance' in 1941, to describe the complex relationship that developed between Britain and America.
14 Lt. Gen. Sir F. Morgan, *Peace and War*, (London, 1961), p. 211.
15 H. Hall, *North American Supply*, (London, 1955), p. 353.
16 S. Ambrose, *The Supreme Commander: The War Years of Gen. Dwight D. Eisenhower*, (Garden City, NJ, 1970), p. 159.
17 FM Lord Alanbrooke, 'Notes On My Life, 3/B/XIII', Alanbrooke Papers, p. 987.

1 INTRODUCTORY STRATEGIC TALKS

1 K. Greenfield, (ed.), *Command Decisions*, (Washington, 1960), p. 11.
2 E. Larrabee, *Commander in Chief*, (New York, 1987), p. 18.
3 Notes on ABC Conference, Washington, 16 Apr. 1941, RG 165, Exec. 8.
4 R. Schaffer, 'Gen. Stanley D. Embick: Military Dissenter', *Military Affairs*, Oct., (1973), p. 92.

5 A. L. Funk, 'Interview with Gen. Eisenhower', Washington, D. C., 31 July 1968.
6 M. A. Stoler, 'The American Perception of British Mediterranean Strategy, 1941–1945', C. L. Symonds (ed.) *New Aspects of Naval History*, (Annapolis, MD, 1979), p. 330.
7 *Ibid.,* p. 326.
8 *Ibid.,* pp. 328–32.
9 Col. J. McNarney & Adm. R. K. Turner, 'Joint Instructions for Army & Navy Representatives', Office of the Chief of Staff, Washington, 21 Jan. 1941, RG 165, Exec. 8.
10 *Time*, (2 June 1941).
11 Marshall to King, Washington, 18 Feb. 1942, RG 165 Book 4, Exec. 8.
12 M. A. Stoler, *Op. cit.,* pp. 30–1.
13 A. D. Chandler, *The Papers of Dwight David Eisenhower,* I, (Baltimore, 1970), p. 112.
14 'Strategic Conceptions and Their Application to the Southwest Pacific', Army War Plans Div., Washington, 28 Feb. 1942, RG 165, Exec. 4.
15 A. Funk, 'The United States and TORCH: Strategy and Intelligence', Special Issue: Operation TORCH and its Political Aftermath: Franco–Anglo–American Relations in 1942, *Franco–British Studies*, (Spring, 1989), p. 16.
16 L. DeJong, *The German Fifth Column in the Second World War*, (Chicago, 1956), pp. 39–143.
17 H. Stimson, 'Diary quote in Pogue', *Op. cit.,* p. 266.
18 *Ibid.,* p. xii.
19 L. Mellet, 'Cantrill Poll', 10–16 Dec. 1941, PPF, FDRL.
20 S. Rosenman, *The Public Papers and Addresses of Franklin D. Roosevelt: The Call to Battle Stations, 1941*, 10, (New York, 1950), pp. 529–30.
21 T. B. Kittridge, *U.S. British Co-operation, 1940–1945,* n. d., Naval Historical Center, Washington.
22 Maj. C. Kirkpatrick, *An Unknown Future and a Doubtful Present*, (Washington, 1990), pp. 38–41.
23 J. Leutze, 'The Secret of the Churchill–Roosevelt Correspondence', September 1939–May 1940', *JCH*, 10, 3, (1975).
24 Adm. G. Dyer, *The Amphibians Came to Conquer*, (Washington, 1969), pp. 156–60; T. Higgins, *Winston Churchill and The Second Front*, (New York, 1957), pp. 43–6.
25 M. Matloff & E. Snell, *Strategic Planning for Coalition Warfare, 1941–1942*, (Washington, 1953), pp. 6–10.
26 *Ibid.,* p. 43.
27 H. Stimson & M. Bundy, *Op. cit.,* p. 214.
28 Roosevelt to Stimson, Washington, 9 July 1941, Rg 165, No. File 1921.
29 'Joint Board Estimate of United States Over-All Production Requirements, Sept. 11, 1941', *FDR Papers*, PSF, Box 1, FDRL.
30 Col. O. Ward, 'Ward Diary', Dec. 1940, quoted in T. Wilson, *Op. cit.,* pp. 41–4.
31 *Ibid.,* 18 Jan. 1941.
32 *Ibid.*, 8 July 1941.
33 R. Schaffer, *Op. cit.,* pp. 89–95.
34 J. Alsop, 'George C. Marshall Interview', Washington Spring 1941, *Joseph Alsop Papers*, Library of Congress, Box 32.
35 Roosevelt to Stimson, Washington, 9 July 1941, RG 165, Box 498.

36 E. Larrabee, *Op. cit.*, p. 11.
37 S. E. Ambrose, *Op. cit.*, pp. 3–4.
38 'Brief of Strategic Concept', Washington, Sept. 1941, RG165, Exec. 4. Note: 'AWPD/1' was based on *ABC-1* and *RAINBOW 5*.
39 C. Kirkpatrick, (ed.), *Op. cit.*, pp. 11–17.
40 R. Cline, *Op. cit.*, p. 60, 130 ['The Victory Program Troop Basis Report' prepared by the Army Resources and Requirements Section in December, 1941 attempted to translate Army strategic and operation plans into terms of troop units so that munitions and supply production could be scheduled in conformity with ultimate Army needs].
41 'The Victory Plan' superseded the 'Protective Mobilization Plan of 1939', which was intended for the defence of the US territory and inadequate for a global war.
42 C. Kirkpatrick, *Op. Cit.*, pp. 112–15.
43 S. Ambrose, *Rise To Globalism*, (London, 1988), pp. 28–31.
44 C. Kirkpatrick, *Op. cit.*, pp. 108–10.
45 P. Seabury & A. Codevilla, *War: Ends and Means*, (New York, 1989), pp. 57, 69.
46 Roosevelt to Morgenthau, 13 Mar. 1941, *Roosevelt Papers*, FDRL.
47 E. Roosevelt, *FDR, His Personal Letters, 1928–1945*, (New York, 1947–1950), pp. 1103–5; E. Roosevelt, *As He Saw It*, (New York, 1950), pp. 42–4.
48 W. Kimball, '*Beggar My Neighbor: America and the British Interim Finance Crisis,* 1940–1941', *JEH*, 58, (1971), pp. 758–72.
49 R. Allen, '*Mutual Aid Between the US and the British Empire*', *JRUSSI,* 109, (1986), p. 245.
50 G. Herring, 'The United States and British bankruptcy, 1944–1945: Responsibility Deferred', *PSQ*, (1971), pp. 260–80, 286.
51 C. Kirkpatrick, *Op. cit.*, pp. 102, 108–9.
52 Gen. A. Wedemeyer, *Wedemeyer Reports!,* (New York, 1958), p. 74. Note: John J. McCloy, Assistant Secretary for War, did not understand Wedemeyer's method of calculation, which began with men before considering material, i.e. amount of soldiers to defeat the Axis, and from such numbers determining the number of weapons.
53 J. Charmley, *Churchill's Grand Alliance*, (London, 1995) p. 23.
54 *Ibid,* pp. 23–7.
55 W. Kimball, *Op. cit.*, Pt. 1., C–9x, R–4x, C–17x, C–19x.
56 J. Charmley, *Op. cit.*, p. 17.
57 B. F. Smith, *The Ultra-Magic Deals* (London 1993) p. 13.
58 W. Kimball, *Op. cit.,* Pt. 1., pp. 91, 93, 101, 115, 182.
59 CAB 65/19, WM 84 (41) 1, Annex, 19 Aug. 1941.
60 M. Peterson, *Thomas Jefferson and the New Nation*, (Oxford, 1970), p. 416.
61 W. Churchill, *Op. cit.*, p. 555.
62 Churchill to Eden, 5 Nov. 1941, PREM 4/ 27/1, .
63 CAB 65/19, WM 84 (41) 1, Annex, 19 Aug. 1941.
64 Adm. W. Leahy 'Letter from Churchill to Roosevelt', London, 19 Sept. 1944, *Leahy Papers*, Library of Congress, Washington.
65 Beaverbrook to Churchill, 26 Dec. 1940, PREM 4/17/1, pp. 104–107.
66 Hull to Roosevelt, L. Pasvolsky, *Pasvolsky File*, Box 2; Washington 19 Nov. 1941 State Dept. 841 24/1073B.

67 C. Taussig, 'Memo', 30 Nov., 1942, *Taussig Papers*, box 46, FDRL.
68 W. Kimball, *The Juggler*, (Princeton, NJ, 1991), pp. 117–18.
69 FM Lord Alanbrooke, 'Notes For My Memoirs', 2/V, 15 January 1943, p. 4.
70 F. Pogue, *George C. Marshall*, III, (New York, 1987), p. 482.
71 R. Hathaway, *Ambiguous Partnership, Britain and American, 1944–1947*, (New York, 1981), p. 8.
72 A. Weinberg, *Manifest Destiny: A Study of Nationalist Expansionism in American History*, (Baltimore, 1935), p. 145; K. Bourne, *Britain and the Balance of Power in North America 1815–1908*, (London, 1967).
73 'Roosevelt Letters: 12 April 1938 & 11 Jan. 1941', E. Roosevelt (ed.), *FDR, His Personal Letters, 1928–1945*, 2, (New York, 1950), pp. 1103–5.
74 Adm. J. McCrea, 'Unpublished Memoirs of John L. McCrea', *McCrea Papers*, Box 1, FDRL.
75 D. Acheson, 'Memo of a Conversation', Washington 28 July, 1941, FRUS, *Conferences at Washington 1941–42*, III, pp. 10–13.
76 FM Lord Alanbrooke, *Op. cit.*, Vol. 3/A/VI, p. 418.
77 R. Sherwood, *Roosevelt and Hopkins*, (New York, 1948), p. 270.
78 J. Coleville, *The Fringes of Power, (London: 1985)*, p. 634.
79 FM Lord Alanbrooke, *Op. cit.*, 2/V, p. 32.
80 W. Churchill, *Marlborough, His Life and Times*, (New York, 1937), p. 62.
81 R. James, (ed.), *Winston S. Churchill: His Complete Speeches*, (New York, 1974), 364 H. Debs, column 1171, 20 August 1940.
82 M. Gilbert, *Road to Victory, Winston S. Churchill, 1941–1945*, (London, 1986), p. 64.
83 R. Hathaway, *Op. cit.*, p. 6.
84 D. Richards, *Portal of Hungerford, (London, 1977)*, pp. 257–8.
85 W. Louis, *Op. cit.*, p. 198.
86 A. Chandler, (ed.), *The Papers of Dwight D. Eisenhower*, (Baltimore, 1970), p. 928.
87 E. Barker, *Churchill and Eden at War*, (London, 1978) p. 138.
88 W. Kimball, '*Churchill and Roosevelt: The Personal Equation', Prologue*, 6, (Fall, 1974), pp. 169–82.
89 A. Turner, *The Unique Partnership: Britain and the US*, (New York, 1971), p. 65.
90 W. Churchill, *Op. cit.*, III, p. 539.
91 Maj. Gen. Sir J. Kennedy, *The Business of War*, (London, 1957), pp. 280–1.
92 Lt. Gen. Sir F. Morgan, *Op. cit.*, pp. 149–50.
93 T. Wilson, *Op. cit.*, p. 41 (note: the term 'immediatist' is used to describe an American who argues for an immediate declaration of war or a changeover to a war footing).
94 Col. J. McNarney, 'Strategic Considerations Peace or War Status', Washington 16 Apr. 1941, RG 319.
95 D. C. Watt, *Succeeding John Bull*, (Cambridge: 1984), pp. 91–3.
96 H. Stimson, *Op. cit.*, 25 Sept. 1941, 'there was a long distance between getting into war and crushing Germany'. FM Lord Brammall & Gen. Sir W. Jackson, *Op. cit.*, p. 208.
97 Brig. Gen. M. MacCloskey, *Planning for Victory in World War II, (New York, 1970)*, p. 96.
98 CCS 32 Meeting, Washington, 24 July 1942, Reel III.

99 Interview with Col. Sir R. Kilner Brown, London, 24 Sept. 1993.
100 Gen. G. Marshall, 'Cable Message to Gen. McNarney', Washington 13 Apr. 1942, Rg 319, CM-IN 3457.
101 FM Lord Alanbrooke, *Op. cit.,* 3/A/IX, p. 775.
102 W. Churchill, *The Second World War,* III, (Boston, 1950), p. 673.
103 Air Vice Marshal E. McCloughry, *The Direction of the War,* (London, 1955), p. 117.
104 Marshall to President, 'Ground Forces', Washington 7 Oct., 1941, RG165, Exec. 4, item 7.
105 S. Huntington, *The Soldier and the State,* (London: 1957), pp. 178–89
106 S. Roskill, *Hankey*, 3, (London, 1974), p. 419.
107 S. Huntington, *Op. cit.,* p. 320.
108 W. Emerson, 'Franklin Roosevelt as Commander-in-Chief in World War II', *JMH*, 22, Winter, (1958–1959), pp. 183.
109 Roosevelt agreed to by-pass the CCS, in 1942, sending his emissaries to argue the case for SLEDGEHAMMER in London with the COS; Churchill followed suit in 1943 when he disregarded the La Marsa agreement (ACCOLADE postponed) and sought further British action in the Eastern Mediterranean through C-in-C Middle East.
110 FM Lord Alanbrooke, 3/A/VI.
111 W. Kimball, (ed.), *Churchill and Roosevelt, The Complete Correspondence*, (Princeton, NJ, 1984), p. 128.
112 R. Steele, *The First Offensive – 1942*, (Bloomington, IL, 1973), p. 38.
113 H. Stimson & M. Bundy, *Op. cit.*, pp. 151–2.
114 R. Steele, *Op. cit.,* pp. 18–45.
115 W. Emerson, *Op. cit.,* p. 183.
116 H. Stimson & M. Bundy, *Op. cit.*, p. 662; Sir A. Bryant, *Op. cit.,* p. 335.
117 T. Buell, *Op. cit.,* pp. 182–3.
118 CAB, 65/25 WM (42), 17 Jan. 1942.
119 R. Cline, *Op. cit.,* pp. 315–17.
120 S. Huntington, *Op. cit.,* p. 318.
121 AF Viscount A. Cunningham, *A Sailor's Odyssey,* (London, 1951), pp. 611–12.
122 Sir A. Bryant, *Op. cit.,* p. 234.
123 V. Davis, *The History of the Joint Chiefs of Staff in World War II: Organizational Development of the JCS Committee Structure*, 2, (Washington, 1972), p. 370–965.
124 S. Huntington, *Op. cit.,* p. 315.
125 R. Sherwood, *Roosevelt and Hopkins,* (New York, 1950), pp. 410ff.
126 JCS 79 Meeting, 10 May 1943, Reel II.
127 Sir M. Howard, *Clausewitz*, (Oxford, 1983), pp. 34–46.
128 M. Matloff, *Op. cit.,* p. 3.
129 W. Emerson, *Op. cit.,* pp. 190–3.
130 FM Sir J. Dill, 'Situation Report', 9 Mar. 1942, RG 165.
131 F. Pogue, Interviews with Marshall, 29 Oct. 1956, 14 Nov. 1956 and 20 Feb. 1957, quoted in Pogue, *Op. cit.*, pp. 329–30.
132 A. Campbell, 'Franklin Roosevelt and Unconditional Surrender', *Diplomacy and Intelligence during the Second World War*, R. Langhorne (ed.), (Cambridge, 1985), pp. 221, 223, 237.
133 W. Emerson, *Op. cit.,* pp. 185, 187–90.
134 FM Lord Alanbrooke, *Op. cit.,* 3/A/VI, Vol. VI, p. 418.

135 E. McCloughry, *Op. cit.,* pp. 238–9.
136 *Ibid.,* p. 160.
137 *Ibid.,* pp. 158–66.
138 H. Macmillan, *Memoirs: The Blast of War, 1939–1945,* (New York, 1968), pp. 169–74.
139 FM Lord Alanbrooke, *Op. cit.,* 3/B/XII, p. 920.
140 F. Loewenheim, H. Langley, M. Jonas, (eds), *Op. cit.,* p. 24.
141 *Ibid.,* pp. 164–6.
142 Gen Lord Ismay, *Op. cit.,* pp. 165–70; J. Leasor, *War At The Top,* (London, 1959), p. 11.
143 FM Lord Alanbrooke, *Op. cit.,* 3/B/XII, p. 901.
144 Gen. Lord Ismay, *Op. cit.,* pp. 158–9.
145 D. Richards, *Op. cit.,* (London, 1978), p. 181.
146 Gen. Lord Ismay, *Op. cit.,* pp. 166–72.
147 R. Lewin, *Churchill as Warlord,* (New York, 1980), p. 34.
148 FM Lord Brammal & Gen. Sir W. Jackson, *Op. Cit.,* p. 200.
149 B. Villa, *Unauthorized Action: Mountbatten and The Dieppe Raid 1942,* (Toronto, 1989), pp 258–9.
150 T. Ben-Moshe, *Churchill: Strategy and History,* (Boulder, 1992), pp. 124–5.
151 A. Marder, *Winston is Back, Churchill at the Admiralty,* (London, 1972), p. 5.
152 J. Colville, *The Churchillians,* (London, 1981), p. 141.
153 A. Danchev, 'Dill', *Churchill's Generals,* J. Keegan (ed.), (London, 1991), p. 226.
154 FM Lord Alanbrooke, 'Documents of a Semi-Official Nature', 7/2/1–17.
155 *Ibid.,* FM Wavell to FM Alanbrooke, 30 May 1946.
156 Lord Moran, *Winston Churchill: The Struggle for Survival 1940–1965,* (Boston, 1966), p. 21.
157 A. Storr, 'Churchill the Man', A. J. P. Taylor (ed.), *Churchill Revised* (New York, 1969), p. 242.
158 Sir B. Liddell Hart, *Op. cit.,* 15/15/1.
159 Lord Moran, *Op. cit.,* p. 29.
160 W. Morgan, 'Lord Alanbrooke', N.D., WDM 1/3, IWM.
161 FM Lord Alanbrooke, *Op. cit.,* 3/A/V, pp. 374–7.
162 Sir A. Bryant, *Op. cit.,* p. 213; J. Coleville, *Op. cit.,* p. 142; J. Kennedy, *Op. cit.,* p. 203; R. Lewin, *Op. cit.,* p. 126.
163 Lord Moran, *Op. cit.,* p. 304.
164 A. Storr, *Op. cit.,* pp. 271–3.
165 FM Lord Alanbrooke, 3/A/X, p. 798.
166 AF Viscount A. Cunningham, *Correspondence,* BL., Add MS 52577, 8 August 1944.
167 FM Lord Alanbrooke, *Op. cit.,* 3/B/XII, p. 895.
168 Gen. Lord Ismay, *Op. cit.,* pp. 164–5.
169 A. Storr, *Op. cit.,* p. 215.
170 Sir B. Liddell Hart, *Op. cit.,* 15/15/1, pp. 1–3.

2 CONFERENCES

1 Brig. Gen. M. MacCloskey, *Op. cit.,* (New York, 1970), p. 96.
2 JSSC to JCS, 'QUADRANT', Washington 24 July 1943, RG. 218, JCS Records.

3 F. Pogue, *George C. Marshall: Ordeal and Hope,* (New York, 1966), p. 58.
4 M. Stoler, *Op. cit.*, pp. 332–6.
5 J. Wheeler-Bennett, *Special Relationships*, (London, 1975), p. 16.
6 'Memorandum of Welles–Cadogan conversation', Washington, 9 Aug. 1941, *FRUS, Conferences at Washington.* 1941, 1:351.
7 Gen. H. Arnold, *Global Mission*, (New York, 1949), p. 240.
8 T. Buell, *Op. cit.*, p. 146.
9 C. Beard, 'Roosevelt Deceived the Public', R. Dallek, (ed.), *The Roosevelt Diplomacy and World War II*, (New York, 1948), pp. 9–16.
10 Lord Moran, *Op. cit.*, p. 21.
11 M. Schoenfeld, *The War Ministry of Winston S. Churchill*, (Ames, IA, 1972), p. 247.
12 R. Dallek, *Franklin D. Roosevelt and American Foreign Policy, 1932–1945*, (Oxford, 1979), p. 324.
13 T. Buell, *Op. cit.*, p. 145.
14 Churchill to Roosevelt, 25 February 1941, *Roosevelt Papers*, Map Room, box 7A, FDRL.
15 COS, 'Review of Future Strategy', A51667, June 1941, PRO WO 193/326.
16 Moffat to Dunn, Washington, 16 July 1941, RG. 59 D.F. 740.0011, European War 1939/13577.
17 FO 371/24329, A3242. W. Scott 'Minutes', 28 Feb. 1940; K. Hancock & M. Gowing, *British War Economy*, (London, 1949), pp. 380–7.
18 'Brief of Strategic Concept of Operations Required to Defeat Our Potential Enemies', *Op. cit.*
19 McNarney and Turner to JPC, *Op. cit.*
20 M. Watson, *Chief of Staff: Prewar Plans and Preparations*, (Washington, 1950), pp. 406–10.
21 D. Haglund, 'George C. Marshall and the Question of Military Aid to England, May–June 1940', *JCH,* 15, (1980), pp. 746–59.
22 Air subcommittee, 'ABC-2', 29 March, 1941, *Letter to CoS, CNO, Br. CoS*, AWPD.
23 Sir B. Liddell Hart, Interview with Gen. F. Morgan, Dep. CoS, formerly 'COSSAC', November 1945, 15/15/24, p. 3.
24 T. Kittridge, 'US Defence Policy and Strategy', *US News and World Report*, 3 (December 1954).
25 R. Lamb, *The Ghosts of Peace, 1935–1945*, (London, 1987), pp. 219–20; T. Wilson, *Op. cit.*, pp. 168–72.
26 J. Conant, *Conant–Douglas Letters*, 4, (9 Oct. 1940). University of Arizona Library.
27 E. Roosevelt, *This I Remember*, (New York, 1949), p. 226; M. Gilbert, *Finest Hour: W. S. Churchill, 1939–1941*, (Boston, 1983), pp. 1176–7.
28 D. Richards, *Portal of Hungerforrd,* (London, 1977), pp. 257–8.
29 Presidential Radio Broadcast to the American Nation, 11 Sept. 1941, FDRL.
30 D. Reynolds, *Op. cit.*, p. 215; Sherwood, *Op. cit.*, p. 368.
31 H. Cantril, *Public Opinion Polls*, 19 August, 13 Sept. 1941, FDRL.
32 CAB 65/19 WM 84 (41), 19 Aug. 1941.
33 Sir A. Bryant, *Turn of the Tide*, (London, 1957), p. 234.
34 COS to JCS, 'HMS Duke of York', Washington, 18 Dec., 1941, RG. 165, Exec. 10.

35 M. Gilbert, *Finest Hour, Winston S. Churchill, 1939–1941*, (London, 1983), p. 358.
36 Sir A. Bryant, *Op. cit.,* p. 225.
37 T. Wilson, *Op. cit.,* p. xii.
38 H. Stimson & M. Bundy, *Op. cit.,* p. 213.
39 Sir B. Liddell Hart, 'Notes of Discussion with Major Gen. Sir Ian Jacob', *Liddell Hart Papers*, 15/15/1, London, 31 Mar. & 15 Apr. 1948.
40 J. Leasor & Gen. S. Hollis, *War At The Top*, (London, 1959), p. 29.
41 COS to JCS, 'American-British Strategy', Washington, 22–24 Dec., 1941, *Arcadia Papers*, RG. 165, Exec. 4.
42 Sir M. Howard, *The Mediterranean Strategy in the Second World War*, (London, 1968), pp. 19–20.
43 W. Kimball, (ed.), 1, *Op. cit.,* p. 326.
44 'Higher Direction of War in ABDA Area to ABC-4/5', Washington, 14–28 Jan. 1942, RG. 165 WDCSA.
45 Gen. G. Marshall, 'Notes GCM', Washington, 23 Dec. 1941, RG. 165 WPD 4402–136.
46 Col. C. Bundy, 'Memo for CoS', Washington, 24 Oct. 1941, RG. 165 ACOS WPD.
47 COS to American COS, Washington, 22 Dec. 1941, RG. 165 Exec. 4.
48 W. Churchill, *Op. cit.,* 'The Campaign of 1943', 18 Dec. 1941, pp. 657–8.
49 Cmdr. K. Edwards, *Operation Neptune*, (London, 1946), p. 23.
50 H. Stimson & M. Bundy, *Op. cit.,* p. 87.
51 H. Stimson, *Op. cit.,* 'Diary (MS)', 25 Dec. 1941.
52 Sir A. Bryant, *Op. cit.,* p. 254.
53 A. Wilt, *Op. cit.,* pp. 40–1.
54 'Second Mtg., COS Conference', Washington, 25 Dec. 1941, RG 165 'ABC 337'.
55 *Ibid.*
56 FM Lord Alanbrooke, *Op. cit.,* 2/V, p. 45.
57 Dill to Brooke', 28 Dec. 1941 quoted in F. Pogue, *Op. cit.,* p.281.
58 *Ibid.,* 3/A/V, p. 355.
59 *Op. cit.*, 2/V, pp. 46–8.
60 'ABC 337', *Op. cit.*
61 'Gen. Strategic Review', Washington, 21 Dec. 1941, RG. 165 Exec. 4.
62 R. Weigley, *Op. cit.,* p. 313.
63 R. Parkinson, *Blood, Toil, Tears, and Sweat*, (London, 1973), p. 342.
64 Adm. J. McCrea, *Op. cit.*
65 F. Pogue, *Op. cit.,* Interview with Gen. G. Marshall, 29 Oct. 1956.
66 *Ibid.*, Interview with Gen. L. Kuter, 10 Nov. 1960.
67 'Operation SUPER-GYMNAST', Washington, 10 Jan. 1942 RG 165 'ABC 337'.
68 'White House Conference', Washington, 4 Jan. 1942, RG 165 'ABC 337'; Churchill, *Op. cit.,* pp. 684–5.
69 C. Kirkpatrick, *Op. cit.,* pp. 114–16.
70 CCS 11 Meeting, Washington, 2 Feb. 1942, Reel III.
71 D. Drew & Col. D. M. Snow, *Making Strategy: An Introduction to National Security and Problems*, (Maxwell Air Force Base, 1988), pp. 27–36.
72 Gen. A. Wedemeyer, *Op. cit.,* pp. 88–92.
73 W. Churchill, *Op. cit.,* III, p. 605.

74 J. Leasor, *Op. cit.,* p.29.
75 W. F. Kimball, (ed.), *Op. cit.,* I, p. 327.

3 EVENTS LEADING TO A JUNE WASHINGTON CONFERENCE

1 'Future Operations', 2 July 1942, WP (42) 278.
2 Molotov to Stalin quoted in R. Edmonds, *The Big Three*, (London, 1991), p. 287.
3 FRUS, *Washington 1941–42*, III, p. 577, (Washington, 1968). R. E. Sherwood, *Op. cit.,* pp. 556–78.
4 'Confidential Protocol of Conference of Allied Representatives', Washington, n. d.; 'Draft of Joint Statement with Draft of Second Protocol', 19 Apr. 1942, RG 165 ABC 400.3295.
5 JSM to COS, 11 May 1942, COS (42) 60th meeting (0) Min. 2.
6 W. Churchill, 20 June 1942 PM/402/3, Argonaut Diary.
7 FRUS, *Op. cit.*, Washington, pp. 582–3; M. Sommers, 'Why Russia Got the Drop On Us', *Saturday Evening Post*, 8 Feb. 1947, p. 25.
8 FM Lord Alanbrooke, *Op. cit.,* 2/V, 4–9 Mar. 1942, p. 367.
9 COS, meetings related to 'Mountbatten, SLEDGEHAMMER, GYMNAST and ROUNDUP', COS meetings on 5, 11, 27 May, 1, 25, 30 June, 1 July 1942.
10 CCS 27 Meeting, Washington, 19 June 1942, Reel III, pp. 1–3.
11 CCS 24 Meeting, Washington, 10 June 1942, *Op. cit.,* p. 4.
12 Dill to Montgomery-Massingberd, 19 Sept. 1941, *Montgomery-Massingberd Papers*, 160/23a.
13 Dill to COS, 15 June 1942, CAB 105/39.
14 J. Terraine, *The Life and Times of Lord Mountbatten*, (London, 1968), pp. 94, 506.
15 H. Stimson, *Op. cit.,* 17, 18, 19, Jan. 1942; R. E. Sherwood, *Op. cit.,* pp. 580–1; 'Winant to FDR', 3 June 1942, PSF, FDRL.
16 CCS 27 Meeting, 19 June, 'CCS 83, Offensive Operations in 1942 & 1943', Washington, 21 June 1942, Reel III.
17 Churchill to Roosevelt, Washington, 20 June 1942, quoted in FRUS, *Washington, 1941–42*, pp. 461–2; W. Churchill, IV, pp. 381–2.
18 K. Sainsbury, *Churchill and Roosevelt at War*, (London, 1994), pp. 24–7, 180.
19 M. Blumenson, 'A Deaf Ear to Clausewitz: Allied Operational Objectives in World War II', *Parameters, US Army War College Quarterly*, XXIII 2, Summer (1993), pp. 16–27.
20 H. Loewenheim, M. Jonas, H. Langley (eds), *Op. cit.*, pp. 254–6; Marshall to Dill 'CCS-94', Washington, 14 Aug. 1942, RG. 165 Exec 10 Box 59; Sir M. Howard, *Op. cit.,* pp. 122–40.
21 *Churchill to Roosevelt, 'Second Front*', London, 28 May 1942, *Churchill–Roosevelt Correspondence*, pp. 495–500, FDRL.
22 P. Ziegler, *Mountbatten*, (London, 1985), p. 184.
23 R. Steele, 'Political Aspects of American Military Planning, 1941–1942', *Military Affairs*, XXXV, 2, (1971), pp. 68–9, 71–2.
24 M. Stoler, *Op. cit.,* pp. 53, 63.
25 F. Pogue, Interview with Gen. G. Marshall, 13 Nov. 1956.

26 CCS 38 Meeting, Washington, 28 Aug. 1942, *Op. cit.*, p. 3.
27 *Ibid.*
28 Churchill to Marshall, Washington, 16 Apr. 1944, RG 165, Item 16 Exec. 8.
29 Marshall & Adm. E. King to Roosevelt, 'Gymnast Operations', 28 July 1942, *PSF*, FDRL.
30 *Battle Summary No. 38, Operation Torch*, (London, 1948), pp. 104–5.
31 R. Sherwood, *Op. cit.*, p. 581.
32 CCS 38 meeting, Washington, 28 Aug. 1942, Reel III.
33 Office of American Secretariat, 'Offensive Operations for 1942–43', Washington, 21 June 1942, RG. 165 WPD Exec. 1 Item 4, Ismay Paper included.
34 COS 942) 97(0), Washington, 13 Apr. 1942, RG. 165, Exec. 1.
35 H. Stimson & M. Bundy, *Op. cit.*, quoting Hopkins, pp. 214–15.
36 Gen. D. Eisenhower to COS, 'BOLERO and Plans for Operations in Northwest Europe', Washington, 25 Mar., 12 Apr. 1942, RG 165 Exec. 1 Box 1 OPD 381.
37 Dill to War Cabinet, 'Operations in Western Europe', Washington, 5 Apr. 1942, CAB 105/39.
38 A. Danchev, *Op. Cit.* He used titles such as 'Broker', 'Fixer' and 'Agitator' for his chapter headings.
39 B. Villa, *Op. cit.*, p. 174.
40 Gen. B. Paget, Adm. Lord Mountbatten, AM S. Douglas, 'Re-entry into France', 21 Mar., 1942, CAB 79/19; CAB-JPS Study, 9 Dec. 1941, 'Operations on Continent in Final Phase' CAB 79/17, JP(41) 1028.
41 CAB 79/19 (42), 112, 9 Apr. 1942.
42 FM Lord Alanbrooke, *Op. cit.*, 2/V, 12–15 Apr. 1942, p. 383.
43 Marshall, 'Notebook', Washington, 13 Apr. 1942, RG 165 Exec. 1 Item 5d.
44 JCS 6 Meeting, Washington, 16 Mar. 1942, Reel I.
45 COS-USCOS Meeting, 'Minutes', London, 14 Apr. 1942, RG. 165 OPD, Exec 1 Box 1 ABC 381 BOLERO.
46 W. Churchill, *Op. cit.*, pp. 323–4; J. Butler, *Grand Strategy*, III, (London, 1964), p. 577.
47 Col. Sir R. Kilner Brown, *Top Brass and No Brass*, (Lewes, 1991), pp. 68, 69, 77.
48 Interview with Sir R. Kilner Brown, London, 24 Sept. 1993.
49 Eisenhower, 'Memo for COS', Washington, 25 Mar. 1942, *Op. cit.*
50 COS-USCOS Meeting, *Op. cit.*
51 H. Loewenheim et al., *Op. cit.*, p. 206.
52 *Ibid.*, p. 222.
53 Ismay, *Op. cit.*, pp. 249–50.
54 F. Pogue, Interview with Gen. Lord H. Ismay, 18 Oct. 1960.
55 CAB, 65/30, 28, 29 Apr. 1942.
56 Roosevelt to COS and Hopkins, Washington, 6 May 1942, PSF., FDRL.
57 FM Lord Alanbrooke, *Op. cit.*, 3/A/VI., 26 June 1942, p. 425.
58 H. W. Wynter, *Op. cit.*, p. 77.
59 Churchill to Roosevelt, London, 23 July 1942, CAB 65/31, p. 26.
60 Marshall & King to Roosevelt, London, 28 July 1942, RG.165 OPD WDCSA 319.1 (TS).
61 Roosevelt to Hopkins, Marshall and King, Washington, 25 June 1942, RG 165, OPD WDCSA 381, 1 (SS).
62 CCS 32 Meeting, 'CCS-94', Washington, 24 July 1942, Reel III.

63 *Ibid.*
64 T. Higgins, *Winston Churchill and the Second Front*, (New York: OUP, 1957), pp. 134–5, 144, 155, 159.
65 Army Secretariat, 'Notes on White House Conference, 30 July 1942', Washington, 1 Aug., 1942, RG 165 Exec. 5, Item 1. for JCS.
66 McNarney to Marshall, Washington, 25 July 1942, RG. 165 OPD, CM-OUT 7303.
67 CAB 79/22, 24 July 1942.
68 Admiral E. King & W. Whitehill, *Fleet Admiral King: A Naval Record*, (New York, 1952), pp. 190–200; H. Stimson & M. Bundy, *Op. cit.*, p. 425.
69 H. Butcher, *My Three Years With Eisenhower*, (New York, 1946), pp. 29, 294.
70 K. Greenfield, *Op. cit.*, p. 7; Sir M. Howard, *The Mediterranean Strategy in the Second World War*, (London, 1968), p. 35.
71 Dill to Marshall, Washington, 14 Aug. 1942, RG. 165 OPD WDCSA.
72 B. Wynter, *Op. cit.*, p. 440.
73 H. Loewenheim, et al., *Op. cit.*, p. 227.
74 Sir M. Howard, *Op. cit.*, pp. 33–5.
75 FM Lord Alanbrooke, *Op. cit.*, 3/A/VI, 24 July, 1942, p. 449.
76 W. Kimball, (ed.), *Churchill and Roosevelt, The Complete Correspondence*, (Princetown, 1984), p. 567.
77 R. Leighton & R. Coakley, *The Logistics of Global Warfare 1940–1943*, (Washington, 1955), p. 487.
78 S. Richardson & H. Steirman, *The Secret History of World War II*, (New York, 1986), pp. 82–3.

4 THE SYMBOL AND TRIDENT CONFERENCES

1 'White House Meeting, 7 January', Washington, 7 Jan. 1943, Rg 165 *OPD*, Minutes Meeting at White House.
2 *Ibid.*
3 A. Wedemeyer, *Op. cit.*, p. 169.
4 Sir M. Howard, *Op. cit.*, p. 35.
5 H. Macmillan, *War Diaries: Politics and War in the Mediterranean*, (New York, 1984), p. 193.
6 CAB 122, CAB 138, JSM 673 'Major Topics for Discussion at Casablanca', London, 8 Jan. 1943.
7 CAB 'Note by the Prime Minister', WP (42) 543; COS (Symbol) 1st Meeting, 13 Jan. 1943; COS (S) 3rd Meeting, 15 Jan. 1943.
8 PRO CAB 122/229 JSM 660, 'Sir J. Dill to COS', 24 Jan. 1943.
9 J. Grigg, *Op. cit.*, p. 68.
10 J. Grigg, *Op. cit.*, p. 71.
11 H. Loewenheim, et al., *Op. cit.*, pp. 284–5.
12 'Anfa Camp Conference Minutes, Casablanca', Washington, 16 Jan. 1943, Reel I.
13 *Ibid.*, CCS 58 Meeting, Washington, 16 Jan. 1943, Reel III.
14 *Casablanca Conference, Papers and Minutes of Meetings*, CCS-151, Office of the CCS, Jan. 1943, pp. 18–19; W. Churchill, IV, p. 606.

15 66 Meeting, *Ibid.*, Washington, 22 Jan. 1943, 'CCS 167 & 169'.
16 A. Wedemeyer, *Op. cit.*, p. 185, 188.
17 *Ibid.*, pp. 165–7.
18 A. Wedemeyer, *Op. cit.*, p. 185, 188.
19 Sir J. Kennedy, *Op. cit.*, pp. 280–1.
20 *Ibid.*, pp. 280–1.
21 K. Greenfield, *Op. cit.*, p. 72.
22 FM Lord Alanbrooke, 3/A/VIII, 16–18 Jan. 1943, pp. 600–8.
23 *Ibid.*, p. 603; CCS 66 Meeting, 22 Jan., 'CCS '155/1 Conduct of the War in 1943', Casablanca, 19 Jan. 1943, Reel III.
24 Sir J. Kennedy, *Op. cit.*, p. 281.
25 J. Grigg, *Op. cit.*, pp. 72–6.
26 A. Wedemeyer, *Op. cit.*, p. 188.
27 'Eisenhower to Gen. T. Handy', A. Chandler, (ed.), *The Papers of Dwight D. Eisenhower*, (Baltimore, 1970); M. Matloff, *Op. cit.*, pp. 75–6.
28 B. Pitt, *Churchill and the Generals*, (Newton Abbot, 1988), pp. 155–8.
29 'Morning Thoughts' represented Churchill's personal views and were not a product of full consultation with the War Cabinet.
30 M. Balfour, 'The Origin of the Formula, Unconditional Surrender in World War II', *Armed Forces and Society,* 5, 2, (1979), p. 283.
31 Sir B. Liddell Hart, 'The Background of Unconditional Surrender', 31 July 1943, *Op. cit.,* 11/1943/50.
32 R. Lamb, *The Ghosts of Peace, 1935–1945*, (London, 1987), pp. 226–7, 'Note by the PM to the War Cabinet', London, 15 Jan. 1944.
33 Sir B. Liddell Hart, 'The Background of Unconditional Surrender', 31 July 1943, *Op. cit.*, 11/1943/50.
34 A. Armstrong, *Unconditional Surrender*, (Westport, CT, 1974), pp. 249–62; M. Matloff, *Op. cit.*, p. 431.
35 T. Ben-Moshe, *The Origins of the Declaration of the Policy of Unconditional Surrender– A New Interpretation*, unpublished, (Hebrew University, 1981).
36 P. Seabury & A. Codevilla, *Op. cit.*, p. 92.
37 S. Ambrose, *Op. cit.*, p. 25
38 A. Campbell, 'Franklin Roosevelt and Unconditional Surrender', R. Langhorne, (ed.), *Diplomacy and Intelligence during the Second World War*, (Cambridge, 1985), pp. 222–5.
39 Sir M. Howard, *Op. cit.*, p. 285.
40 R. Lamb, *Op. cit.*, p. 223.
41 J. Grigg, *Op. cit.*, pp. 72–5.
42 JSSC, 'Effect of 'Unconditional Surrender' Policy on German Morale', Washington, 10 Mar. 1944, RG165.
43 Adm. J. McCrea, 'Roosevelt–de Gaulle Conversation – President's Villa', Casablanca, 22 Jan. 1943, Unpublished papers of J. L. McCrea, FDRL; Sir M. Howard, *Op. cit., Grand Strategy*, pp. 279–80.
44 Gen. C. de Gaulle, *Mémoires de Guerre*, (Paris, 1954–1959), p. 256.
45 Roosevelt to C. Hull, Washington, 18 Jan. 1943, PSF, FDRL.
46 Gen. C. de Gaulle, *Op. cit.*, pp. 241, 251. J. Grigg, *Op. cit.*, pp. 156–60.
47 H. Kissinger, *Diplomacy*, (New York, 1994), p. 401.
48 CAB 65/19 WM(41) 80, 81, 11 Aug. 1941.
49 E. Roosevelt & J. Brough, *A Rendevous With Destiny*, (New York, 1975).

50 J. Grigg, *Op. cit.,* pp. 78–80.
51 J. Grigg, *Op. cit.,* pp. 78–80.
52 T. Higgins, *Op. cit.,* pp. 76–87.
53 Lord Ismay, 'QUADRANT Directive', London, 15 July 1943, *Op. cit.,* VI6/13.
54 J. A. Isley & P. Crowl, *The US Marines and Amphibious War,* (Princeton, 1951), pp. 37–8; Brig. A. Head, 'Amphibious Operations', *RUSI,* XCI, (1946), pp. 485–94.
55 'Interview with J. G. Christiansen', Washington, 12 May 1944, RG 319, Box 19.
56 C. Gabel, *The Lorraine Campaign: An Overview, September–December 1944,* (US Army Command and Gen. Staff College, 1985), p. 30, Combat Studies Institute.
57 Sir M. Howard, *Op. cit.,* pp. 251–5.
58 M. Matloff, *Strategic Planning for Coalition Warfare, 1943–1944,* (Washington, 1959), p. 25.
59 CCS 67 Meeting, Washington, 22 Jan. 1943; 3rd Anfa Meeting, 23 Jan. 1943, Reel III.
60 M. Matloff, *Op. cit.,* pp. 254, 278.
61 E. Larrabee, *Op. cit.,* p. 185.; B. Liddell Hart, *Op. cit.,* 15/15/1.
62 *Ibid.*, p. 85.
63 CCS 58 meeting, Anfa, 16 Jan. 1943, Reel III.
64 Sir M. Howard, *Op. cit.*, p. 35.
65 P. Seabury & A. Codevilla, *Op. cit.,* p. 120.
66 M. Matloff & E. Snell, *Op. cit.,* p. 382.
67 W. Emerson, *Op. cit.,* p. 199.
68 P. Seabury & A. Codevilla, *Op. cit.,* pp. 222–3.
69 M. Matloff, *Op. cit.,* p. 30.
70 K. Greenfield, *Op. cit.,* pp. 32–3.
71 JCS 71 Meeting, Washington, 30 Mar. 1943, p. 6, Reel 1.
72 CCS 81 Meeting, Washington, 23 Apr 1943, 'Supplementary Minutes', p. 2, Reel III.
73 Sir W. Jackson, *Op. cit.,* pp. 56–7.
74 FM Lord Alanbrooke, 3/A/IX, 10 May 1943, p. 86.
75 F. Pogue, *Op. cit.,* p. 310 'Brooke Interview', 18 Apr. 1961.
76 T. Wilson, 'The United States Leviathan', *Allies At War,* W. Reynolds & A. Chubarian, (eds), (London, 1994), pp. 186–8.
77 JCS 79 Meeting, Washington, 10 May 1943, p.2.
78 R. Schaffer, *Op. cit.,* pp. 89–95.
79 JCS 8 Meeting, Washington, 7 Nov. 1943, Reel I.
80 V. E. Davis, *The History of the Joint Chiefs of Staff in W.W. II, Organization Development,*, 2, (Washington, 1972), pp. 370–95.
81 CCS 79 Meeting, *Op cit.*
82 JCS 78 Meeting, Washington, 8 May 1943, Reel I .
83 JCS 80 Meeting, Washington, 12 May 1943, p. 7, Reel I.
84 JCS 78 Meeting, Washington, 8 May 1943; JCS 79 Meeting, Washington, 10 May 1943, Reel I.
85 JCS 81 Meeting, Washington, 14 May 1943, p. 3, Reel I.
86 CCS 83 Meeting, Washington, 13 May 1943, Reel III.
87 K. Greenfield, *Op. cit.,* p. 33.
88 CCS 83 Meeting, *Op. cit.*

89 FM Lord Alanbrooke, *Op. cit.*, IX, 19 May 1943, p. 9.
90 CCS 83 Meeting, *Op. cit.*, 'Annex A', p. 12.
91 *Ibid.*, p. 8.
92 Gen. Lord H. Ismay, *Op. cit.*, pp. 269, 298.
93 Dill to Alanbrooke, 9 February 1944, Alanbrooke Papers, 14/39/B, KCL.
94 H. Kissenger, *A World Restored*, (Boston, 1973), p. 109.
95 C. Jenkins & B. Sherman, *Collective Bargaining*, (London, 1977).
96 H. Nicholas, *The United States and Britain*, (Chicago, 1975), p. 4.
97 B. Spector, 'Negotiation as a Psychological Process', *Journal of Conflict Resolution*, 21, 4, (1977), pp. 613–14.
98 'CCS 242/6: TRIDENT Final Report to President and Prime Minister', 25 May 1943, *Papers and Minutes*, Washington, 1943.
99 *Ibid.*, 'Annex B', p. 13.
100 *Ibid.*
101 'CCS 242/6: Final Report to the President and Prime Minister', 25 May 1943, *TRIDENT Papers*, Office of CCS, Washington, 1943.
102 FM Lord Alanbrooke, *Op. cit.*, 3/A/VIII, 19 May 1943, p. 703.
103 CCS 96 Meeting, Washington, 25 May 1943, Reel III.
104 'CCS 251/1: Proposals for Improving Combined Planning', 25 May 1943, *Ismay Papers*, VI/II.
105 JCS 84 Meeting, Washington, 18 May, 1943, Reel I.
106 FM Lord Alanbrooke, *Op. cit.*, 3/A/VIII, 25 May 1943, p. 704.
107 J. Kautsky, 'Myth, Self fulfilling Prophecy, and Symbolic Reassurance in the East–West Conflict', *Conflict Resolution*, IX, 1, (1965), pp. 1–2.
108 'Analysis of Trident and Anfa Conferences', Washington, 25 May 1943, RG 165 OPD, Tab SS 106, ABC 381, SS Papers 96–126/3.
109 FM Lord Alanbrooke, *Op. cit.*, 3/A/VIII, 25 May, 1943, p. 705.
110 Sir B. Liddell Hart, 'The Higher Strategic Decisions of the War', n.d., 15/15/24, p. 17.
111 'Minutes of the Algiers Conference', 7 June 1943, JCS Document, MR File, FDRL.
112 Lord Moran, *Op. cit.*, pp. 121–2.
113 Minutes, '1st meeting in Algiers', 29 May 1943, Official TRIDENT Conference Book, Office of the CCS, Washington.
114 W. Churchill, *The Second World War*, III, *Op. cit.*, pp. 816–30; Gen. D. Eisenhower, *Op. cit.*, pp. 185–7. See the 'Marshall Memorandum'.
115 R. Edmonds, *Op. cit.*, p. 328: Sov-Angl. O, 1. 'Document 131'.
116 W. Kimball, *Op. cit.*, II, 'C-328', 25 June 1943, pp. 278–9.
117 *Ibid.*, 'R-297', 28 June 1943, pp. 283–4.
118 *Ibid.*, 'C-582', 19 Feb., 1944, pp. 733–4.
119 PREM 3 476 W.O. paper, 'Anglo–American Relations in Washington in the Autumn of 1942. Lord Halifax, 'Anglo–American Relations, Quarterly Report July, Aug., Sept. 1944', Washington, 1943, CAB 122/1035, p. 4.

5 QUADRANT: THE QUEBEC CONFERENCE

1 JCS Meetings 100–102, and White House, Washington, 6, 7, 9, 10 Aug. 1943, Reel I.

2 JCS 103 Meeting, 'Pre QUANDRANT: Agenda Priority', Washington, 10 Aug. 1943., Reel I.
3 JCS Meetings 100–102, *Op. cit.*
4 White House Meeting, 'Letter to Roosevelt', Washington, 10 Aug. 1943.
5 *Ibid.*
6 JCS Meetings, 100–102 *Op. cit.*
7 Stimson Diary, *Op. cit.,* May, Aug. 1943.
8 White House Meeting, 10 Aug. 1943, Washington Reel I.
9 White House Meeting, *Op. cit.*
10 *Ibid.*
11 *Ibid.*
12 C. Peek, (ed.), *Five Years, Five Countries, Five Campaigns*, 141 Infantry Regiment, (Munich, 1945), p. 72.
13 JCS meetings 100–102, *Op. cit.*
14 *Ibid.*
15 *Ibid.*, 'CCS 289' and '289/1', '242/6', 'CCS 300/1', 'CCS 303', 'JCS 443', 'JCS 442' & '442/1' (papers presented on European strategy during CCS meetings between 5–17 Aug. 1943), Reels III and IV.
16 'CCS 381: Conduct of the War, 1943–1944', Washington, 17 May 1943 RG. 165 JWPC.
17 C. Wilson, *Introduction to the New Existentialism*, (London, 1966), pp. 39–50.
18 I. Myers, *Gifts Differing*, (Palo Alto, CA, 1980), pp. 65, 118.
19 FM Lord Alanbrooke, *Op. cit.,* 3/A/IX, 24 July 1943, p. 746.
20 CCS 106 Meeting, 'QUADRANT Conference', Washington, 14 Aug. 1943, Reel IV.
21 *Ibid.*, pp. 2–3.
22 *Ibid.*
23 Interview with Lt. Gen. J. Doolittle, 14 Dec. 1981: When Gen. Doolittle assumed command of the 8th Air Force in Jan. 1944, he instituted procedures to lessen air accidents over the UK and improved the manpower replacement system.
24 CCS 106 Meeting, *Op. cit.*
25 Lt. Gen. Sir F. Morgan, 'Operation OVERLORD', QUADRANT Conference, appendix B, Washington, Aug. 1943, Ismay File.
26 *Ibid.*
27 CCS 108 Meeting,QUADRANT Conference, Washington, 15 Aug. 1943, Reel IV.
28 *Ibid.*, 'CCS 303', 'CCS 304'.
29 FM Lord Alanbrooke, 3/A/IX, 15 Aug., 1943, p. 764.
30 JCS 104 Meeting, QUADRANT Conference, Washington, 15 Aug. 1943, Reel II.
31 *Ibid.*
32 *Ibid.*, p. 3.
33 *Ibid.*
34 J. Grigg, *Op. cit.,* p. 105.
35 CCS 109 Meeting, QUADRANT Conference,Washington, 16 Aug. 1943, Reel IV.
36 N. Parrish, *Behind the Sheltering Bomb*, (New York, 1979), p. 18.
37 CCS 108 Meeting, *Op. cit.*

38 JCS 105 Meeting, QUADRANT Conference, Washington, 16 Aug.1943, Reel II.
39 *Ibid.*, p. 2.
40 Gen. Sir W. Jackson, *Op. cit.*, pp. 104–5.
41 CCS 110 Meeting, QUADRANT Conference, 'CCS 303/3: Strategic Concept for the Defeat of the Axis in Europe',Washington, 17 Aug. 1943, Reel IV.
42 FM Lord Alanbrooke, 3/A/IX, 19 Aug. 1943, p. 776.
43 *Ibid.*, 'Notes For My Memoirs', 2/XI, 19 Aug. 1943, pp. 7–8.
44 *Ibid.*
45 *Ibid.*, p. 2.
46 '328/1: Directive to Gen. Eisenhower', Washington, 27 Aug. 1943 RG. 165 OPD.
47 CAB 79 (COS) 43 273 Meeting, 8 Nov. 1943.
48 J. Ehrman, *Grand Strategy*, V, (London, 1956), p. 9.
49 Minutes, 1st Meeting, CCS, 'President and Prime Minister', QUADRANT Conference, Washington, 19 Aug. 1943, Office of the CCS. CCS 116 Meeting, 'CCS 319/5: Final Report to the President and Prime Minister', Washington, 24 Aug. 1943, Reel IV.
50 'CCS 319/5, 'Final Report to the President and Prime Minister', QUADRANT Conference, Washington, 24 Aug., 1943, Reel IV.
51 'JCS 108 Meeting', *Op. cit.*, p. 2.
52 M. Matloff, *Op. cit.*, p. 398.
53 Minutes, 2nd Meeting: CCS, President and Prime Minister, QUADRANT Conference, Washington, 23 Aug, 1943, Reel IV.
54 FM Lord Alanbrooke, 3/A/IX, 23, Aug. 1943, p. 775.
55 *Ibid.*, 'Notes On My Memoirs', *Op. cit.*, 24 Aug. 1943, pp. 8–10.
56 'Papers and Minutes', QUADRANT Conference, Washington, Aug. 1943, pp. 87, 227, 24, Reel IV.
57 M. Matloff, *Op. cit.*, pp. 242–3.
58 JCS 108 Meeting, *Op. cit.*, p. 5.
59 AM Sir J. Slessor, *The Central Blue: Recollections and Reflections*, (London, 1956), p. 358.

6 TEHRAN: THE SECOND FRONT, THE FRENCH RESISTANCE AND THE FRENCH ARMY

1 J. Harvey, (ed.), *The Diplomatic Diaries of Oliver Harvey, 1937–1940*, (Eden's Secretary), (London, 1970), pp. 313–14; FO 371/370, 31 Oct. 1943; 20 Oct. 1943, PREM 3/172/5.
2 R. Lewin, *Churchill as Warlord*, (New York, 1973).
3 *The Documents of the Tehran, Yalta and Potsdam Conferences*, (Moscow, 1969), pp. 23–5.
4 Gen. F. Walker, *From Texas to Rome: A Gen.'s Journal*, (Dallas, 1969), pp. 288–90; B. Holden Reid, 'The Italian Campaign 1943–45: A Reappraisal of Allied Gen.ship', *Journal of Strategic Studies*, 13 1, (1990), pp. 143–4.
5 *The Documents of the Tehran, Yalta and Potsdam Conferences*, *Op. cit.*, p. 14.

6 'Eisenhower to CCS', Washington, 24 Oct. 1943, RG. 165 NAF 486 WD Cable log.
7 C. d'Este, *The Fatal Decision*, (New York, 1991), p. 413 .
8 J. Ehrman, (ed.) *Grand Strategy*, V, (London, 1956), pp. 109–11.
9 CCS 131 Meeting, Washington, 26 Nov. 1943, Reel IV.
10 COS (43)(0), 'CCS 409: 'OVERLORD and the Mediterranean', EUREKA Conference, Washington, 25 Nov. 1943, Reel IV.
11 *The Documents of the Tehran, Yalta and Potsdam Conferences, Op. cit.*, pp. 13–14.
12 Sir M. Howard, *Op. cit.*, pp. 55–8.
13 'Aegean Operations', 5–15 Oct. 1943, Map Room Papers 310, FDRL.
14 M. Stoler, *Op. cit.*, pp. 143–54.
15 R. Weigley, *Op. cit.*, p. 330.
16 *Ibid.*, p. 330.
17 'CCS 426/1: Report to the President and Prime Minister', p. 301, 6 Dec. 1943, Reel IV.
18 'CCS 398 Minutes and Papers', EUREKA Conference, 18 Nov. 1943, p. 77, Reel IV.
19 M. Foot, *SOE, The Special Operations Executive, 1940–1946*, (London, 1984), pp. 19–21; 'Subversive Activities in Relation to Strategy', Gen. Directive from the COS, 25 Nov. 1940, COS (40) 27 (0), CAB 80/56, CAB 65/14; CAB 65/8 WM (40) 209, 22 July, 1940.
20 N. Bethell, *The War Hitler Won*, (London, 1972), pp. 5–6.
21 Lord Selborne, 'SOE Assistance to OVERLORD', 13 Oct 1944, WP(44) 570, CAB 66/56.
22 B. Sweet-Escott, 'SOE in the Balkans', P. Auty & R. Clogg, (eds.), *British Policy towards Wartime Resistance in Yugoslavia and Greece*, (London, 1975), p. 5.
23 H. R. Kedward, *Occupied France*, (Oxford, 1993), pp. 46–7.
24 OSS/London, p. 12, Reel I.
25 Gen. Sir C. Gubbins, 'Resistance Movements In The War', *JRUSSI*, (3 May 1948), pp. 213.
26 'SOE Charter', CAB 65/14; CAB 65/8 WM (40) 209, 22 July 1940.
27 M. Foot, *Op. cit.*, pp. 46–8.
28 Lord H. Dalton, *Memoirs 1931–1945; The Fateful Years*, 2, (London,1957), p. 368.
29 D. Stafford, *British and European Resistance: 1940–1945*, (Oxford, 1983), p. 38.
30 CAB 84/85 JIC (42) 156 (0) 29 Apr. 1942.
31 J. Moffat to J. Dunn, Washington, 16 July 1941, DF 740.0011, RG. 59.
32 'The Distant Future', CAB 79/12 JP(41) 444, 14 June 1941.
33 'Review of Future Strategy', WO, JP (41)144, 14 June 1941.
34 *Dalton Diaries*, No. 4, 1941, 18/2 46.
35 J. Sweets, *The Politics of Resistance in France, 1940–1944*, (De Kalb, IL, 1976), pp. 231–3.
36 A. Funk, *Hidden Ally*, (New York, 1992), pp. 6–7.
37 OSS War Diary, 'Preamble to January 1944', p. xix, Reel I.
38 *Ibid.*, Major Gen. R. Barker to COS ETOUSA, p. xiv.
39 D. Stafford, *Op. cit.*, pp. 89–91.
40 Interview with Sir R. Brook, London, 29 Mar. 1994.

41 'Progress Report Operation OVERLORD', Washington, 10 Sept. 1943, RG. 331 SHAEF G-3 file 322–7 II, Ops C.
42 D. Eisenhower, *Eisenhower at War, 1943–1945*, (New York, 1986), pp. 162–6.
43 RG 165 OPD 336 France (Sec. III), Case 169, Washington, Jan. 1944, Kimball, *Op. cit.,* Churchill to Roosevelt, 30 Jan. 1944.
44 A. Funk, 'Churchill, Eisenhower and the French Resistance', *Military Affairs*, XLV, 1, Feb. 1981, (1981), p. 30.
45 *Ibid.,* p. 30; pp. 29–33; PREM 3 185/127, Jan. 1944.
46 RG 165, OPD 336, *Op. cit.*
47 RG 165, ABC 400.3295 Sec. 2A, Eisenhower to McCloy, Washington, 2 Aug. 1943.
48 RG. 331 SHAEF (44) 25, Operation Directive to SFHQ, Washington, 23 Mar. 1944, SHAEF G-3 File 322–8, Ops C.
49 *Ibid.,* 'SHAEF Mes. S-51120', Washington, 2 May 1944, p. 20.
50 J. Beevor, *Recollections and Reflections, 1940–1945*, (London, 1981), pp. 84–5.
51 Interview with Sir D. Dodds-Parker, London, 24 Mar. 1994.
52 J. Beevor, *Op. cit.,* pp. 84–5.
53 OSS War Diary, *Op. cit.,* 1., p. 28.
54 RG. 331 SHAEF, G-3 File, Outline OVERLORD, Report: 'Analysis of the Resistance Movement', 9 Dec. 1943.
55 R. Brook, *Op. cit.,* 1994.
56 Cowell to Weiss, *Allied OVERLORD Planning*, 17 Mar. 1994.
57 Maj. H. Warren, *Special Operations: AAF Aid to European Resistance Movements*, (Washington, US Air History Office, 1947).
58 Sir D. Dodds-Parker, *Op. cit.*.
59 OSS War Diary, *Op. cit.,* I, p. 39.
60 Sir D. Dodds-Parker, *Op. cit.*
61 JCS to Eisenhower, Washington, 17 Apr. 1944, RG. 331 SHAEF SGS File, 370.64 I.
62 G. Harrison, *Cross-Channel Attack*, (Washington, 1951), p. 203.
63 Gen. C. Gubbins, *Op. cit.,* pp. 211–15; P. Wilkinson & J. Astley, *Gubbins and SOE*, (London, 1993), pp, 88, 94.
64 Sir D. Dodds-Parker, *Op. cit.*
65 A. Funk, 'American Contacts with the Resistance in France, 1940–1943', *Military Affairs*, XXXIV, 1, (1970), p. 20.
66 M. R. D. Foot, IHR Seminar, London, 23 May 1995.
67 OSS War Diary, *Op. cit.*, p. xxxvii.
68 Sir R. Brook, *Op. cit.*
69 *Ibid.*
70 OSS War Diary, *Op. cit.*, 2, pp. 34–8.
71 A. Funk, *Op. cit.*; Interview with R. Brook, *Op. cit.*
72 P. Wilkinson & J. Astley, *Op. cit.,* p. 196.
73 CAB 106/982, File SGS 319/1/10, 'Monthly SFHQ Reports, June, July 1944'.
74 Lord Selborne, 'SOE Activities: Summary for the Prime Minister', Quarter: July to Sept. 1944', PREM 3, 408/1, 24 Oct. 1944.
75 OSS War Diary, *Op. cit.,* 3, p. xxiv.
76 *Ibid.,* Preamble to 1 Jan. 1944, p. 24.
77 *Ibid.,* vol. 13, Book 8.

78 *Ibid.*, p. xxiv.
79 CAB 106/982, 'SAC Eisenhower's Despatch: French Resistance Miscellanea', SGS File 337/11, 9 June, 1944.
80 OSS War Diary, *Op. cit.*, 3 'Signals of 8, 18 June 1944', pp. 229–30
81 *Ibid.*, 1, p. 26.
82 CAB 106/982; *Op. cit.*, Eisenhower: 'Relations with the French', 31 Aug. 1944.
83 W. Mack, 'Mack to Cadogan', PRO, 31 May 1944, FO 371/41993.
84 OSS War Diary, *Op. cit.*, 12, p. 75.
85 CAB 106/982, *Op. cit.*, SCAF 45, 4 June 1944.
86 D. Dilks, *Cadogan Diaries, 1938–1945*, (London, 1971), p. 635.
87 OSS War Diary, *Op. cit.*, Bross Interview 3 Dec. 1944, 1, p. 25.
88 Lord Selborne, *Op. cit.*, 'Summary, Jan. to Mar. 1944'.
89 D. Eisenhower, *Op. cit.*, p. 165.
90 J. Beevor, *Op. cit.*, pp. 154–5.
91 M. Foot, *SOE in France*, (London, 1966), pp. 257, 266, 289–90; D. Stafford, *Op. cit.*, pp. 127–30.
92 OSS War Diary, *Op. cit.*, 3, p. xviii.
93 *Ibid.*, p. xix: 'The Maquis Plan': Maquis' Memo No. 3, 26 Oct. 1943.
94 *Ibid.*, p. xxi.
95 *Ibid.*, 2, p. xiii; vol. 3.
96 *Ibid.*, 1, pp. 80–4.
97 Gen. C. Gubbins, *Op. cit.*, p. 217; D. Stafford, *Op. cit.*, pp. 154–5; G. Garrison, *Op. cit.*, pp. 206–7.
98 OSS War Diary, *Op. cit.*, 1, p. 68, 85.
99 P. Abrahams, 'Bitter Memories of the Resistance', *Financial Times*, 12 Nov. 1995, pp. 1–2.
100 O. Paxton, *Vichy France, 1940–1944*, (N.Y. 1972).
101 CAB 106/892, *Op. cit.*, File SGS 370.64 'France, Employment of FFI Agreement between Eisenhower and Koenig', 26 Aug. 1944.
102 Gen. C. Gubbins, *Op. cit.*, p. 218.
103 Lord Selborne, *Op. cit.*, Summary from July–Sept. 1944.
104 Battle of Gheluvelt Crossroads, 29 Oct. 1914.
105 Sir D. Dodds-Parker, *Op. cit.*; Interview with Lt. Col. Sir P. Thorne, London, 17 May 1994.
106 A. Burn, *The Fighting Captain*, (London, 1993), pp. 146, 160.
107 Sir R. Brook, *Op. cit.*
108 Gen. C. de Gaulle, *Mémoires de Guerre*, 'Note établie par le Cabinet du Général de Gaulle et du général Eisenhower, à la villa des Glycines, le 30 Décembre 1943', (Paris, 1956), p. 676.
109 CCS 13 Meeting, Washington, 24 Mar. 1942, Reel III.
110 J. Vernet, 'Les Projets de réorganisation de l'Armée de terre Française de 1945 à 1946', *Revue historique des Armées*, (1979), p. 228.
111 *Ibid.*
112 Marshall to Hull Washington, 20 Nov. 1943, Rg 165 OPD, 336, France, Sec. 1.
113 FRUS, *Washington and Quebec*, 1943, 159–60.
114 M. Vigneras, *Rearming the French*, (Washington, 1957), pp. 9–13.
115 Gen. J. Deane to JCS, 22 Washington, Apr. 1943, RG. 165 OPD 400 France, Sec. 1.

116 Churchill to Roosevelt, Doc. 216, 24 Mar. 1943, FDRL.
117 CCS Meeting 75, Washington, 12 Mar. 1943, Reel III.
118 CCS, Special Meeting, 'Giraud', Washington, 8 July 1943, Reel III.
119 CCS 75 Meeting, Washington, 12 Mar. 1943, Reel III..
120 CCS 87 Meeting, 'TRIDENT', Washington 18 May 1943, Reel III.
121 M. Vigneras, *Op. cit.,* p. 58.
122 *Ibid.,* p. 39.
123 Eisenhower to OPD and Marshall, 17 Feb. 1943, Rg 165 Message 1453.
124 Roosevelt to Murphy, Washington, 20 Feb. 1943, RG 165, OPD. Exec. 1.
125 CCS, Special Meeting, 'Giraud', 8 July 1943, *Op. cit.*
126 JCS Meeting with the President, Washington, 15 Nov. 1943.
127 Eisenhower to Marshall, 18 Feb. 1943, Murphy to Sec. of State for President, 20 Feb. 1943; Marshall to Eisenhower, 20 Feb. 1943, JRC 902/II 'Rearmament Plan', RG. 165 Exec. 1.
128 JCS Meeting with the President, *Op. cit.*
129 *Ibid.*
130 Hopkins to Monnet, Washington, 22 Feb. 1943, JRC 902/II 'Rearmament Plan', RG. 165. Exec. 1.
131 JCS 101 Meeting, 'Bessell Report', p. 3, Washington, 7 Aug. 1943, Reel III.
132 *Ibid.,* p. 3; Wedemeyer to COS, 28 April, 1943 RG. 165 OPD 381 Security, 118.
133 Col. V. Lockhart, *T-Patch to Victory*, (Canyon, TX, 1981), pp. 131–7; C. Gabel, *Op. cit.,* pp. 30–4.
134 JCS 101 Meeting, *Op. cit.,* p. 4.
135 Interview with A. Funk, 29 Sept. 1994, Rennes, France.
136 Marshal A. Juin, *Mémoires*, (Paris, 1960), pp. 300–2.
137 Gen. J. de Tassigny, *Histoire de la Première Armée Française*, (Paris, 1949).
138 Steyer to Eisenhower, Msg. 2627, 16 Nov. 1943, RG 165, JRC 400.1/007 'Substituting From Theater Stocks'.
139 Marshall to Eisenhower, Washington, 18 May 1943, RG. 165, Messages 6213 & 8565, Eisenhower to Marshall, 1 May 1943, JRC Cable Log.
140 RG 165 Memo, G-2 MIS WD for ACOS OPD, 28 Aug. 1943, OPD 226.2 France, Sec. 1.
141 M. Vigneras, *Op. cit.,* p. 404.

7 ANVIL, OVERLORD AND THE ITALIAN CAMPAIGN

1 F. Loewenheim, et al., (eds.), *Op. cit.,* pp. 386–8.
2 CAB 79 (COS), 14, 19 Oct. 1943.
3 F. Loewenheim, et al., *Op. Cit.,* pp. 370–4, pp. 312–13.
4 JCS 117 Meeting, Washington, 5 Oct. 1943, Reel II.
5 FRUS *Cairo and Tehran*, 1943, Washington, 22 Nov. 1943, pp. 301–3, 327–30.
6 *Ibid.*
7 J. Holland, *The Aegean Mission*, (New York 1988), pp. 169, 172.
8 FM Lord Alanbrooke, *Op. cit.,* 3/A/X 1 Nov. 1943, 808.
9 K. Sainsbury, *Op cit.,* p. 177.
10 Lord Moran, *Op. cit.,* p. 152.

11 FM Lord Alanbrooke, *Op. cit.,* 3/A/X, 18 Nov. 1943, 823.
12 J. Eisenhower to Author, 2 Aug. 1994.
13 JCS 120 Meeting, Washington, 26 Oct. 1943, Reel II.
14 Richard Collins Papers, 'Details for SEXTANT', quoted in T. Parrish, *Roosevelt and Marshall,* (New York, 1989), p. 374.
15 JCS 131 Meeting, Washington, 26 Nov. 1943, Reel II.
16 *Ibid.*
17 *Ibid.*
18 *Ibid.*
19 CCS 128 Meeting, SEXTANT Conference, Washington, 24 Nov. 1943, Reel IV; F. Pogue Interview with Marshall quoted in T. Parrish, *Op. cit.,* p. 390.
20 FM Lord Alanbrooke, *Op. cit.,* 3/A/X, 26 Nov. 1943, 830.
21 J. Stilwell, T. White, (ed.), *The Stilwell Papers*, (New York, 1948), p. 245.
22 Col. C. Donnelley, quoted in T. Parrish, *Op. cit.,* pp. 384–6.
23 CCS 132 Meeting. EUREKA Conference, 30 Nov. 1943, Washington, Reel IV; G.A. Harrison, *Op. cit.,* p. 125.
24 CAB 65/40 WM(43)169, 13 Dec. 1943.
25 Gen. T. Handy Interview Washington, 28 Sept. 1956, RG 165, 'Plan for Invasion of Southern France'; JPS 249, Washington, 5 Aug. 1943, 'Study, Operation Against Southern France'; 'ABC 384 Europe' (5 Aug. 1943), 9-A, 29 Nov. 1943, RG 165 WPD.
26 'Papers and Minutes of Meetings', SEXTANT Conference, (Washington 1943).
27 FRUS, *Cairo and Tehran, Op. cit.,* pp. 699–705.
28 FM Lord Alanbrooke, *Op. cit.,* 3/A/X, 4 Dec. 1943, p. 858.
29 'Papers and Minutes of Meetings', SEXTANT Conference, *Op. cit.*
30 R. Parkinson, *Alamein to VE Day,* (London, 1974), pp. 197–208.
31 'Preparation for Future US–British Conferences', Washington, 31 Dec. 1943, Rg 218.
32 A. Perlmutter, *FDR and Stalin,* (London, 1993), p. 55.
33 D. Kaiser, 'Churchill, Roosevelt and the Limits of Power', *International Security,* 10:1, (Summer, 1985), 204–21.
34 H. Bruenn, MD, 'Clinical notes on the Illness and Death of President Franklin D. Roosevelt', *Annals of Internal Medicine,* (April 1970).
35 COSSAC (44) 5, Op. ANVIL, Washington, 6 Jan. 44, RG. 331, SHAEF SGS FILE 370.2/2 I.
36 CCS 142 Meeting., Washington, 21 Jan. 1944, Reel IV; J. Hobbs, *Dear Gen.: Eisenhower's Wartime Letters to Marshall,* (Baltimore, 1971), pp. 131–48.
37 'Firm Recommendations with Regard to Operations ANVIL and OVERLORD', RG. 331, SGS File 370.2/2 I; CCS Meeting 144, 'CCS 465/4', Washington, 4 Feb. 1944, Reel IV.
38 FM Lord Alanbrooke, *Op. cit.,* 3/B/XI, 19 Jan. 1944, p. 895.
39 JCS 'Record of SHAEF on OVERLORD and ANVIL', Washington, 5 Feb. 1944, Reel II.
40 Eisenhower to CCS, 'Meeting, London', 8, 9 Feb. 1944, RG. 165, Exec. 10, Box 54.
41 CCS 145 Meeting, Washington, 11 Feb. 1944, Reel IV.
42 Eisenhower, Memo 'OVERLORD/ANVIL Conference', London, 11 Feb., 1944, RG 165, Exec. 10, Box 54.

43 Col. P. Munch, 'Gen. George C. Marshall and the Army Staff', *Military Review*, lvxxiv, 8, (Aug.,1994),14–23.
44 J. Charmley, *Op. cit.*, p. 92.
45 P. Winfield, *Bye Bye Baby*, (London, 1992), p. 3.
46 D. Reynolds, *The American Occupation of Britain, 1942–1945*, (N. Y., 1995); G. Smith, *When Jim Crow Met John Bull,* (London, 1987), pp.1–4, 186.
47 FM Lord Wilson, *Report by the SACMED to the CCS on Ops in So. France August 1944*, p. 8.
48 FM Lord Alanbrooke, *Op. cit.*, 3/B/XI, 16 Feb. 1944, 902.
49 Eisenhower to Marshall, Washington, 6 Feb. 1944, RG. 331 'OVERORD/ANVIL' SHAEF SGS file 381.
50 Marshall to Eisenhower, *Op. cit.*, Washington, 7 Feb. 1944, CM-OUT 277; J. Hobbs, *Op. cit.*, 134, 138–41.
51 JCS 147 Meeting; 'Meeting with the President', Washington, 21 Feb. 1944, Reel II.
52 *Ibid.*
53 *Ibid.*
54 *Ibid.*
55 *Ibid.*
56 *Ibid.*
57 Special Meeting, 'OVERLORD/ANVIL', London, 17 Feb. 1944, RG. 331 SHAEF SGS File 381 I.
58 Interview with Sir R. Kilner Brown, London, 22 Oct. 1994.
59 'Battle of Numbers', Washington 8 Feb. 1944, RG. 165 OPD Exec. 10. Item 522.
60 Lord Moran, *Op. cit.*, p. 180.
61 F. Hinsley, *British Intelligence in the Second World War*, III, Pt. I, (London, 1984), p. 185; CAB 121/592, NAF 577, 3 Jan. 1944.
62 Maj. Gen. J. Lucas, 'Meeting. Alexander's Headquarters', 8 Jan. 1944, *J. P. Lucas Papers,* as quoted in D. Graham & S. Bidwell, *Tug of War,* (London, 1986), p. 138.
63 F. Hinsley, *Op. cit.*, pp. 173, 176.
64 FM H. Wilson, *Report by SACMED to the CCS on the Italian Campaign, May to December 1944*, Pt. II, 1946, p. 2.
65 G. Boulle, *Le Corps Expéditionnaire Français en Italie, 1943–44*, (Paris, 1973), p. 310.
66 F. Hinsley, *Op. cit.*, pp. 173–81.
67 R. Bennett, 'Intelligence and Strategy in World War II', K. G. Robertson, (ed.), *British and American Approaches to Intelligence*, (London, 1987), pp. 142–3.
68 Maj. F. Galgano, 'The Landings at Anzio', *Military Review*, (Jan. 1994), pp. 69–71.
69 A. Horne & Lord D. Montgomery, *Monty, The Lonely Leader*, (London, 1994), pp. 78–9.
70 'Gen. B. Somervell and Adm. F. Horne to Roosevelt: Landing Craft for BOLERO', Washington, 14 May 1942, RG 165 WDCSA 400 (S); R. Weigley, *Op cit.*, pp. 330–1.
71 R. Lewin, *Montgomery As Military Commander*, (New York, 1971), pp. 175–6.
72 Gen. G. Marshall, 'Shipping', Washington, 18 Feb. 1942, PSF, box 3, FDRL.

73 *Ibid.*, Horne, p. 79; N. Hamilton, *Monty, Master of the Battlefield 1942–1944*, (London, 1983), p. 526.
74 COS to JSM, 'Landing Craft', Washington, 19 Feb. 1944, RG 165 OPD CM-IN 14255.
75 F. Hinsley, *Op. cit.*, pp. 24–6.
76 Montgomery to Eisenhower, Washington, 21 Feb. 1944, RG. 165, Exec. 9, Book 15, Box 45.
77 Eisenhower to Montgomery, *Op. cit.*
78 FM. H. Wilson, *Op. cit.*, pp. 7, 11–12.
79 CCS 147 Meeting, Washington, 25 Feb. 1944, Reel IV.
80 Eisenhower to Marshall, Washington, 21 Mar. 1944, RG 165 OPD CM-IN 15429.
81 CCS 151 Meeting, 'OVERLORD and ANVIL' CCS 465/14, Washington, 24 Mar. 1944, Reel IV.
82 Sir M. Howard, *Op. cit.*, p. 69.
83 CCS 158 Meeting, Washington, 28 Mar. 1944, Reel IV.
84 *Ibid.*
85 CCS Meeting, Washington, 29 Mar. 1944, Reel IV.
86 *Ibid.*
87 FM Lord Alanbrooke, 3/B/XII, 22 Mar. 1944.
88 Brig. Gen. F. Roberts to Gen. T. Handy, 'What Shall We Do About ANVIL?', Washington, 23 Mar. 1944, RG. 165 OPD Exec. 9 Book 16.
89 B. H. Reed, 'The Italian Campaign 1943–45: A Reappraisal of Allied Generalship', *JSS*, 13 1, (1990), pp.128–61.
90 D. Graham & S. Bidwell, *Op. cit.*, pp. 398–404.
91 PREM 3/333/19, Churchill to Gen. Ismay for COS, 19 July 1943.
92 Sir M. Howard, *Op. cit.*, pp. 61–2.
93 T. Barker, 'The Ljubljana Gap Strategy: Alternate to Anvil/Dragoon or Fantasy?', *JMH*, 56, (1 Jan. 1992), pp. 73–4.
94 D. Graham. &. S. Bidwell, *Op. cit.*, p. 400.
95 Brig. C. Molony, *Official History of the Second World War*, VI, Pt. I, (London, 1956), p. 313.
96 Eisenhower to Marshall, 29 June 1944, RG. 218, JCS, Box 4, Chair. File.
97 R. Weigley, *Eisenhower's Lieutenants*, (Bloomington, IL, 1981), p. 332.
98 T. Barker, *Op. cit.*, p. 61.
99 'JCS Operations to Assist OVERLORD', Washington, 29 June 1944, Reel VII.
100 Dr Kehrig, Director of German Military Archives, 'Le Débarquement de Provence; Le Point de Vue Allemand', *Terre*, 57, (Sept. 1994), pp. 22–3.
101 T. Barker, *Op. cit.*, p. 83.
102 JSM 1613, JSM to COS, 31 Mar. 1944, CAB 105/45; FMD 183, Dill to COS, 1 Apr. 1944, CAB 105/85.
103 Dill to COS, Washington, 1 Apr. 1944, RG 165 Exec. 10 Item 66; Churchill to Dill for Marshall, Washington, 16 Apr. 1944, Rg 165 Exec 3 OPD.
104 Sir R. Kilner Brown, *Op. cit.*, London, 22 Oct. 1994.
105 Adm. E. Cochrane, 'Additional Landing Craft Program', CCS 560, Sec. 2', Washington, 17 Aug. 1943, RG. 218, JCS.
106 T. Wilson, 'The United States Leviathan', W. Reynolds & A. Chubarian, (eds), *Allies At War*, (London, 1994), p. 191.
107 S. Parker, *Op. cit.*, p. 140; Rg 331 SHAEF SGS Files 381 1, '387/11'.
108 'CCS: OVERLORD and ANVIL', Washington, 8 Apr. 1944, Reel IV.

109 FM Lord Alanbrooke, *Op. cit.*, 3/B/XII, 19 Apr. 1944, p. 937.
110 *Op. cit.*, ADD, MSS 52577, *Cunningham Papers.*
111 'CCS 465/22', Washington, 17 Apr. 1944, Reel IV.
112 CAB 105/45 JSM 1620, JSM to COS, 10 Apr. 1944.
113 CCS 154 Meeting, Washington, 8 Apr. 1944, Reel IV; CAB 105/85, Dill to COS, 4 Apr. 1944.
114 CCS 158 Meeting, Washington, 28 Apr. 1944, Reel IV.
115 'CCS 561': 'Operations in Support of OVERLORD', Washington, 27 Apr. 1944, Reel IV.
116 *Ibid.*, 1 May 1944.
117 *Ibid.*, 7 May 1944.
118 FM H. Wilson, *Report by the SACMED to the CCS on Ops in So. France August 1944*, (London, 1946), pp. 21–5.
119 CCS 160 Meeting, 'CCS 454/6: Review of Conditions in Europe', Washington, 26 May 1944, Reel IV.
120 Eisenhower to Marshall, 29 June 1944. *Op. cit.*
121 *Op. cit.*, 10 June 1944, 'CCS 561/5': from AFHQ, Wilson in COSMED 120 is aiming at a target date of 15 August for ANVIL and CCS 162 Meeting, 'CCS 561/5', Washington, 10 June 1944, Reel IV.
122 CAB 122/1246, B 12995 Wilson to Eisenhower, 19 June 1944.
123 Lt. Col. R. Leigh, *48 Millions Tons to Eisenhower*, (Washington DC, 1945), pp. 17–21.
124 FM H. Wilson, *Report by SACMED to the CCS on the Italian Campaign*, II (London, 1948), pp. 33–6; Wilson to COS, AFHQ, Washington, 24 June, 1944, RG. 218, Box 4, JCS Chairman's File.
125 A. Chandler, (ed.), *Op. cit.*, p. 1938.
126 LETOD 150, Redman to Hollis, CAB 122/1246, 27 June 1944.
127 Ike to CCS, CAB 122/1246 SCAF 53, 23 June 1944.
128 CCS 166 Meeting, 15 June, 1944, Reel IV and 'CCS 603 Operations to Assist OVERLORD', Washington, 24 June 1944.
129 *Ibid.*
130 COS to JSM, CAB 122/1246COS (W), 26 June 1944.
131 JSM 114, JSM to COS, CAB 122/1246 27 June 1944.
132 *Ibid.*
133 'CCS Ops to Assist OVERLORD', Washington, 27 June 1944, Reel IV.
134 *Ibid.*
135 *Ibid.*
136 *Ibid.*
137 S.L. Parker, *Attendant Lords: A Study of the British JSM in Washington, 1941–1945*, (unpublished doctoral thesis, University of Maryland, 1984), p. 263.
138 FM Lord Alanbrooke, *Op. cit.*, Vol. 3/B/XII, 28 June 1944; ADD, MSS 52577, *Cunningham Papers*, BL.
139 R. Bennett, *Ultra and Mediterranean Strategy, 1941–45*, (London, 1989), p. 362.
140 135, COS to JSM, CAB 122/1246 COS (W) 134, COS (W), 28 June 1944.
141 R. Bennett, *Op. Cit.*
142 JSM 118, JSM to COS, CAB 122/1246, 29 June 1944.
143 *Cunningham Papers*, *Op. cit.*
144 W. Kimball, et al., *Op. cit.*, 'C-717', 'C-718', 28 June 1994.

145 *Ibid.,* 'R-573', 28 June 1944.
146 *Ibid.,* 'C-721', 1 July 1944.
147 *Ibid.,* 'R-577', 1 July, 1944.
148 FM Lord Alanbrooke, *Op. cit.,* 3/B/XII, 29 June 1944, p. 971; Roosevelt to Churchill, 'R-574', 29 June 1944.
149 Churchill to Roosevelt, *Op. cit.,* 'C-721'.
150 *Ibid.,* 30 June, 1944, p. 971.
151 COSMED 139, Box 310 (ANVIL), 2 July 1944, FDRL.
152 *Cunningham Papers, Op. cit.,* 5 July 1944.
153 John Ehrman, *Op. cit.,* p. 361.
154 H. Macmillan, *Op. cit.,* p. 420.
155 Winant to Roosevelt, Box 310 (ANVIL), 3 July 1944, FDRL.
156 Sir A. Bryant, *Triumph in the West,* (New York, 1959), p. 168.
157 M. Gilbert, *Winston S. Churchill, Road to Victory, 1941–1945,* (London, 1986), p. 843.
158 166, COS to JSM CAB 122/1308, COS (W.), 12 July 1944.
159 Redman to Noble, CAB 122/1308, 18 July 1944.
160 Noble to COS, CAB 122/1308: JSM 142, 19 July 1944, COS (W) 183, COS to Noble, 20 July.
161 CCS 168 Meeting, 28 July 1944, Reel IV; JSM 159, JSM to COS, 27 July 1944, 'Excerpt of Min. of Operations to Assist OVERLORD'; CAB 122/1308; JSM 163 JSM to COS, 28 July 1944.
162 W. Churchill, *The Second World War,* VI, (London, 1953), p. 58.
163 CAB 122/1308 MEDCOS 167, 5 Aug. 1944.
164 M. Matloff, *Op. cit.,* p. 473.
165 W. Kimball, *Op. cit.,* 'C to R', C-742, 4 Aug. 1944.
166 FM Lord Alanbrooke, *Op. cit.,* 3/B/XII, p. 992.
167 Lord Moran, *Op. cit.,* p. 181.
168 M. Miller, *Ike the Soldier,* (New York, 1987), p. 674.
169 R. Ferrell, (ed.), *The Eisenhower Diaries,* (New York, 1981), pp. 111–25.
170 F. Harbutt, 'Churchill, Hopkins and the "Other" Americans: An Alternative perspective on Anglo–American Relations, 1941–1945', *IHR,* VIII, (May 1986), p. 252.
171 W. Churchill, *Op. cit.,* pp. 58–9.
172 W. Kimball, III, *Op. cit.,* R to C, 'R-596', 8 Aug. 1944.
173 JSM to COS, CAB 105/46, JSM 180, IZ 5728, 7 Aug. 1944.
174 Eisenhower to Marshall, Washington, Aug. 1944, RG. 165 CM-IN.
175 CCS to Eisenhower, CAB 122/1309, 10 Aug. 1944.
176 T. Ben-Moshe, *Op. cit.,* p. 264; J. Strange, 'The British Rejection of Operation SLEDGEHAMMER, An Alternative Motive', *JMA,* 46, (February 1982), pp. 6–15.
177 *US Seventh Army: Report of Operations in France and Germany,* (Heidelberg, 1946), pp. 1–29.
178 A. Wilt, *The French Riviera Campaign of August 1944,* (Carbondale, IL) pp. 50–3.
179 J. Turner & R. Jackson, *Destination Berchtesgarden,* (London, 1975), pp. 28–38.
180 Author's personal experience: 15 Aug. 1944.
181 Gen. Sir H. Wilson, 'DRAGOON', 16 Aug. 1944, Sp. Files, box 300, FDRL.
182 Adm. H. Hewitt, 'DRAGOON', 15 Aug. 1944, Sp. Files, box 300, FDRL.

183 Gen. Sir H. Wilson, *Op. cit.*
184 J. Clarke & R. Smith, *From the Riviera to the Rhine*, (Washington, 1993), pp. 80, 142.
185 J. Hobbs, *Op. cit.*, p. 203.
186 J. Clarke & R. Smith, *Op. cit.*, pp. 197–8; R. Weigley, *Op. cit.*, p. 237.
187 W. Gould, *The Campaign in Southern France*, Air Ministry, London, AHB/II/117/13, p. 90.
188 A. Wilt, *Op. Cit.*
189 Lt. Col. R. Leigh, *Op. cit.*, p. 46.
190 Gen. Sir W. Jackson et al., *Op. cit.*, p. 200.
191 J. Carke & R. Smith, *Op. cit.*, pp. 59–61.
192 R. Bennett, *Op. cit.*, pp. 296–7.
193 W. Deakin et al., *Op. cit.*, p. 9.
194 Maj. G. Higgins, 'German and US Operational Art: A Contrast in Maneuver', *Military Review*, (Oct. 1985), pp. 22–9; R. Weigley, 'To the Crossing of the Rhine: American Strategic Thought in World War II', *Armed Forces and Society*, 5, 2, Feb., (1979), pp. 303–20.

8 CONCLUSIONS

1 L. Kennett, *The American Soldier in World War II,* (New York, 1987), pp. 15–17.
2 D. Reynolds, *Op. cit.*, p. 182.
3 T. Ben-Moshe, *Op. cit.*, p. 111.
4 O. A. Rzbesbevsky, 'The Soviet Union – The Direct Strategy', D. Reynolds, W. F. Kimball & A. O. Chubarian (eds.), *Op. cit.*, pp. 41–3.
5 T. Wilson, 'The United States Leviathan', *Op. cit.*, pp. 175.
6 G. Crowther, *Paying for the War*, (Oxford, 1940), p. 3.
7 FM Lord Alanbrooke, *Op. cit.*, 3/A/VIII, 21 Jan. 1943, p. 610.
8 Maj. D. Bolger, 'Zero Effects', *Military Review*, (May 1991), pp. 61–72.
9 Maj. G. Scott, 'British and German Operational Styles in World War II', *Military Review*, (Oct. 1985), pp. 38–41.
10 Interview with Keith Sainsbury, London, 14 Mar. 1995.
11 Jackson to Author, *Op. cit.*, p. 5.
12 R. Bennett, *Op. cit.*, pp. 296–7.
13 W. Jackson, et al., *Op. cit.*, p. 200.
14 A. Wilt, *Op. cit.*, p. 168.
15 M. Matloff, 'The Anvil Decision, Crossroads of Strategy', *US Naval Institute Proceedings,* (Annapolis MD, 1958), p. 389.
16 Jackson, *Op. cit.*
17 M. Stoler, *Op. cit.*, pp. 325–6.
18 Sir B. Liddell Hart, *Op. cit.*, 15/15/1, p. 5.
19 Interview with Mark Stoler, 4 Nov. 1994, FDRL.

Bibliography

UNPUBLISHED MATERIAL

Official documents

Great Britain
Prime Minister's Office: Operational papers, PREM 3. (PRO)
Prime Minister's Office: Confidential papers, PREM 4. (PRO)
Cabinet Minutes and Memoranda, CAB 65, 66. (PRO)
Chiefs of Staff Committee Minutes and Memoranda, CAB 79, 80. (PRO)
Minister of Defence, Secretariat files, CAB 120. (PRO)
Joint Staff Mission, Washington, CAB 122. (PRO)
Minister of Defence, Historical Section of the Cabinet: *The Higher Strategic Decisions of the War*, 1939–45, 4 volumes (MoD)

United States
Records of Joint Chiefs of Staff, *Minutes*, RG 218. (NARA)
US Army: War Department Operations Division, RG 165. (NARA)
Office of Strategic Services: Standard Files, RG 226. (NARA)
Office of Strategic Services: *OSS London, War Diaries*, (KCL)
Records of the Joint Chiefs of Staff: *The European Theater*, (KCL)

Private papers

Great Britain
Alanbrooke, Field Marshal Lord, (KCL)
Cunningham, Admiral of the Fleet Lord, (BL)
Harvey, Oliver, (BL)
Kirkman, Lt. General Sir Sidney, (KCL)
Ismay, General Lord, (KCL)
Liddell Hart, Sir Basil, (KCL)
Montgomery, Field Marshal Lord, (IWM)
Montgomery-Massingberd, Field Marshal Sir (KCL)
Slessor, Marshal of the RAF, Sir John, (AHB)

United States
Biddle, Francis, (FDRL)
Conant, J. B., *Conant–Douglas Letters,* (University of Arizona Library)
Hopkins, Harry L., (FDRL)
Leahy, William D., Fleet Admiral, (LoC)
McCrea, John L., Vice Admiral, (FDRL)
Mellett, Lowell, (FDRL)
Roosevelt, Franklin D., (FDRL)
Rosenman, Samuel, L., (FDRL)

PUBLISHED OFFICIAL DOCUMENTS

International

Kimball, W. F., *Churchill and Roosevelt: The Complete Correspondence*, I–III, (Princeton, 1984)

Great Britain

Principal War Telegrams and Memoranda, 1940–43: Washington/America, UK and Europe, (London, 1976)

United States

Foreign Relations of the United States:

Conferences at Washington, 1941–42, and Casablanca, 1943, (Washington, 1968)
1942, II, (Washington, 1962)
Conferences at Washington and Quebec, 1943, (Washington, 1970)
Conferences at Cairo and Tehran, 1943, (Washington, 1961)
1943, II, (Washington, 1964)
1943, III (Washington, 1963)

Russia

The Tehran Yalta & Potsdam Conferences (Documents), (Moscow, 1969)

MEMOIRS, COLLECTED LETTERS, PUBLISHED DIARIES, ETC.

Great Britain

Bryant, A., *The Turn of the Tide, 1939–43,* (London, 1957),
—— *Triumph in the West, 1943–46*, (London, 1959)
Churchill, W. S., *The Second World War*, III, (London, 1950); IV, (London, 1951); V, (London, 1952)
Colville, J., *The Fringes of Power: Downing Street Diaries, 1939–1955*, (London, 1985)
Danchev, A. (ed.), *Establishing the Anglo-American Alliance: The Second World War Diaries of Brigadier Vivian Dykes*, (Oxford, 1990)
De Gaulle, C., Gen., *The Complete War Memoirs of Charles de Gaulle*, (New York, 1964)
De Tassigny, J. L., *Histoire de la Premiére Armée Française*, (Paris, 1949)
Dilks, D. (ed.), *The Diaries of Sir Alexander Cadogan, 1938–1945*, (London, 1971)
Gladwyn, Lord, *Memoirs*, (London, 1972)
Harvey, J. (ed.), *The War Diaries of Oliver Hardy, 1941–45*, (London, 1978)
Ismay, Lord, *Memoirs*, (London, 1960)
Juin, A., *Mémoires*, (Paris, 1960)
Kennedy, J., *The Business of War*, (London, 1957)
Macmillan, H., *The Blast of War*, (London, 1967)

Moran, Lord, *Winston Churchill: The Struggle For Survival, 1940–1965*, (London, 1966)
Pimlott, B. (ed.), *The Second World War Diary of Hugh Dalton, 1940–1945*, (London, 1986)
Slessor, J., *The Central Blue*, (London, 1956)
Wheeler–Bennett, J. (ed.), *Action This Day: Working With Churchill*, (London, 1968)
—— *Special Relaltionships*, (London, 1975)

United States
Blum, J. M. (ed.), *From the Morgenthau Diaries: Years of War, 1941–1945*, (Boston, 1967)
Butcher, H., *My Three Years With Eisenhower*, (London, 1946)
Chandler, A. D. (ed.), *The Papers of Dwight David Eisenower: The War Years*, I–III, (Baltimore, 1970).
Clark, M., *Calculated Risk*, (London, 1951)
Eisenhower, D. D., *Crusade in Europe*, (London, 1948)
Ferrell, R. H. (ed.), *The Eisenhower Diaries*, (New York, 1981)
Leahy, W. D., *I Was There*, (London, 1950)
Murphy, R., *Diplomat Among Warriors*, (London, 1964)
Stilwell, J. W., *The Stilwell Papers*, T. H. White, (ed.), (New York, 1948)
Stimson, H. L. & Bundy, M., *On Active Service In Peace and War*, (New York, 1948)
Truscott, L. K., *Command Missions Wedemeyer Reports!*, (New York, 1958)
Wedemeyer, A. C.,*Wedemeyer Reports!*, (New York, 1958)

Secondary Works: Books

Acheson, D., *Present At The Creation*, (New York, 1969)
Ambrose, S. E., *The Supreme Commander: The War Years of Gen. Dwight D. Eisenhower*, (Garden City, 1970)
—— *Eisenhower*, vol. 1, (New York 1983)
—— *Rise To Globalism*, (London, 1988)
Armstrong, A., *Unconditional Surrender*, (Westport, 1974)
Arnold, H. H., *Global Mission*, (New York, 1949)
Barker, E., *Churchill and Eden at War*, (London, 1978)
Barnett, C., *The Collapse of British Power*, (London, 1972)
—— *The Audit of War*, (London, 1987)
Beard, 'C. A., Roosevelt Deceived the Public', *The Roosevelt Diplomacy and World War II*, Dallek, R., (ed.), (New York, 1948)
Beevor, J. G., *SOE, Recollections and Reflections, 1940–1945*, (London, 1981)
Beloff, M., 'The Special Relationship: An Anglo American Myth', *A Century of Conflict*, M. Gilbert, (ed.), (London, 1966)
Ben-Moshe, T., *Churchill: Strategy and History*, (Boulder, 1992)
—— 'The Origins of the Declaration of the Policy of Unconditional Surrender: A New Interpretation', (unpublished study, Hebrew University, 1981)
Bennett, R., 'Intelligence and Strategy in World War II', *British and American Approaches to Intelligence*, K. G. Robertson, (ed.), (London, 1987)
—— *Ultra and Mediterranean Strategy 1941–1945*, (London, 1989)

—— *Behind the Battle*, (London, 1994)
Bethell, N., *The War Hitler Won*, (London, 1972)
Bond, B., *Liddell Hart: A Study of His Military Thought*, (London, 1977)
Boulle, G., *Le Corps Expéditionnaire Français en Italie, 1943–44*, (Paris, 1973)
Bourne, K., *Britain and the Balance of Power in North America 1815–1908*, (London, 1967)
Brammal, Field Marshal Lord & Jackson, General Sir, *The Chiefs*, (London, 1992)
Brook, Sir R., 'The London Operation: The British View', *The Secrets War: The OSS in WWII*, G. C. Chalou, (ed.), (Washington, 1992)
Brown, Sir R. K., *Top Brass and No Brass*, (Lewes, 1991)
Buell, T. B., *Master of Sea Power*, (Boston, 1980)
Burn, A., *The Fighting Captain*, (London, 1993)
Butler, J. R. M., *Grand Strategy*, III, (London, 1964)
Campbell, A. E., 'Franklin Roosevelt and Unconditional Surrender', *Diplomacy and Intelligence during the Second World War*, R. Langhorne, (ed.), (Cambridge, 1985)
Cantrill, H. (ed.), *Public Opinion, 1935–1946*, (Princeton, 1951)
Carlton, D., *Britain and the Suez Crisis*, (Oxford, 1988)
Calvocoressi, G.W. P. et al., *Total War*, (New York, 1989)
Chandler, A. D. (ed.), *The Papers of Dwight D. Eisenhower*, (Baltimore, 1970)
Charmley, J., *Churchill's Grand Alliance*, (London, 1995)
Churchill, W. S., *The World Crisis*, (London, 1931)
—— *Marlborough, His Life and Times*, (New York, 1937)
—— *The Second World War*, (Boston, 1950)
Clark, W., *Less Than Kin*, (London, 1957)
—— *Special Relationship*, (Boston, 1968)
Clarke, J. J. & Smith, R. R., *From the Riviera to the Rhine*, (Washington, 1993)
Clayton, A., *Three Marshals of France*, (London, 1992)
Cline, R. S., *Washington Command Post: The Operations Division*, (Washington, 1951)
Cohen, W. I., *The American Revisionists – The Lessons of Intervention in World War I*, (Chicago, 1967)
Coleville, J., *The Fringes of Power*, (London, 1985)
—— *The Churchillians*, (London, 1981)
Craig, G. A., 'The Political Leader As Strategist', *Makers of Modern Strategy*, P. Paret, (ed.), (Oxford, 1990)
Cray, E., *General of the Army: George C. Marshall, Soldier & Statesman*, (New York, 1990)
Crefeld, M. V., *Fighting Power, German and US Army Performance, 1939–1945*, (London, 1983)
Cunningham, A. B., Admiral of the Fleet Viscount, *A Sailor's Odyssey*, (London, 1951)
D'Este, C., *The Fatal Decision*, (New York, 1991)
Dallek, R., 'The Roosevelt Diplomacy & WWII', *The Roosevelt Diplomacy & WWII*, R. Dallek, (ed.), (New York, 1970)
—— *Franklin D. Roosevelt and American Foreign Policy, 1932–1945*, (Oxford, 1979)
Danchev, A., *Very Special Relationship*, (London, 1986)
'Dill', *Churchill's Generals*, J. Keegan, (ed.), (London, 1991)
Darman, P., *A–Z of the SAS*, (London, 1992)

Davis, V. E., *The History of the JCS in WW II, Organization Development*, 2, (Washington, 1972).
Deakin, W., *British Political & Military Strategy in Central, Eastern, & Southern Europe in 1944*, (London, 1988)
Deane, J. R., *The Strange Alliance*, (New York, 1947)
De Jong, L., *The German Fifth Column in the Second World War*, (Chicago, 1956)
Dimbleby, D. & Reynolds, D., *An Ocean Apart*, (New York, 1988)
Dodds-Parker, D., *Setting Europe Ablaze*, (London, 1983)
Dyer, G. C., *The Amphibians Came to Conquer*, (Washington, 1969)
Eckes, Alfred E., Jr, *The United States and the Global Struggle for Minerals*, (Austin, 1979)
Edmonds, R., *The Big Three*, (New York, 1991)
Edwards, R. N. K., *Operation Neptune*, (London, 1946)
Ehrman, J., *Grand Strategy*, V, (London, 1956)
Eisenhower, D., *Eisenhower at War, 1943–1945*, (New York, 1986)
Eisenhower, D. D., *Crusade in Europe*, (London, 1948)
Ferrell, R. H. (ed.), *The Eisenhower Diaries*, (New York, 1981)
Foot, M. R. D., *SOE in France*, (London, 1966)
—— *SOE, The Special Operations Executive, 1940–1946*, (London, 1984)
—— 'A Comparison of SOE and OSS', *British and American Approaches to Intelligence*, K. G. Robertson, (ed.), (London, 1987)
Fry, R. & Ury, W., *Getting to Yes*, (London, 1991)
Fuller, J. F. C., *On Future Warfare*, (London, 1928)
—— *The Second World War*, (London, 1948)
Funk, A. L., *Hidden Ally*, (New York, 1992)
Gallop, G. H., *The Gallop Poll: Public Opinion, 1935–1971*, I, (New York, 1971)
Germains, V., *The Mechanization of War*, (London, 1927)
Gilbert, M., *Finest Hour: W.S. Churchill, 1939–1941*, (Boston, 1983)
—— *Winston S. Churchill, Road to Victory, 1941–1945*, (London, 1986)
Gottman, J., *Why Marriages Succeed Or Fail*, (New York, 1994)
Graham, D. & Bidwell, S., *Tug of War*, (London, 1986)
—— *Coalitions, Politicians and Generals*, (London, 1993)
Greenfield, K. R. (ed.), *Command Decisions*, (Washington, 1960)
—— *American Strategy in WWII: A Reconsideration*, (Baltimore, 1963)
Griffin, P., *Less Than A Treason*, (Oxford, 1990)
Grigg, P., *1943 The Victory that Never Was*, (New York, 1980)
Hall, H. D., *North American Supply*, (London, 1955)
Hamilton, H., *Monty, Master of the Battlefield 1942–1944*, (London, 1983)
Hancock, W. K., & Gowing, M. M., *British War Economy*, (London, 1949)
Hankey, L., *The Supreme Command*, (London, 1961)
Harbutt, F. J., *The Iron Curtain: Central America and the Origins of the Cold War*, (New York, 1986)
Harrison, G. A., *Cross-Channel Attack*, (Washington, 1951)
Hathaway, R. M., *Captain, Ambiguous Partnership, Britain and America, 1944–1947*, (New York, 1981)
Hearden, P. J., *Roosevelt Confronts Hitler*, (DeKalb, IL, 1987)
Heinl, R. D., Jr, 'Inchon', *Assault from the Sea: Essays on the History of Amphibious Warfare*, M. L. Bartlett (ed.), (Annapolis, 1983)
Higgins, T., *Winston Churchill and the Second Front*, (New York, 1957)

—— *Soft Underbelly*, (New York, 1968)
Hinsley, F. H., *British Intelligence in the Second World War*, III, I, (London,1984)
Hobbs, J. B., *Dear General: Eisenhower's Wartime Letters to Marshall*, (Baltimore, 1971)
Holland, J., *The Aegean Mission*, (New York, 1988)
Horne, A. with Montgomery, D., *Monty, The Lonely Leader*, (London, 1994)
Howard, M., *The Mediterranean Strategy in the Second World War*, (London, 1968)
—— *Studies in War and Peace*, (New York, 1970)
—— *Grand Strategy, August 1942–September 1943*, (London, 1972)
—— *Clausewitz*, (Oxford, 1983)
Howard, M. & Paret, P. (eds), *On War*, (Princeton, 1976)
Hunt, D., 'British Military Planning and Aims in 1944', *British Politics & Military Strategy in Central, Eastern and Southern Europe in 1944*, E. B. W. Deaken & J. Chadwick (eds), (London, 1988)
Huntington, S. P., *The Soldier & The State*, (Cambridge, 1957)
Hurstfield, J. G., *America and the French Nation, 1939–1945*, (Chapel Hill, 1986)
Isley, J. & Crowl, P., *The US Marines and Amphibious War*, (Princeton, 1951)
Jackson, W., *'OVERLORD': Normandy 1944*, (London, 1978)
Jacobi, J., *The Psychology of C.C. Jung*, (New Haven, 1968)
James, R. R., (ed.), *Complete Speeches*, (London, 1974)
Jary, S., *18 Platoon*, (London, 1988)
Jenkins, C. & Sherman, B., *Collective Bargaining*, (London, 1977)
Kennett, L., *The American Soldier in World War II*, (New York, 1987)
Kersaudy, F., *Churchill and De Gaulle*, (London, 1981)
Kimball, W. F., *The Juggler*, (Princeton, 1991)
King, E. J., & Whitehill, W. M., *Fleet Admiral King – A Naval Record*, (New York, 1952)
Kirkpatrick C. E., *An Unknown Future and a Doubtful Present*, (Washington, 1990)
Kissinger, H., *A World Restored*, (Boston, 1973)
—— *Diplomacy*, (New York, 1994)
Lamb, R., *The Ghosts of Peace, 1935–1945*, (London, 1987)
Larabee, E., *Commander in Chief*, (New York, 1987)
Leasor, J., *The Clock with Four Hands*, (New York, 1959)
—— *War At The Top*, (London, 1959)
Leigh, R., *48 Millions Tons to Eisenhower*, (Washington, 1945)
Leighton, R. M. & Coakley, R. W., *The Logistics of Global Warfare 1940–1943*, (Washington, 1955)
Lesser, I. O., *Resources and Strategy*, (London, 1989)
Lewin, R., *Montgomery as Military Commander*, (New York, 1971)
—— *Churchill as Warlord*, (New York, 1973)
Lewis, L., *Sherman: Fighting Prophet*, (New York, 1932)
Liddell Hart, B. H., *When Britain Goes to War, Adaptability and Mobility*, (London, 1932)
—— *The Strategy of the Indirect Approach*, (London, 1941)
—— *A Short History of the Second World War*, (London, 1967)
—— *The Rommel Papers*, (London, 1984)
Littlejohn, D., *The Patriotic Traitors*, (London, 1972).
Lockhart, V. M., *T-Patch to Victory*, (Canyon, 1981)

Loewenheim, F. L., et al., (eds), *Roosevelt and Churchill, Their Secret Wartime Correspondence*, (New York, 1990)
Louis, W. R., *Imperialism at Bay*, (Oxford, 1977)
MacCloskey, M., *Achieving Victory in World War II*, (New York, 1970)
—— *Planning for Victory in World War II*, (New York, 1970)
MacDonald, C., 'Deterrent Diplomacy: Roosevelt and the Containment of Germany, 1938–1940', *Paths to War*, R. B. & E. M. Robertson, (eds), (New York, 1989)
Macmillan, H., *War Diaries: Politics and War in the Mediterranean*, (New York, 1984)
Matloff, M., *Strategtic Planning for Coalition Warfare, 1943–1944*, (Washington, 1959)
Matloff, M., & Snell, E., *Strategic Planning for Coalition Warfare, 1941–42*, (Washington, 1953)
Mayle, P. D., *Eureka Summit:Agreement in Principle and the Big Threat Teheran*, (Newark, 1987)
McCloughry, E. J. K., *The Direction of the War*, (London, 1955)
Mearscheimer, *Liddel Hart & the Weight of History*, (London, 1988)
Miller, M., *Ike the Soldier*, (New York, 1987)
Millet, A. R. & Murray, W. (eds), 'The United States Armed Forces in the Second World War', *Military Effectiveness*, III, (Boston, 1988)
Mings, S. D., 'Stategies in Conflict, Britain and the Anglo–American Alliance, 1941–1943', (PhD thesis, University of Texas, 1975)
Molony, C. J. C., *British Official History, WW II, Grand Strategy, The Mediterranean and the Middle East*, (London, 1956)
Morelock, J. D., *Generals of the Ardennes*, (Washington, 1993)
Morgan, F., *Overture to Overlord*, (New York, 1950)
—— *Peace and War*, (London, 1961)
Morrison, S. E., American Contribution to the Strategy of World War II, (London, 1958)
Mosley, L., *Marshall, Organizer of Victory*, (London, 1982)
Murphy, R. D., *Diplomat Among Warriors*, (New York, 1964)
Myers, I. B., *Gifts Differing*, (Palo Alto, 1980)
Nicholas, H. G., *The United States and Britain*, (Chicago: 1975)
Parker, S. L., 'Attendant Lords: A Study of the British Joint Staff Mission in Washington, 1941–1945', (PhD thesis, University of Maryland, 1984)
Parkinson, R., *Blood, Toil, Tears, and Sweat*, (London, 1973)
—— *Alamein to VE Day*, (London, 1974)
Parrish, N. F., *Behind the Sheltering Bomb*, (New York, 1979)
—— *Roosevelt and Marshall*, (New York, 1989)
Paxton, O., *Vichy France: Old Guard and New Order*, (N.Y., 1972)
Pearson, M., *Tears of Glory*, (New York, 1978)
Peek, J. C. H., (ed.), *Five Years, Five Countries, Five Campaigns*, (Munich, 1945)
Perlmutter, A., *FDR & Stalin*, (London, 1993)
Peterson, M. D., *Thomas Jefferson and the New Nation*, (Oxford, 1970)
Pogue, F. C., *George C. Marshall: Ordeal and Hope*, (New York, 1966)
—— *Organizer of Victory*, (New York, 1973)
Reid, B. H., *J. F. C. Fuller, Military Thinker*, (London, 1987)
Reynolds, D., *The Creation of the Anglo–American Alliance, 1937–41: A Study in Competitive Cooperation*, (London, 1981)

—— 'Roosevelt,Churchill & the Wartime Anglo–American Alliance 1939–1945: Towards a New Synthesis', *The Special Relationship: Anglo–American Relations Since 1945*, Louis, W. R. and. Bull, H., (eds), (Oxford, 1986)
—— *The American Occupation of Britain, 1942–1945*, (N. Y., 1995);
Richards, D., *Portal of Hungerford*, (London, 1977)
Rock, R., *Chamberlain and Roosevelt*, (Columbus, 1988)
Rommel, E., *Infantry Attacks*, (London, 1990)
Roosevelt, E., *As He Saw It*, (New York, 1946)
—— *This I Remember*, (New York, 1949)
Roosevelt, E.(ed.), *FDR, His Personal Letters, 1928–1945*, (New York, 1950)
Rose, M., *Industrial Behavior*, (London, 1978)
Rosenman, S. I., *The Public Papers and Addressess of Franklin D. Roosevelt: The Call to Battle Stations, 1941*, (New York, 1950)
Roskill, S., *Hankey*, (London, 1974)
Ruge, F., *Rommel in Normandy*, (London, 1979)
Rzbesbevsky, O. A., 'The Soviet Union: The Direct Strategy', D. Reynolds, W. F. Kimball, and A. O. Chubarian (eds), *Allies at War*, (London, 1994)
Sainsbury, K., *The Turning Point*, (Oxford, 1986)
—— *Churchill and Roosevelt at War*, (London, 1994)
Sayers, R. S., *Financial Policy, 1939–1945*, (London, 1956)
Schoenfeld, M. P., *The War Ministry of Winston S. Churchill*, (Ames, 1972)
Seabury, P. & Codevilla, A., *War: Ends and Means*, (New York, 1989)
Sherwood, R. E., *Roosevelt and Hopkins*, (New York, 1948)
Slessor, J., *The Central Blue: Recollections and Reflections*, (London, 1956)
Smith, B. R., *The Ultra-Magic Deals*, (London, 1993)
Smith, G.,*When Jim Crow Met John Bull*, (London, 1987)
Snow, D., & Drew, M., *Making Strategy: An Introduction to National Security & Problems*, (Maxwell Air Force Base, 1988)
Stafford, D., *British and European Resistance: 1940–1945*, (London, 1983)
Steele, R. W., *The First Offensive – 1942*, (Bloomington, 1973)
Stoler, M. A., *The Politics of the Second Front*, (Westport, 1977)
—— *George C. Marshall*, (Boston, 1989)
—— 'The American Perception of British Mediterranean Strategy, 1941–1945', *New Aspects of Naval History*, C. L. Symonds (ed.), (Annapolis, 1979)
Sweet-Escott, B., 'SOE in the Balkans', *British Policy towards Wartime Resistance in Yugoslavia and Greece*, P. Auty & R. Clogg, (eds), (London, 1975)
Sweets, J, *The Politics of Resistance in France, 1940–1944*, (De Kalb, 1976)
Talbott, S., *Deadly Gambits*, (London, 1985)
Taylor, F., *The Principles of Scientific Management*, (London, 1972)
Terraine, J., *The Life and Times of Lord Mountbatten*, (London, 1968)
Thomas, R. T., *Britain and Vichy: The Dilemma of Anglo–French Relations, 1940–1942*, (London, 1979)
Thorne, C., *Allies of a Kind*, (London, 1978)
Turner, A. C., *The Unique Partnership: Britain and the US*, (New York, 1971)
Turner, J. F. & Jackson, R., *Destination Berchtesgarden*, (London, 1975)
Vigneras, M., *Rearming the French*, (Washington, 1957)
Villa, B. L., *Unauthorized Action: Mountbatten & The Dieppe Raid 1942*, (Toronto, 1989)
US Army, *US Seventh Army: Report of Operations*, (Heidelberg, 1946)

Walker, F. L., *From Texas to Rome: A General's Journal*, (Dallas, 1969)
Warren, H. G., *Special Operations: AAF Aid to European Resistance Movements*, (Washington, 1947)
Watt, D. C., *Succeeding John Bull*, (Cambridge, 1984)
Weigley, R. F., *The American Way of War*, (Bloomington, 1973)
—— *Eisenhower's Lieutenants*, (Bloomington, 1981)
Weinberg, A. K., *Manifest Destiny: A Study of Nationalist Expansionism in American History*, (Baltimore, 1935)
Weinberg, G., *World in the Balance: Behind the Scenes in World War II*, (Hanover, 1981)
Wilmot, C., *The Struggle for Europe*, (London, 1952)
Wilson, A., *Churchill: Taken from the Diaries of Lord Moran*, (Boston, 1966)
Wilson, C., *Introduction to the New Existentialism*, (London, 1966)
Wilson, T. A., *The First Summit: Roosevelt & Churchill At Placentia Bay, 1941*, (Lawrence, 1991)
—— 'Coalition: Structure, Strategy and Statecraft', *Allies at War*, Kimball, W., Chubarian, O. & Reynolds, D., (eds), (London, 1994)
—— 'The United States Leviathan', *Allies At War*, Kimball, W., Chubarian, O. & Reynolds, D., (eds), (London, 1994)
Wilkinson, P. & Astley, J. B., *Gubbins and SOE*, (London, 1993)
Wilt, A. F., *War From The Top*, (London, 1990)
Winfield, P., *Bye Bye Baby*, (London, 1992)
Ziegler, P., *Mountbatten*, (London, 1985)

SECONDARY WORKS: ARTICLES, MONOGRAPHS, ETC.

Abrahams, P., 'Bitter Memories of the Resistance', *Financial Times*, 12 Nov. 1995, pp. 1–2.
Allen, R. G. D., 'Mutual Aid Between the US and the British Empire', *Royal Statistical Society*, 109, (1986)
Alsop, J., 'Interview with George C. Marshall', Spring, *Joseph Alsop Papers*, LoC, Washington, Box 32.
Balfour, M., 'The Origin of the Formula, "Unconditional Surrender", in World War II', *Armed Forces and Society*, Vol. 5, No. 2, (1979), pp. 281–308.
Barker, T. M., 'The Ljubljana Gap Strategy: Alternate to Anvil/Dragoon or Fantasy?', *Journal of Military History*, 56, January 1, (1992), pp. 57–85.
Blumenson, M., 'A Deaf Ear to Clausewitz: Allied Operational Objectives in World War II', Parameters, *US Army War College Quarterly*, XXIII, 2, (Summer 1993), pp. 16–27.
Brogan, D., 'The Americans', *The Spectator*, (3 July 1942).
Bruenn, H. G., 'Clinical notes on the Illness and Death of President Franklin D. Roosevelt', *Annals of Internal Medicine*, (April 1970).
Buckley, C., 'Salient Points about the Sicilian Campaign', *Daily Telegraph*, (24 August 1943).
Davies, A., 'Geographical Factors in the Invasion and Battle for Normandy', n. d., *LHMA*.

Doubler, M. D., 'Busting the Bocage: American Combined Arms Operations in France, 6 June–31 July 1944', *Combined Studies Institute*, USACGSC (1988).

Emerson, W. R., 'Franklin Roosevelt as Commander-in-Chief in World War II', *Military Affairs*, 22, (Winter 1958–59), pp. 181–207.

Feagin, J. R. & Riddell, K., 'The State, Capitalism, and World War II: The US Case', *Armed Forces and Society*, 17, (Fall 1990), pp. 53–79.

Funk, A. L., 'American Contacts with the Resistance in France, 1940–1943', *Military Affairs*, XXXIV, 1, (1970), pp. 15–21.

—— 'Churchill, Eisenhower and the French Resistance', *Military Affairs*, XLV, 1, (February 1981), pp. 29–33.

—— 'The United States and Torch: Strategy and Intelligence', *The British Institute in Paris*, 7, Spring: Operation TORCH and its Political Aftermath: Franco–Anglo–American Relations in 1942, (1989), pp. 15–29.

Gabel, C. R., 'The Lorraine Campaign: An Overview, September–December 1944', *Combat Studies Institute*, USCGSC, (1985)

Galgano, Jr, F. A., 'The Landings at Anzio', *Military Review*, (January 1994), pp. 69–71.

Gubbins, C., 'Resistance Movements In The War', *Journal of Royal United Services Institute*, 93, (May 1948), pp. 210–23.

Haglund, D. G., 'George C. Marshall and the Question of Military Aid to England, May–June 1940', *Journal of Contemporary History*, 15, (1980), pp. 746–59.

Harbutt, F., 'Churchill, Hopkins and the "Other" Americans: An Alternative perspective on Anglo–American Relations, 1941–1945', *International History Review*, VIII, (May 1986), pp. 236–62.

Head, A. H., 'Amphibious Operations', *Journal of Royal United Services Institute*, XCI, (February to November 1946), pp. 485–94.

Heinl, J. R. D., 'The US Marine Corps: Author of Modern Amphibious Warfare, M.L. Bartlett, (ed.), *Assault from the Sea*, (Annapolis, 1983), pp. 1977:1310–23.

Herring, G., 'The United States and British bankruptcy, 1944–1945: Responsibility Deferred', *Political Science Quarterly*, 86, (1971), pp. 260–80

Higgins, G. A., 'German and US Operational Art: A Contrast in Maneuver', *Military Review*, (October 1985), pp. 22–9.

Higgins, T., 'The Anglo–American Historians' War in the Mediterranean 1942–1945', *Military Affairs*, (October 1970), pp. 84–8.

Irwin, W. W., 'Origin and Development of the Jedburgh Project In Support of Operation Overlord', (unpublished MA thesis, US ACGSC, 1975).

Kaiser, D. E., 'Churchill, Roosevelt and the Limits of Power', *Journal of International Security*, 10: 1, (Summer 1985), pp. 204–21.

Kautsky, J. H., 'Myth, Self fulfilling Prophecy, and Symbolic Reassurance in the East–West Conflict', *Journal of Conflict Resolution*, IX, 1, (1965), pp. 1–2.

Kehrig, Dr., 'Le Débarquent de Provence; Le Point de Vue Allemand', *Terre*, 57, (1994), pp. 22–3.

Kimball, W. F., 'Beggar My Neighbor: America and the British Interim Finance Crisis, 1940–1941', *Journal of Economic History*, 29, (1969), pp. 758–72.

—— 'Churchill and Roosevelt: The Personal Equation', *Prologue*, 6, (Fall 1974), pp. 169–82.

Kittridge, T. B., 'US Defense Policy and Strategy', *US News and World Report*, (3 December 1954).

Leutze, J., 'The Secret of the Churchill–Roosevelt Correspondence, September 1939–May 1940', *Journal of Contemporary History*, 10, 3 (July 1975), pp. 465–94.

Matloff, M., 'Was the Invasion of Southern France a Blunder?', *US Naval Institute Proceedings*, (1958).

—— 'Wilmot Revisited: Myth and Reality in Anglo–American Strategy for the Second Front', D-Day, *The Normandy Invasion in Retrospect, Eisenhower Foundation* (ed.), (Lawrence, KS, 1971).

—— 'Mr. Roosevelt's Three Wars: FDR as War Leader', *The Harmon Memorial Lectures in Military History*, 1959–1987, L. C. H. R. Borowski, (ed.), (Washington, 1988)

Maund, L. E. H., 'The Development of Landing Craft', *Journal of the Royal United Services Institute*, XC, (May 1945), pp. 212–17.

Munch, P. G., 'General George C. Marshall and the Army Staff', *Military Review*, LVXXIV, 8, (1994), pp. 14–23.

Reid, B. H., 'The Italian Campaign 1943–45: A Reappraisal of Allied Generalship', *Journal of Strategic Studies*, 13, 1, (1990), pp. 128–61.

Rowan-Robinson, H., 'The Surrender of Italy: Political and Military Implications', *Journal of the Royal United Services Institute*, LXXXVIII, (February to November 1943).

Schaffer, R., 'General Stanley D. Embick: Military Dissenter', *Military Affairs*, (October 1973), pp. 89–95.

Scott, G. L., 'British and German Operational Styles in World War II', *Military Review*, (October 1985), pp. 37–41.

Sendall, W. R., 'The Sea Flank Was Open: Lost Opportunities', *Military Review*, (1953), pp. 107–9.

Silkett, W. A., 'Alliance and Coalition Warfare', *Parameters*, XXIII, 2, (Summer 1993), pp. 74–85.

Smith, W. B., 'Problems At An Integrated Headquarters', *Journal of the Royal United Services Institute*, LXXXVIII, (February to November 1945), pp. 455–62.

Sommers, M., 'Why Russia Got the Drop On Us', *Saturday Evening Post*, (8 February 1947).

Spector, B. I., 'Negotiation as a Psychological Process', *Journal of Conflict Resolution*, 21, 4, (1977), pp. 607–18.

Steele, R. W., 'Political Aspects of American Military Planning, 1941–1942', *Military Affairs*, XXXV, 2, (1971), pp. 68–74.

Stoler, M. A., 'The "Pacific-First" Alternative in American World War II Strategy', *The International History Review*, (July 1980).

Strange, J. L., 'The British Rejection of Operation SLEDGEHAMMER, An Alternative Motive', *Military Affairs*, 46, (February 1982), pp. 6–15.

Sutherland, J., 'The Story General Marshall Told Me', *US News & World Report*, (2 November 1959).

Thorne, P., 'Hitler and the Gheluvelt Article', *Guards Magazine*, (1994).

Time, (2 June 1941).

Vernet, J., 'Les Projets de réorganisation de l'Armée de terre Française de 1945 à 1946', *Revue Historique des Armées*, (1979), pp. 228.

Weigley, R. F., 'To the Crossing of the Rhine: American Strategic Thought in World War II', *Armed Forces and Society*, (5 February 1979), pp. 303–20.

Wilt, A. F., 'The Summer of 1944: A comparison of Overlord and Anvil', *Journal of Strategic Studies*, 4, 2, (1981), pp. 188–95.
—— 'The Significance of the Casablanca Decisions, January 1943', *Journal of Military History*, 55, 4, (1991), pp. 517–29.
Wilson, H. M., 'Report by SACMED to the CCS on the Italian Campaign', I, II, January–August 1944, AFHQ, (1946).
—— 'Report by the SACMED to the CCS on Operations in Southern France, August 1944', AFHQ, (1946).

INTERVIEWS WITH CONTEMPORARIES

General François Binoche (2 February 1991)
Sir Robin Brook (29 March 1994)
Sir Ralph Kilner Brown (24 September 1993), (17 February 1995)
General Jacques Brûle (13 August 1994)
General J. P. de Lassus St-Geniès (20 February 1994)
Sir Douglas Dodds-Parker (24 March 1994)
General James Doolittle (14 December 1975)
Arthur L. Funk (29 September 1994)
General Sir William Jackson (6 January 1993)
Geoffrey Jones (14 August 1994)
Robert Reigle (15 April 1994)
Keith Sainsbury (15 March 1995)
Mark Stoler (4 November 1994)
Peter Thorne (17 May 1994)

Index

ABC talks, 1, 7, 64–6, Paper, *ABC–1*, 5, 7, 9, 11
Abrahams, Paul, 120–1
Adriatic, *see* Istria
Aegean, 50, 88, 106–7, 132, 134–5
'Agreement in principle', 22–3, 60–2, 66, 100, 124–6; '*oui, en principe*', 125
Alexander, F-M Sir Harold, 136, 141, 143, 145–6, 153, 155
Allied Air Operations:
1943 appraisal, 96, 99
Allied Armies Italy (AAI), 146, 166
Ambrose, Stephen, E., 75, 138
Anfa Plan, 124–5
Anglo–American relationship: definitions, 2–3, 19; distrust within, 5–6, 11, 14, 16, 18, 21, 24, 98, 103, 167–8; language usage within, 21, 37, 84–5, 100, 125–6; negotiating conditions within, 88–7, 95–103, 139–40; officer experience related to, 21–2, 37–9, procedural differences within, 22, 38, 82–3, 145
ANVIL, Assessment of, 159, 166–7; Alternative to, 139–40, 145–6; Cancellation, 144; Conception, 101–2; Debate, 1; Execution of, 158–9; Plans, 157–8; and Resistance in Southern France, 112–13, 119–20
Anzio, 105–6, 165; and Alistair Horne, 142; Casualties, 142; Gen. Eisenhower, 142; Gen. Alphonse Juin, 142; Plan, 141–2
ARCADIA Conference, Agreement, 44–5; American proposals, 43; British proposals, 43–4; Churchill at, 43, 46–7, 50–1; Gen. Hollis's view of, 51; Plan, 46
ARMPIT, *see* Istria
Arnold, USAF Gen. Henry, 7, 27; Air War, 103; at ARCADIA, 46, 49; at Placentia Bay, 38–9; on Policy, 103
Atlantic Charter, 41, 50, 77
AVALANCHE, 94
Balkans, 114, 149, and ARCADIA agreement, 45, 50; F-M Sir Alan Brooke, views of, 103, 132; Churchill, 156; Gen. D. Eisenhower, 133; Adolf Hitler, 142; Italian troops in, 96; F-M Henry M. Wilson, 150
Barker, Gen. Ray, *see* Morgan
BAYTOWN, 94
Beaverbrook, Lord, Minister of Supply, 42
Bessell, Col. William, 127
Blumenson, Martin, 55
BOLERO, 48, 54; and American interests 92, 95, 138; BRIMSTONE, 69; British interests, 60, 63–4, 71; and Churchill, 54–5, 70; and MODICUM, 59; TORCH, 57, 65
BRIMSTONE, 69
Britain, Great, 1–3; and America's defense, 16–17, 21, 42; American attitudes toward, 5–6, 9–12, 42, 167; and *Atlantic Charter*, 77; and the French Resistance, 107–10, 115–21; Governmental structures, 24, 30, 29–33, 160–2; and Lend-Lease, 13–15, 40, 42; and Russia, 52, 55, 67–8, 70, 86, 91,105, 135–6, 161; and 'Unconditional Surrender', 74–6
Brook, Sir Robin, 111
Brooke, F-M Sir Alan, 4, 18–19; and Americans, 23, 46–9, 67, 166–7; relations with Churchill, 23, 29–30, 34–5; and Gen. Lord Hastings Ismay, 31–2; personality, 62, 65, 100–3, 132, 163, 165; SLEDGEHAMMER, 54–5, 60, 63; TORCH, 66; TRIDENT, 83, 86, 88–90; QUADRANT, 95–7, 100–3
BUCCANEER, 134–6

Cadogan, Sir Alexander, 38, 40, 118
Cairo Conference (SEXTANT), 131–7
Canterville Ghost (Oscar Wilde), 21
Casablanca Conference (SYMBOL), 69; American handicap, 80–1;

British preparations and plans, 70–1; French leadership problems, 76–7; 'Unconditional Surrender', 74–6; Results, 79–80
Cavendish-Bentinck, William, 75–6
Charmley, John, 15–16, 138
Chiang Kai-shek, *see* Roosevelt
Chiefs of Staff: British, 31–8, 105–6, 163; Cabinet Secretariat, 31; Churchill, 29–36, 88–9; Defense Committee, 31; and Dill, 28–9, 34, 48, 53, 58–9; and the French, 124; and Minister of Defence, 30–1, 33; Special Operations, 9, 11, 17–18; and Strategy, 39, 48–9, 52, 60–3, 81–2, 86, 96–8, 103; War Cabinet, 30
Chiefs of Staff: Combined, Conferences, 70, 73, 88, 136; Creation of, 32, 37, 45, 47–8, 50, 163; Eisenhower, 137–8, 157; Paper, *CCS–94*, 64–6; Meetings, 132–3, 148–9, 154–5; Negotiations, 54, 56, 58, 61, 82, 86, 90; Second Front, 88, 96–7, 100–3, 107; Special Operations, 113, 115, 118
Chiefs of Staff: US (Joint), 6; and ANVIL, 140, 152; and Churchill, 90, 131, 156; at Conferences, 70–1, 76, 79, 133; and COS, 37, 57–8, 95, 163; creation, 25–6; Eisenhower, 112, 114, 139, 150; Negotiating skills, 84–5, 89. 95; and Roosevelt, 43, 53, 56, 69, 93–4, 100, 140; Strategy, 92, 94, 97–9, 127, 133, 148, 151; TORCH, 65;
Chief of Staff to the Supreme Allied Commander (COSSAC), 80, 92, 97, and French Resistance, 111, 114–15; 41–3
Christiansen, Gen. James, 79
Churchill, Winston S., Prime Minister, 1, 69; Anzio, 141–2; Conferences, 37–8, 43–5, 50, 83, 101; and the COS, 2, 7, 9, 64–5, 88–9; De Gaulle, 76–7, 110, 114, 118, 123; Landing Craft, 57, 102; as Minister of Defence, 30–1, 33; Personality, 35–6, 62, 132, 134–5, 154–5; and Roosevelt, 2, 7, 9, 39, 43, 54–5, 58, 61–2, 71, 73, 79, 91, 131, 135–7, 153–4; Second Front, 52, 55, 58–9, 66, 88, 100, 105; Special Operations, 107, 109, 112, 118; Special Relationship, 15–21, 160–1; Stalin, 67–8, 90–1, 105, 137; Strategy, 21, 37, 39–40, 46–7, 50, 55, 63, 102, 146, 158; 'Unconditional Surrender', 74–6; View of Americans, 23, 39, 56, 62; War Leader, 24, 29–33, 43, 70, 90, 106, 131–2, 160, 164
Clark, Gen. Mark, 123, 146, 149
Conant, James B., 41–2
Congress, US, 14, 16–17, 25, 43
Cooke, Adm. Charles ('Savvy'), 92
COSSAC, *see* Morgan
Crusade in Europe, (Eisenhower), 159
Cunningham, Adm. Sir Andrew, 32–3; 136–7, 152, 154; on Churchill, 35; on Adm. E. J. King, 26

Dalton, Hugh, Minister of Economic Warfare (MEW), 108–10. 115
Danchev, Alex, 59
Darlan, Adm. Jean, 75
De Gaulle, Gen. Charles, ANVIL, 157–8; at Casablanca, 76–7, and French rearmament, 122–3, 130; Gen. Henri Giraud, 76–7; and the Résistance, 108, 110–11
Devers, Gen. Jacob L., 146, 157
DIADEM, 145, 149, 150–1
Dill, F-M Sir John, 32, 39, 165; American preparedness, 26, 43; and ANVIL, 144, 148; as Chief of Joint Staff Mission, 53, 58–9, 70, 72; On Churchill, 33–4, 38; Friendship with Gen. George C. Marshall, 53–4, 66; On Strategy, 18, 41, 48, 65, 73
Dodds-Parker, Col. Sir A. D., 113–14
Donovan, Gen. William J., 111–13
Douglas, Lewis W., 41–2
DRAGOON, 155–6

Eastern Mediterranean, 5, 106–7, 131, 133–5; ACCOLADE, 106, 131; Crete, 132, 134; Dodecanese, 132,

135; Rhodes, 132, 134;
HARDIHOOD, 106, 131
Economic Warfare, Ministry of, 107–8
Eisenhower, Gen. Dwight D. ('Ike'), ANVIL, 101, 137, 139–40, 143–4, 148, 150, 158–9; and Churchill, 81, 89–90; on Co-operation, 5, 7, 20, 23, 13, 140; and Adm. Jean Darlan, 75; and De Gaulle, 117–18, 122; and Marshall, 133, 138–9, 146, 149–50; Paper, 'Eisenhower Memorandum', 58; French Résistance, 111–12, 115–16, 119, 121; OSS, 112; OVERLORD, 136–8, 140–3, 146; Planning, 58, 61, 92, 105, 133, 149; as Supreme Commander, 139; 'Unconditional Surrender', 74
'Emasculation', 98
Embick, Gen. Stanley D., 5–7, 11, 39, 84, 167

Foot, M. R. D., 115
France, 9, 15, and Allied controversy, 133, 137, 139, 142–3, 148–50, 156, 159; in Allied planning, 52, 54–5, 59, 67, 78–9, 96–7, 101–2, 105–7; Rearmed, 122–3, 145; Stalin, 106; Vichy, 111
French: Committee of National Liberation, 110–11, 130; Communists, 115; and Eisenhower, 112; Liberation, 120; North Africa, 77, 122–3, 130, 165; North African Army, 123, 125, 128; Résistance, 108–10, 114–15, and SHAEF, 111–14, 116–19
Funk, Arthur, L., 128

General Staff Division (GSD), 6
Germany, 6–10, 12, 14–15, 17, 40–2, 44, 55, 59, 63–4, 66, 71–3, 75–6, 78, 80, 86, 88–9, 92, 96, 99–103, 107, 109, 112, 121–2, 133, 145, 147, 161, 164
'Germany First', policy of, 1, 7, 45, 51, 60–1, 83, 164–5, 168
Gerow, Gen. Leonard T., 15
Giraud, Gen. Henri, 117, 124–6, 129; and De Gaulle, 76–7; and Roosevelt, 76–7
Global war: ABDA, 47–9
Gothic Line, 146, 166
Graf Spee, 17
Grant, Ulysses S., 48, 74, 163
Grigg, John, 77–8
Gubbins, Gen. Sir Colin, 109, 113, 116
GYMNAST, Plan, 44, 49, 57–8, 63–5; and Adm. Lord Louis Mountbatten, 52–5

HABBAKUK, 100–1
Halifax, Lord E. F., Foreign Secretary, 15
Hamilton, Nigel, 143
Harding, Gen. Sir John, 146
Harriman, Averell, Dir. of Lend-Lease, 39, 91
Hewitt, Adm. H. Kent, 146
Hitler, Adolph, 5, 14–16, 54, 108, 115, 121, 141, 160, 165; and Roosevelt, 42; as strategist, 10, 67, 97, 142–3, 158–9, 166
Hollis, Gen. Sir Leslie, 50–1
Hopkins, Harry, L, as Roosevelt's personal adviser, 26, 39, 52–4, 64, 132, 156; as negotiator, 58–9, 61–3
Horne, Alistair, 142
Howard, Michael, 80
Hull, Cordell, US Secretary of State, 13–14, 74
HUSKY, compared to OVERLORD, 78–9; Plan, 79–80, 84, 124

IMPERATOR, 55
'Indirection', 99
Intelligence, 53, 54, 107, 109, 111, 115, 120, 143, 152,
Ismay, Gen. Lord ('Pug'), 31–3, 62, 86
Istria (Adriatic), 143–4, 146–7, 149
Italian: Armistice, 75, 104; Campaign, 88, 105, 127, 130, 133, 137–41, 144, 146, 149, 165; defeat, 38, 71, 165; Foreign policy, 9; landings, 94; soldiers, 78
Italy, 9, 89, 92–4, 96–9, 101–3, 164

Jacob, Gen. Sir Ian, 70, 80, 167
Japan, and Allied strategy, 73, 94–5, 168; American strategy, 60, 64–6, 86, 164; attitude of American public toward, 8, 10, 16, 42
Japanese: and Allied concerns, 40, 78; Pacific expansion, 17, 40, 45–7, 49, 160–1; armed forces, 9, 12, 21, 43, 60
Joint Planning Committee (JPC), 10
Joint Staff Mission, 17; and ANVIL, 145, 147, 150, 155; and the COS, 52; Dill, head of, 18, 26; and Adm. Mountbatten, 53
Joint Staff Planners (JPS), 84, 148
Joint Strategic Survey Committee (JSSC), 5, 84, 167
Joint War Plans Committee (JWPC), 6, 84
Juin, Gen. Alphonse, 142
JUPITER, 35, 101

Kennedy, Gen. Sir John, 21, 72
Kennedy, Joseph P, US Ambassador to Great Britain, 15
Keynes, John Maynard, 37–8
King, Adm. Ernest J., anti-British, 39, 71, 86, 90, 92, 96, 165; and ANVIL, 147; and GYMNAST (TORCH) 53, 57–8, 65; and Japanese 7, 46, 72, 83, 90; and JCS, 25–6, 39; Landing craft, 144, 147–8; Paper, 'CCS–94', 66; OVERLORD, 86, 90, 96; personality, 7, 26, 39, 49, 95; SLEDGEHAMMER, 52, 57–8
Kirkman, Gen. Sir Sidney, 146
Kissinger, Henry, 87
Knox, Frank, Secretary of the Navy, 10
Koenig, Gen. Pierre, 114–16
Kuter, Gen. Lawrence, 49, 93, 99

Landing craft, and ANVIL, 133, 137, 139, 143; BUCCANEER, 134; British seamanship, 92; and Churchill, 46–7, 132, 142; designations, 102, 143; OVERLORD, 132, 139; production, 147; shortages, 53, 57, 80, 90, 102, 133; SEXTANT agreement, 136; and southern France, 101; theater transfer, 144, 147–8
de Lattre de Tassigny, Gen. Jean, 157
Leahy, Adm. William D., and De Gaulle, 126; role of, 26–7, 101; strategy, 57, 65, 97
Leasor, James, 51
Lend-Lease, 13–4, 18, 122; and Harriman, 39; and Hitler, 42; and Hull, 13–14; and Morganthau, 13–14
Liddell Hart, Sir Basil, 158–9, 167
Ljubljana Gap, 146, 150

Macmillan, Harold, impression of Roosevelt and Churchill, 70; on ANVIL, 154
Marshall, Gen. George C, as CoS, 1, 11, 13, 15, 37, 39, 41, 43, 45, 79, 94, 164; on ANVIL, 105–6, 144; Brooke, 60, 62, 97, 165; and CCS, 47–8, 50; Churchill, 134, 147; COS 37, 92, 133; Congress, 37; Dill, 39; Eisenhower, 58, 139, 143; French rearmament, 123, 126–7, 129; Hopkins, 58–9; JCS, 25–6, 93; King, 38, 66; on leaders in democracy, 56; Mediterranean options, 54, 81, 86, 106, 137–8, 148; OVERLORD, 98–9, 105; Pacific strategy, 7, 61, 83; Plans to invade France, 54–5, 59, 80, 90; Politics, 11–12; Roosevelt, 10, 25, 28–9, 47, 57, 63, 65, 74, 93, 103; Western hemisphere defense, 8, 28
'Marshall Memorandum', 58, 61
McCloy, John, J., 112
McCrea, Capt John L., 49, 76
McNarney, Col. Joseph T., 6, 21
Mediterranean Allied Air Forces (MAAF), 92
Mediterranean strategy, 5–6; American reactions, 57, 65–6, 70, 80–1, 93–4, 97–8; and ARCADIA, 44–6, 50; Churchill, 55, 70, 81, 105, 131–2, 155, 155; COS, 72–3; Marshall, 69, 81, 148; Pacific, 71; Roosevelt, 72
Mobilization Day, (M Day), 10

Montgomery, F-M Sir Bernard L., 142; amphibious operations, 137, 139; Eisenhower, 107, 143, 164; generalship, 145; loyalty, 4
Moran, Lord, 38–9, 141
Morgan, Gen. Sir Frederick, 3, 41; and Barker, 97; as COSSAC, 80, 96–7, 101–2; as planner, 78, 88
Morganthau, Henry, Secretary of the Treasury, 3–14
Moulin, Jean, 118–19
Mountbatten, Adm. Lord Louis, 32, 52–4, 56, 59
Murphy, Robert D., 125–6

Neutrality Act, 42
Noble, Adm. Sir Percy, 155
Normandy, 165; and the French Résistance, 105, 107, 112–13, 116, 119–22; alternatives to, 137, 143, 146, 152, 155
North Africa, early American objections to operations in 1; Tobruk falls, 18; Allied presence, 30, 111, 113, 123, 126; fighting in Russia compared, 73–4; proposed landing in, 44, 50, 55–7, 67; training facilities for French soldiers, 129–30

'Off the record', 100–1
On War, Clauzwitz, 28
Operations Division (OPD), 6
OSS, 111, 113; and John Bross, 118; operational groups (OG), 116–17; Special Operations Branch (SO), 111–12, 114; and Special Projects Operations Center (SPOC), 113–14, 119; War Diary, 117; and Vichy, 111; *also see* SOE
OVERLORD, 78; American to command, 93, 139; British alternative to, 106, 131, 133; linchpin of American strategy, 107; plans for, 101, 143; support by French Résistance, 116, 120; as ROUNDHAMMER, 88; Stalin, 106, 135

Patch, Gen. Alexander, 120, 129
Pearl Harbor, 2, 8, 13, 15, 39, 43–4, 50–1
Placentia Bay, 38–9, 41, 46
POINTBLANK, 96, 99
Portal, ACM Sir Charles, 20, 32, 46, 96, 99; and ANVIL, 137; and Brooke, 48; and Churchill, 34; personality, 49
Pound, Adm. Sir Dudley, 38, 46, 48; and Churchill, 33

QUADRANT Conference, 93–4, 101–2, 131

Rainbow 5, 8, 44
Ramsay, Adm. Sir Bertram, 138–9
Reynolds, David, 138
RIVIERA meeting, *see* Placentia Bay
Rommel, F-M Erwin, 3
Roosevelt, Franklin D., administrative style, 10, 24–5, 28–9, 31, 56, 65, 126, 132, 162; aid to Britain, 7, 9, 14; and Arnold; *Atlantic Charter*, 41, 50, 77; and CCS, 47, 53, 56; Chiang Kai-shek, 131, 134; and Churchill, 47, 52, 77, 91, 112, 132, 136, 146, 153–4; Conferences, 37, 43, 50, 69, 79; and De Gaulle, 76–7, 117, 123–4; and Eisenhower, 110, 140 ; his impressions of Britain, 16, 18, 39, 140; and Hopkins, 64; isolationism, 16, 42, 160; JCS, 28, 38, 69, 85, 93; and leadership, 24, 27–8, 38, 40–1, 45, 75, 83, 99, 117, 161; and Lend-Lease, 14, 160; and Marshall, 25, 45–8, 103; Mountbatten, 53; politics, 43, 50, 56, 99, 162; and second front, 52, 55, 57, 63, 65, 73, 85, 105, 165; and Stalin, 75, 105, 107, 135; and Stimson, 67; and 'Unconditional Surrender', 75; Woodrow Wilson, 29, 75
ROUNDHAMMER (*see* OVERLORD)
ROUNDUP, 48, 53, 55, 57, 59, 64–5, 71
Russia, 9–10, 12, 42–3, 50, 160; Balkans, 93, 105; and France, 115,

119; and Lend-Lease to, 52, 161; and second front, 50, 55–7, 69, 78, 80, 86, 131–2, 135
Russian: front, 6, 10–11, 44, 48, 53,–4, 63–4, 68, 70, 73–4, 78, 161

SACMED, 157; *see* Wilson
Sainsbury, Keith, 165
SCAEF, 136–7
Selective Service, 37, 160
SHAEF, 143; *see* French
Sherwood, Robert, 19
Sicily, *see* HUSKY
SLEDGEHAMMER, 52; and Churchill, 54–5; and Marshall, 59–60; and MODICUM talks, 59–60; and Roosevelt, 65; and SUPER-GYMNAST, 44, 57; and TORCH, 55
Smith, Gen. Walter B. ('Beetle'), 65, 104, 137–8
Smith, Graham, 138
Somervell, Gen. Brehon, 84–5
Special Operations Executive (SOE), 107–12; and Bank of England, 116, CARPETBAGGER, 115; and deception plans, 121–2; and Jedburghs, 115–16, Maquis Plan, 119; MASSINGHAM, 113; and Special Force Headquarters (SFHQ), 112–13; and various Résistant movements, 110, 114
'Stalemate', 102
Stalin, *see* Churchill; France; OVERLORD; Mountbatten; Roosevelt
Stark, Adm. Harold ('Betty'), 39; and 'Plan Dog', 9; and American policy, 28
Stillwell, Gen. Joseph ('Vinegar Joe'), 8
Stimson, Henry L., Secretary of War, and strategy: American, 10, 48, 53–4, 58, 65, 92–3; British, 6; and Grant, 163; and Roosevelt, 10, 25, 47, 67
Strategy and Policy Group (S&P), 6, 167
Styer, Gen. Wilhelm D., 128

Taft, Robert, Senator, 15–16
Tehran (EUREKA) Conference, 37, 105–6, 132, 135
Tobruk, 18–19
TORCH, 78–9, *see* BOLERO, Brooke, King, SLEDGEHAMMER
TRIDENT conference, 83, 85; and Americans, 89
Tunisia, 77
Turner, Adm. Richmond K., 6–7, 40

ULTRA, *see* Intelligence
Ultra Magic Deals (Bradley Smith), 16
'Unconditional Surrender', 74–7
United Nations, 50

Victory Program, 6, 10, 12–14, 79, 127
Villa, Brian L, 59

Ward, Col. Orlando,10–11
War Plans Division (WPD), 12, 15
Washington Conference, 52, 58
Wavell, F-M Sir Archibald, 34
Wedemeyer, Gen. Albert C., 165; in Washington, 6, 12–13, 84; at conferences, 71–3, 93, 98
Welles, Sumner, 39–40
Western Hemisphere: American defense of, 7–8, 45; and Britain, 7, 16, 41–2; and Canada, 9; and Eisenhower, 7; German threat to, 8, 10, 44; and Hitler, 9–10; and Isolationism, 8, 42
Wilkinson, Col. Peter, 146
Wilson, F-M, Henry M., and ANVIL, 141, 143, 149–50, 155–6, 158; as SACMED, 142
Winant, John, US Ambassador to Great Britain, 131–2
WORKSHOP, 35

Yamamoto, Adm. Isoroku, 13

Welles, Sumner, 39–40
Western Hemisphere: American defense of, 7–8, 45; and Britain, 7, 16, 41–2; and Canada, 9; and Eisenhower, 7; German threat to, 8, 10, 44; and Hitler, 9–10; and Isolationism, 8, 42
Wilkinson, Col. Peter, 146
Wilson, F-M, Henry M., and ANVIL, 141, 143, 149–50, 155–6, 158; as SACMED, 142
Winant, John, US Ambassador to Great Britain, 131–2
WORKSHOP, 35

Yamamoto, Adm. Isoroku, 13